MY FBI

MY FBI

Bringing Down the Mafia,
Investigating Bill Clinton, and
Fighting the War on Terror

LOUIS J. FREEH

With Howard Means

St. Martin's Press ❧ New York

To my mom and dad,
who taught me all the good things I know and how to live

To my true hero and best friend, Marilyn,
who taught me how to love

To our six sons,
Justin, Brendan, Sean, Connor, Liam, and Colin,
who taught me how to give

Finally, to the men and women of the FBI,
who taught me the meaning of sacrifice

www.stmartins.com

ISBN 0-312-32189-9
EAN 978-0-312-32189-5

First Edition: October 2005

10 9 8 7 6 5 4 3 2 1

CONTENTS

CONTENTS

PREFACE

When I retired from the FBI in June 2001 I decided not to write this book. As director I had never sought publicity or the spotlight that sometimes corners public officials. In fact, I had intentionally shunned that role to the point that I declined the perfunctory gala retirement party that traditionally pays tribute to exiting heads of agencies. Instead, on my last day in office, June 25, 2001, I went down to the central FBI courtyard—where I was sworn in as director on September 1, 1993—and together with my family said thank you to the men and women of the FBI for the privilege of serving with them twice.

I had a most interesting and historic tenure as director. I was only the fifth occupant of that office since J. Edgar Hoover took over the Bureau in 1924. I was appointed by a Democrat after a Republican had appointed me as a federal judge. I had absolutely no political connections for the position, did not want to be considered, said no to the job at first, and made not a single effort to be appointed. Because of that I was able to serve with total independence.

I spent most of the almost eight years as director investigating the man who had appointed me. Although I served in one of the most sensitive positions during one of the most politically polarized times in the nation's history, no member of Congress called for my removal on grounds of partisanship or unfairness. I gave thousands of speeches and made hundreds of public appearances before Congress, the media, and under the glare of critical scrutiny from the FBI, the United States, and sixty-eight foreign countries. Never once did I say or do anything that embarrassed or caused harm to the FBI or the nation. Nobody inside or outside the FBI ever credibly questioned my honor or integrity. And in over eighty years, I am the only FBI director who, without any pressure whatsoever, voluntarily relinquished that powerful office and returned to civilian life. According to President Bush, my retirement took him "by surprise," which I clearly had not intended. I had been trusted with the country's deepest secrets, which even today I would not divulge.

What brought me back to the FBI from the bench, and kept me there for almost eight years, was simple. It was what made me want to be an FBI agent as early as when I was twelve years old. And it was with me when at twenty-five I took my first of many oaths of office to protect and defend our country. My respect and affection for the men and women of the FBI and the extraordinary integrity and sacrifice of their daily work never ceases to overwhelm me. As director, I spent as much time with them as I could. I went to every FBI division several times during my tenure and on those daylong visits I met, listened to, and took photos with every one of our people who was there. I spent time with each separate squad—without the division chiefs being present—so I could understand and learn about what they were doing and needed.

In all the meetings, briefings, crises, and events in which I participated, never once did I lose my temper or yell or treat any member of the FBI disrespectfully or unprofessionally. I had too much respect for the most fundamental tenet of their service—each of them was ready to give up his or her life at any time for our country. This is very sobering.

I went to Quantico—the FBI training academy—several times each month. There, I would jog with the classes of new agents, take pictures with them, teach them, and shoot with them, and I made it a point to be at their graduations. I only missed three of them in eight years. At the graduations I would meet all of their families and thank them for also serving the FBI.

I did the same with all of our FBI National Academy classes: more than 8,000 senior police officers in four sessions each year—local, state, federal, and foreign—who attended the FBI Academy during my tenure. When overseas I always visited—and jogged—with the FBI agents, Marine Corps embassy details, and host country police officers who met with us.

My respect for the men and women of the FBI remains immense. I took every opportunity to thank and praise them. If one of them suffered a loss or personal tragedy, I would go see that person, make a telephone call, or send a note. I did the same for every law enforcement officer in the United States who was killed in the line of duty while I was director. Those calls to the various police chiefs, sheriffs, and agency chiefs were among the most difficult things I did.

More difficult were the tragic deaths of four FBI agents killed in the line of duty while I led them. I will never lose the sense of grief and responsibility I feel for the loss of these heroes: Martha Dixon Martinez, Mike Miller, Billy Christian, and Chuck Reed. The FBI and the nation will always be grateful to them and their families for making the supreme sacrifice to protect all of us. To honor them and the other thirty FBI agents killed in the line of duty since 1924, I commissioned a Martyr Memorial that is prominently displayed in every FBI office.

In the end, I left the FBI with great pride, gratitude, and a sense of privilege. Over the eight years, I had probably received hundreds of awards, plaques, honors, degrees, etc., on my travels. All of them were important yet none of them adorned my office on the seventh floor at FBI headquarters. Instead, I had a few personal photos and, by the time I left, an entire wall of drawings and sketches done by our six sons from 1993 to 2001. They were taped up on the wall without much design or order right next to my desk. I chose that wall so I could look at them during phone calls or meetings when I needed to keep my focus on reality and what, at the end of any Washington, D.C., day, is really important. I did that pretty well. I promised myself when I became director that I wouldn't be one of those D.C. types who would announce—usually when things were going south—that they were leaving government in order to spend more time with their family. I actually spent all the time I needed with them while director. When a reporter asked me my two most important accomplishments in Washington, without hesitation I said, "Liam and Colin."

But none of the above was the impetus behind writing this book. I decided to write *My FBI* to tell the story of very special heroes: the men and women of the FBI. These extraordinary Americans are best described by the FBI Core Values (see page xiii), which I helped to write and define. The consistent dedication, sacrifice, honesty, and grace under pressure that they exhibit in the most stressful and dangerous of circumstances are a model for all of us. They inspired me every day, and the honor of serving with them will remain the pride of my professional life.

The cases and anecdotes, triumphs and tragedies in these pages will help Americans to understand and honor their very special service. It will also serve to correct the many mistaken, sometimes even craven, interpretations of what the FBI has actually achieved against almost insurmountable odds with both honor and skill. Various know-nothing Talking Heads who have inaccurately portrayed what the FBI does best also require this rebuttal. But mostly, and I reiterate, *My FBI* has much less to do with me than with the men and women of the FBI whom I honor and love. Their story can be told through my experiences with them. All Americans and people of liberty can join in my celebration of their good work.

A Message from the Director

FBI CORE VALUES

The strategic plan for accomplishing the FBI's mission must begin by identifying the core values which need to be preserved and defended by the FBI in performing its statutory missions. Those values are: rigorous obedience to the Constitution of the United States; respect for the dignity of all those we protect; compassion; fairness; and uncompromising personal and institutional integrity. These values do not exhaust the many goals which we wish to achieve, but they capsulize them as well as can be done in a few words. Our values must be fully understood, practiced, shared, vigorously defended and preserved.

Observance of these core values is our guarantee of excellence and propriety in performing the FBI's national security and criminal investigative functions. Rigorous obedience to constitutional principles ensures that individually and institutionally we always remember that constitutional guarantees are more important than the outcome of any single interview, search for evidence, or investigation. Respect for the dignity of all whom we protect reminds us to wield law enforcement powers with restraint and to recognize the natural human tendency to be corrupted by power and to become callous in its exercise. Fairness and compassion ensure that we treat everyone with the highest regard for constitutional, civil and human rights. Personal and institutional integrity reinforce each other and are owed to the Nation in exchange for the sacred trust and great authority conferred upon us.

We who enforce the law must not merely obey it. We have an obligation to set a moral example which those whom we protect can follow. Because the FBI's success in accomplishing its mission is directly related to the support and cooperation of those whom we protect, these core values are the fiber which holds together the vitality of our institution.

Louis Freeh

Louis Freeh
Director
Federal Bureau of Investigation

CHAPTER 1

Khobar Towers

Shortly before 10:00 P.M. local time on June 25, 1996, a Datsun driven by Hani al-Sayegh, a prominent member of the Saudi branch of Hezbollah, or "Party of God," pulled into the far corner of a parking lot adjacent to Building 131 at the King Abdul Aziz Airbase in Dhahran, along the oil-rich Persian Gulf coast of Saudi Arabia. The eight-story apartment structure was part of a housing complex known collectively as Khobar Towers, then home to more than two thousand American, British, French, and Saudi troops. Building 131 was occupied almost exclusively by members of the U.S. Air Force, enforcing the no-fly zone that had been in effect over southern Iraq ever since the end of the first Gulf War. With al-Sayegh in the Datsun was Abdallah al-Jarash, who had been recruited into Hezbollah at the Sayyeda Zeinab shrine in Damascus.

A few minutes later, a white, four-door Chevrolet Caprice entered the parking lot and waited for the Datsun to blink its lights—the all-clear signal. When it did, a tanker truck followed the Chevy into the lot. The truck had been purchased earlier that month from a Saudi dealership for approximately 75,000 Saudi riyals and taken to a farm outside Qatif, twenty minutes or so from Dhahran. There it had been outfitted with some five thousand pounds of explosives and turned into a massive bomb.

After the truck backed up to a fence just in front of the north side of Building 131, the driver, Ahmed al-Mughassil, commander of the military wing of the Saudi Hezbollah, and his passenger, Ali al-Houri, a main Hezbollah recruiter, leaped from the cab, raced to the Chevy, and drove off, followed by the Datsun.

Sgt. Alfredo Guerrero was pulling sentry duty on the rooftop at Building 131 when he saw the driver and passenger abandon the truck and the two cars speed away. Almost certain that they were staring at a bomb in the lot below them, Guerrero and two other sentries sounded an alarm. Then Guerrero, who had been stationed in Dhahran for only a month, began to race through the top floors of Building 131, warning people to leave. The sergeant had cleared the better part of two floors when the tank truck exploded, ripping a crater thirty-five feet deep and eighty-five feet wide and shearing off the north face of the apartment building.

Despite the heroism of Alfredo Guerrero, who escaped without serious injury, nineteen Americans were murdered at Khobar Towers and more than five dozen others were hospitalized. In all, 372 U.S. military personnel suffered wounds in the explosion. Khobar was the most deadly attack on American citizens abroad in thirteen years, since the October, 1983 explosion at a U.S. Marine barracks in Beirut, Lebanon, killed 241 marines. And the totals might have been far higher. In his haste, the driver of the truck had parked perpendicular to Building 131. Had he parked parallel and delivered the impact of the explosion along a broader front, he might have succeeded in toppling the entire structure, with a catastrophically greater loss of life.

My wife, Marilyn, and I and our children were visiting my parents at their home in North Bergen, New Jersey, when the Khobar terrorists struck. June 25, 1996, was a Tuesday, not a Saturday or a

Sunday, but the day afforded a rare chance to get everyone together. I'd kept my schedule light. Just as important, schools had let out only a few days earlier, and summer camps and other activities would soon kick in. Marilyn and I grabbed a small window of opportunity, and as so often seems to happen in hyperbusy lives, the window closed before we were ever quite through it. My mother was preparing dinner for the family when the FBI command center called to tell me that the attack had taken place a half hour earlier. (Saudi Arabia is seven hours ahead of East Coast time.) I'd never heard of Khobar Towers, but that was irrelevant. Marilyn and I immediately began to refill the car with the kids and their gear.

My predecessor as director of the Federal Bureau of Investigation, William Sessions, had traveled with a large security detail, including a driver. He might have been wise to do so: the world is full of nuts. But I had been an FBI agent myself, one of the grunts, and I didn't choose to live in the grand style now that I ran the place. Nor did Marilyn and I want our children to grow up thinking they were in protective custody or that they had to travel in a convoy to see their own grandparents.

I was at the wheel of my own car, heading unaccompanied down the New Jersey Turnpike, when I first discussed the attack with Attorney General Janet Reno, my direct boss and first line of communication with the Clinton administration. I also talked with then Deputy National Security Adviser Samuel R. "Sandy" Berger in those early hours after the attack. Sandy, who would take over as the principal adviser the next year with the resignation of Anthony Lake, was helping coordinate the national-security response, and the FBI was a vital part of that. I was on an unsecure car-phone line, though, and if Janet and Sandy did have more information than I had already picked up, they were unable to share it with me. In those early hours and for months to come, we all had far more questions than answers.

Six and a half hours after Khobar Towers was hit and Building

131 destroyed—about 10:00 P.M. East Coast time—Marilyn and I were pulling into our driveway in Great Falls, Virginia, just as Bill Clinton first announced the attack to the public, in a brief address from the Oval Office.

"The explosion appears to be the work of terrorists," the president explained. "If that's the case, like all Americans I am outraged by it. The cowards who committed this murderous act must not go unpunished. Within a few hours, an FBI team will be on its way to Saudi Arabia to assist in the investigation. . . ."

The president closed by echoing a point he had made earlier: "Let me say it again: We will pursue this," he said with a stern voice. "America takes care of our own. Those who did it must not go unpunished."

Those were words—and a promise—I would not forget.

For the FBI, the Khobar Towers attack was indeed a call to action. The Bureau's primary responsibilities were and remain domestic, but during my first three years as director, we had been expanding our global presence. Crime and terrorism had gone multinational, and we had to do so ourselves if we were to combat it effectively within our own borders. The Bureau also had specific extraterritorial responsibility for bombings where Americans were killed. That gave us jurisdiction, and we needed to exercise it as quickly as possible.

Crime scenes can grow stale in a hurry. Evidence is lost, or it decays beyond any useful capacity. Well-meaning efforts to clear up the site of a human disaster can destroy vital information about angles of impact, the size of an explosion, and the nature of the explosive materials themselves. Often, too, the smallest and most easily lost remnants can be the most telling. A piece of circuit board no bigger than a fingernail found in the fields around Lockerbie, Scotland, ultimately led us to the Libyans who had blown Pan Am flight 103 out of the sky. We didn't want to miss something similar in this instance.

All that is standard operating procedure for any crime scene, but from the very beginning it was clear that the attack on Khobar Towers was no ordinary criminal event. For one thing, it had occurred in an extraordinary place. Although it has long been one of America's most vital allies in the Middle East, Saudi Arabia ranks among the world's most closed societies. The usual problems of gaining access to a crime scene on foreign soil and establishing liaison with local authorities—never easy when you fly agents in to work an investigation—were compounded in this case not just by the secrecy that surrounds everything on the Arabian Peninsula but also by the special evidentiary needs of a legal system based on Islamic religious law, the Sharia. Just as Saudi overzealousness at the crime site could destroy evidence for us, so insensitivity on our part could destroy the admissibility of evidence for the Saudis.

The real possibility existed, too, that wherever the attack had been planned and whoever had carried it out, local fundamentalists might well be involved. Saudi Arabia's able ambassador to the United States, Prince Bandar bin Sultan, had been quick to announce a reward of 10 million riyals (then about $3 million in U.S. dollars) for information leading to the arrest of the bombers. But the kingdom exists in a delicate balance between its vast ruling monarchy and the Wahhabis, the more conservative Muslims who control the streets and mosques. Were the attackers foreign or homegrown terrorists? Either way, we were walking into the middle of an incendiary arrangement, to the discomfort of both sides.

The previous fall, following a similar bombing attack on a Riyadh compound where U.S. civilian contractors were training members of the Saudi National Guard, authorities had rounded up several suspects and questioned them over a period of many months.

Just about a month before the Khobar attack, Saudi authorities had broadcast the subjects' confessions on state-controlled television, then beheaded the penitents before we had a chance to interview them, or even sit in on interviews the Saudis conducted. Again, the haste of the executions raised questions in the Clinton administration over what was being served: justice or expediency?

We had more jurisdiction in the crime this time than we'd had in that earlier bombing—nineteen dead U.S. servicemen, as opposed to five murdered Department of Defense contractors—but there was no guarantee the Saudi royal family would see it that way or cooperate to any greater degree even if they did. Without that cooperation, we would end up once again spinning our wheels in the sand.

Marilyn and I had no sooner unloaded the kids and their bags than I turned around and headed the two dozen miles back into Washington, to the command center at the FBI headquarters on Pennsylvania Avenue. In those days, the official name of the facility—the Strategic Investigations and Operations Center—was almost as large as the space itself: three rooms on the third floor, maybe two thousand square feet in all, crammed with monitors and secure phones with direct lines to the White House, the Central Intelligence Agency, the Department of Defense, the National Security Agency, and elsewhere.

Even before Khobar Towers, we were spilling out of the space. An eighty-one-day siege in Jordan, Montana, had ended less than two weeks earlier with the surrender of the sixteen remaining "Freemen" antigovernment extremists who had holed themselves up in a rural compound. The long memory of the fiery end of the fifty-one-day siege at the Branch Davidian compound at Waco, Texas, three years earlier had kept us on high alert throughout the Montana ordeal. (The eleven-day siege ignited by the U.S. Marshals

Service at Ruby Ridge in Idaho in 1992 was also much on our minds.) Khobar itself would soon seem a trigger to a summer of crises. Three weeks later, on July 17, TWA flight 800 exploded off Long Island minutes after taking off from John F. Kennedy International Airport, killing all 230 passengers aboard. No one knew what had brought it down: mechanical failure, a bomb, a ground-to-air missile all seemed possible in the early stages. Ten days after, a bomb exploded in Atlanta's Centennial Park during the height of the summer Olympic Games. With crisis piled on crisis, we had agents stashed in the hallway, working highly sensitive investigations on open phone lines. We had no choice. A new command center ten times larger (named by me after "Bush 41") would finally be ready in 1999, but that was three years down the road. For now, we had to make do with what was, and that was cramped beyond belief.

My national security adviser, Robert "Bear" Bryant, was waiting for me. So were John O'Neill, Bryant's section chief in charge of terrorism, and a few other agents of similar rank. (John would take over as chief of security for the World Trade Center in September 2001. He was killed September 11 of that year when the North Tower collapsed.) Bryant was in my view the best agent we ever had for counterintelligence and counterterrorism cases. Rock-solid, smart, and incredibly talented, he cared more about the people who worked for him than anyone else I know. As midnight came and went, we pored over intelligence reports, trying to work out theories of the attack.

Information was still scarce, which was telling in its own right. When something like Khobar Towers is the work of a loose confederation or of rank amateurs, listening posts at the CIA and NSA tend to light up with related chatter: participants phoning their wives and brothers to celebrate the great event or, better still, calling each other to plan a rendezvous or a next attack. The more disciplined the planners and bombers, the more silent the listening stations. For the moment, at least, the Khobar attackers and their masters were being quiet as a tomb, a strong hint that they were among the pros of global mayhem.

As for a working theory, the best we could do on short notice was to assume that this attack was a continuation of the earlier one on the Saudi National Guard headquarters. That one had been carried out, so we were told, by disaffected Sunnis, young men in their twenties and thirties who were resentful of the royal family and in league with Osama bin Laden, the black sheep of one of the kingdom's richest families. We had, of course, no direct confirmation of that. The men in question had had their heads removed, with no consultation from us, but in the absence of other leads to pursue, we began to pull in intelligence from a variety of sources on Sunni radicals and the networks that supported them.

None of that, though, began to solve what for all of us in the room was the most pressing need: access. The Bureau had been true to Bill Clinton's word: 150 FBI pros—including agents, lab analysts, and forensic experts—were headed for Riyadh. But we could fly another ten thousand agents there and it wouldn't do a bit of good unless we could get them to the crime site and secure the cooperation of our hosts. That required the intervention of the royal family, and the only person I even faintly knew who fit that description was the Saudi ambassador, Prince Bandar. I picked up the phone and called him.

The prince took my call that night, and he couldn't have been more gracious. We need to work together, I told him, and we want to cooperate with the Saudis on the ground in the kingdom. First, though, we need your help. His answer was what I'd hoped to hear: please come out to see me.

Prince Bandar lives at the crest of Washington diplomatic and political society. Other ambassadors wait in line to see the president; Bandar practically has his own key to the Oval Office. Thanks to the special relationship with the Saudis, and because of threats against him, he is the only ambassador to the United States assigned

State Department protection. Bandar's parties are legendary; the mansion in McLean, Virginia, where he lives and entertains, is epic. Passing between the enormous iron gates just off Virginia Route 123 that guard his driveway, I wondered who and how many people were waiting for me. I had come alone because I felt that the more the prince and I could put matters on a personal footing, the greater progress we would make, now and in the future. As it turned out, Bandar had only his highly competent principal deputy with him, Rihab Massoud, in effect the Saudi deputy chief of mission to the United States.

Over the course of perhaps two hours, including lunch, the three of us kicked around more working theories of the attack. The prince and Massoud, both excellent analysts, seemed to have no more idea than the Bureau did about who might be responsible, but Bandar did have new background information to offer. I learned for the first time that Hezbollah was active in the Sunni-dominated Eastern Province of Saudi Arabia, where the bombing had occurred. Although the Hezbollah is based in Lebanon, it takes its orders and draws financial and logistic support from Tehran, particularly Iran's two security services, the Islamic Revolutionary Guards Corps (IRGC) and the Intelligence and Security Ministry (MOIS). That raised the specter that the Iranian government had known of and backed the bombing of Khobar Towers. Bandar agreed it was possible, but he doubted that was the case. For Iran to officially sanction an attack in the Saudi kingdom would be very serious, he said—a grave turn of events.

"I'll work with you and the FBI to get what you need. President Clinton told me you are in charge," the prince said near the end of our meeting. It turned out Prince Bandar was true to his word—the beginning of a friendship that grew stronger as I came to know and trust him.

"What we need first," I said, "is access for the contingent we are sending over there. We also want to talk and work directly with your police."

Bandar promised to call Prince Nayef, the Saudi interior minister, to pave the way for the small army of agents we were flying into the kingdom.

"Do you know our police?" he asked.

"Well"—I laughed—"we have an agent in Rome. . . ."

Rome was, in fact, as close as we had been able to get to stationing one of our own in the kingdom. He dealt with Riyadh the way circuit preachers used to deal with tiny remote hamlets in the Old West: twice a year or so. With Bandar's intervention, we would soon have an Arab-speaking agent living permanently in Riyadh, a huge leap forward.

As helpful as he was, Prince Bandar was not able to be completely forthright with me at that first meeting. He knew that two months earlier the Saudis had arrested a Qatif native named Fadel al-Alawe as he attempted to cross into the kingdom over the Jordanian border in a car loaded down with thirty-eight kilograms of plastic explosives. Under questioning, al-Alawe admitted to Saudi authorities that he had been involved in a series of surveillances at Khobar Towers. The car and its hidden explosives, he said, had been given to him in Beirut, and he had driven from Lebanon through Syria and Jordan to the border. By early April, three other plotters had been rounded up inside Saudi Arabia. As Bandar parceled the story out to me over the next several weeks, it became evident that the Saudis felt they had intercepted the plan and excised the terrorist cell that was to carry it out. In fact, the kingdom harbored numerous Hezbollah cells. With one rolled up, the plotters simply activated another.

Had we known about the earlier arrests, we certainly would have stepped up security at Dhahran. Quite possibly, we could have intercepted the tanker truck before it could be detonated. The nineteen dead might still be living. There's a terrible potential price for holding that type of information so close to the vest. But secrecy is a way of life in that part of the world, and Bandar, I suppose, could argue that he had let out all he could by telling me at our first meeting about the Hezbollah presence in the Eastern Province. Besides, hindsight is always 20/20. We had to deal with what was, not what could have been.

When I got back to my office, I phoned Janet Reno and Sandy Berger and told them that I'd had a very productive discussion with Bandar. The table had been set for the team we were sending. Our lab analysts and forensic experts would have access to the crime site. I met that afternoon with John Deutsch, then head of the CIA, and told him the same thing. In both instances, I passed on Prince Bandar's mention of the Hezbollah presence in eastern Saudi Arabia. That knowledge added to the stew, but in the absence of any stronger evidence, our working theory stayed as it was: Khobar was home grown, possibly connected to the earlier attack on the national guard building; for the Saudis, at least, an internal matter.

A little more than a day later, Bear Bryant, John O'Neill, a few others, and I boarded a plane at Andrews Air Force Base and followed our agents to the desert.

I would visit Saudi Arabia on multiple occasions over the next several years, but this was my first time. Until you've been there, I think, nothing can prepare you for the heat. After a seventeen-hour flight that took us through Frankfurt, Germany, in air-conditioned comfort—thanks to the Air Force's elite 89th Squadron, the same people who fly the president—I walked off the plane wearing my standard blue suit into what felt like a wall of fire. Local time was about two in the afternoon. The thermometer stood at nearly 120 degrees Fahrenheit, just another day in Dhahran.

The ultimate goal of our visit was 225 miles west, in Riyadh.

Prince Bandar had arranged for our small group to meet with the royal family, including King Fahd and Prince Nayef. Bandar had even arrived in advance of us to serve as translator. But that was for later in the evening—much later, I was to learn. For now, I wanted to visit what remained of Building 131.

The U.S. commander at the airbase, a one-star general, was on hand to greet us and escort us to Khobar Towers. He had been up, I would guess, for three straight days. Fatigue was written all over him, and a deep sense of personal responsibility that he had not done enough to protect the men and women under his charge. (And indeed he would later see his career derailed for allegedly failing to take adequate security measures at the base.)

At the crime site, the Saudis had laid down carpeting so people could watch the agents work—ours and theirs—without having to stand ankle-deep in the sand. The scene itself was staggering. The broad crater where the truck had exploded had a slick of mud-colored water across its bottom. Beyond, Building 131 looked as if some giant had ripped the front off.

The blast, clearly audible twenty miles away in Bahrain, had torn apart and scattered everything in its path. The human remains that had been discovered but not yet retrieved had been circled with red paint, a horrifying reminder of how fragile human life can be. The crime scene was littered with hairbrushes, photo frames, pieces of clothing—objects blown out of barracks rooms that no longer were surrounded by four walls.

As we approached the crime site from a distance, it seemed to be crawling with busy worker bees scurrying this way and that. Up close, the bees got a more human face. Most of them—our own agents, FBI personnel, and the Saudi police who were working alongside them—had been at it virtually nonstop for a day and a half: dealing with the body parts, using giant sifters to cull through the sand for any forensics that might be embedded there. The work is hard enough in normal conditions, physically and emotionally. Remember, people are looking for the smallest pieces of evidence; the strain on the eyes alone is monumental. Meanwhile, the temperature was slowly dropping from 120 to 110 as the afternoon wore on. I could see the exhaustion on all their faces. Some already had been treated for dehydration. Others would be. The unique smell of decaying human flesh was overwhelming, especially in the intense heat, but there was no way to hurry retrieval either. The evidentiary needs were too great.

I gathered our own people together to thank them for everything they were doing. I would be meeting with the king and his ministers later that evening, I told them, and I'd get the FBI all the help they needed and deserved. It seemed to be a boost they needed and appreciated.

An emergency hospital had been set up nearby, no more than a few hundred yards from the crater, and I went there next. The place was filled with the walking wounded—splints and bandages, facial wounds from the flying glass—and those still being examined and treated. I talked to as many of them as I could muster, mostly in smaller groups. I wanted them to know that their government was on the case, that we weren't going to rest until we found out who had done this and had brought them to justice. I was still in my midforties then, but as always when I'm around soldiers and sailors and airmen in situations like that, I was struck by how young so many of them seemed.

The images of those wounded servicemen and -women were still with me at two the next morning when our small party was finally received by King Fahd at his palace in Riyadh.

We had been flown by helicopter to Riyadh from Dhahran late that afternoon. Prince Bandar, who all of a sudden seemed to be everywhere, greeted us at the airport and led us to a "waiting palace"—in effect, a large, very modern hotel where we were to cool our heels until King Fahd sent for us. (Specific appointments are out of the question: no one is the king's equal, and thus no one can command his time. He commands yours.) For our side, at least, the break was welcomed. We had been gone for twenty-four hours by then. Most of us hadn't had a chance to shower or shave, much less change clothes or get any meaningful sleep.

I used part of the time to get an intelligence briefing from John Brennan, the CIA's chief of station in Saudi Arabia. Amazingly, John had also grown up in North Bergen, across the Hudson River from Midtown Manhattan. Now here we were, halfway around the world, swapping leads about a bombing at the eastern edge of the Arabian desert. Meanwhile, a squadron of limousines and their drivers sat in front of our holding palace, waiting to whisk us into King Fahd's presence whenever the summons came.

When the call finally did arrive, about ninety minutes after midnight, we piled into the limos only to be delayed further by what seemed like innumerable checkpoints along our route. Better than anyone else, the Saudi royals understand the perilous world they live and rule in. The king's palace, or more accurately, the palace complex, was out of a storybook: a grand and ornate confection of marble, glass, and towering minarets, all centrally air-conditioned and so secure that a mouse would have trouble sneaking in. One of the members of the royal family met us and showed us eventually to the throne room, where King Fahd was waiting.

The U.S. contingent sat to one side of the king. John Brennan hadn't come along for obvious reasons, but the acting ambassador to Saudi Arabia, Ted Kattouf, joined us. On the king's other side were Crown Prince Abdullah and most of the senior princes. Although King Fahd held the place of honor among us all, he said little other than to welcome us and express condolences for the American losses. Fahd had suffered a debilitating stroke the previous November. Succession battles within the family had been anything but easy, but the crown prince appeared to be speaking for the king.

On behalf of our side, I thanked the king and his family for receiving us, assured them all that we were here to work in cooperation with but under the aegis of the Mubahith, the Saudi equivalent of a combined FBI and CIA, and expressed our condolences for the Saudi losses at Khobar Towers. As so often is the case in terrorist attacks, these dead had been minding their own business in a park across the street from the compound when the truck bomb went off.

As I had a few days earlier with Prince Bandar, we talked about who might be responsible for the bombing and why. No one on the Saudi side even hinted that members of a Hezbollah terrorist cell were then being held on suspicion of planning a similar attack, although, like Bandar, they all must have known about the arrest on the Jordanian border. For my part, I stated the U.S. position very carefully: we didn't know who was responsible, and we didn't want to make rash assumptions. That's why we needed to conduct an investigation on Saudi soil and why we needed the maximum cooperation from the Mubahith and other agencies under the royal family's control. At a minimum, I said, we would need to have our own agents in place in Saudi Arabia for months. By now, my American colleagues had heard me make the point so often—and the hour was so late and our small party so sleep-starved—that several of them seemed on the verge of falling over where they sat. Not so on the Saudi side. They've learned to adjust to life in an arid land under a broiling sun by being nocturnal. The night was still young. As if to prove it, the king, through the crown prince, assured me that leaving FBI agents on Saudi soil would be no problem. Then he suggested that Prince Nayef and I adjourn to the Interior Ministry to discuss details.

The sort of parity of office that diplomats fret over is nearly impossible to achieve with the Saudis. As interior minister, Nayef and I shared many similar duties and responsibilities, but I was almost halfway through a ten-year appointment. His position was held by blood, for life, so long as he didn't end up on the wrong side of whoever was occupying the throne. Still, unequals that we were, we did manage to hammer out some working arrangements along with several senior Mubahith officers who had accompanied us. And then, around four o'clock in the morning, we finally sat down to dinner, a seven- or eight-course affair with blessedly few culinary surprises. I was well past hunger.

The arrangement wasn't perfect. So long as we were unable to directly question suspects—or even sit in while Saudi authorities did the questioning—we would always be investigating a vicious multiple murder with one hand tied behind our back. What's more, indictments would be hard to come by and convictions even harder to win without being able to offer such critical testimony. That, after all, is what the United States of America had promised its citizens and the world, as well as the families and loved ones of those who had been killed and grievously injured: that justice would be done. Seeing justice done was always the carrot dangling in front of our eyes.

But within the confines of a secretive and deeply conflicted culture, the Saudis, I thought, had probably gone as far as they could toward accommodating us. Pushing them further into our camp, getting them to see the investigation more through our eyes, would take pressure from the very top of our own government. And that, as the investigation wore on and more and more new information bubbled to the surface, was precisely where I found myself most stymied: not halfway around the world on the Arabian Peninsula but at home, a half dozen blocks up Pennsylvania Avenue.

Let me try to explain.

I was probably still suffering from jet lag from that initial trip to Saudi Arabia when I had my first serious conversations with Sandy Berger on how to handle the bombing. All things being equal, I told the then-deputy national security adviser, we would expect to undertake the criminal investigation. That was our statutory duty. We had the resources and talent to undertake the job, and the will to see it through. Just as important, we had the Saudis about as lined up as we were likely to get them on the front end. But all things weren't equal. That was obvious. Even though the attack had occurred on foreign soil, this had been an act of war against the United States of America. Saudis were killed, to be sure, but American military personnel had been targeted. If the president decided to take military or other action against the perpetrators, I didn't want the criminal investigation to get in the way, and I certainly didn't want the president deferring to the Department of Justice or the FBI just because he would be preempting our investigation.

In retrospect, the point I was trying to make sounds almost petty. An American military barracks was in ruins; people had been left blown apart in the blistering Saudi sun. I'd seen them there, and I would never forget the sight. To me, though, the matter I was raising was crucial, and in the months that followed, I repeated it constantly. The FBI was going after the killers with everything at our disposal. I couldn't guarantee we would ever bring them to trial, but we would continue to pursue them until we had run every last one of them to ground. But we understood that in the hierarchy of possible responses, ours was second tier. Bill Clinton was commander in chief. If he decided that we were getting in the way of more appropriate action, we would step aside.

Bill Clinton had courted me to become FBI director three years earlier, but by the early summer of 1996, fault lines were showing in our relationship. Maybe I was, in Clinton's eyes, too much the altar boy I once had been, or too insensitive to the nuances of politics. Whatever had driven a wedge between us, the strain was an open secret within the inner circle of the administration. That, too, was on my mind as I sought to clarify the Bureau's position relative to the Khobar Towers investigation: I'd fallen off the A-list at 1600 Pennsylvania Avenue. But Sandy Berger knew all that, and he was very definitive in his response every time I raised the matter: The president is clear on this, he would tell me. He wants you to conduct the investigation, and he has told the Saudis that. The FBI is in charge; Louis Freeh is the point man. The Bureau, I was assured, had the president's complete cooperation and authority on this. I remember the phrase exactly because the administration was still repeating it three years later: we were to leave "no stone unturned" in finding the killers and bringing them to justice. Trouble was, the administration's actions didn't come close to matching its rhetoric.

I traveled twice again to Saudi Arabia during the months just after that first visit. On one of those trips, Prince Bandar took me aside and told me, "Listen, we have the goods," and slowly, very slowly, with many fits and starts, the "goods" did begin to come together. As they did, they pointed ineluctably toward Iran.

(On that same trip, during a dinner at Bandar's Riyadh palace, the elegant Saudi ambassador to the U.S. reached his well-manicured hand into a roast baby camel's hump, drew out a fistful of meat, and deposited it on my plate—a great honor, he assured me. It was my one and only experience with baby camel's hump, but it was good: closer to tenderloin than chicken in flavor.)

In March 1997, in the first truly big break in the case, Canadian authorities acting on a tip from the Saudis arrested the driver of the Datsun used in the Khobar Towers bombing, Hani al-Sayegh. Al-Sayegh, who had been living in Canada since August 1996 under a false passport, denied any part in the attack, but that May, under questioning in an Ottawa detention center by an assistant U.S. attorney and several FBI agents, he did admit to having once been a member of the Hezbollah cell that carried it out. He had been recruited for the cell, he said, by the Iranian Revolutionary Guard and had taken part in two operations directed by one of the Guard's brigadier generals, Ahmad Sherifi.

Two months later, in mid-July, the Syrian government turned over to the Saudis Mustafa al-Qassab, another member of the Hezbollah cell responsible for the Khobar attack and like many of them a Qatif native. Not long after that, at a meeting in Pakistan, outgoing Iranian president Hashemi Rafsanjani essentially admitted to Saudi crown prince Abdullah that the Khobar attack had been planned and carried out with the knowledge of the Iranian supreme ruler, Ayatollah Khamenei.

Simultaneously, the Saudis were sending the same signals to the administration. Within the first months after the attack, Prince Bandar and Rihab Massoud had met with Tony Lake, still then the national security adviser, and Sandy Berger to prepare them for the likelihood of an Iranian connection to the Khobar Towers attack and to hash over the implications. This was four years before 9/11, remember. The bombing appeared to be the work of Hezbollah, Iran's exclusive terrorist agent, and at that point, Hezbollah, not al Qaeda, held the grim distinction of having slaughtered more Americans than any other terrorist organization.

A blind pig couldn't have missed the outlines, but to flesh out the connections and put the dots together, we needed permission for FBI agents to sit in on and help conduct the questioning of suspects held in Saudi custody. That, we were told time and again—by Bandar and others—could happen only if the president and his top people exerted pressure on Crown Prince Abdullah and King Fahd to make it happen.

In the White House, though, and at the State Department in Foggy Bottom, interest was headed in another direction. In May 1997, Mohammad Khatami was elected to succeed Rafsanjani as president of Iran. "Moderate" is a relative term in a country as radicalized at the top as Iran, but to the Clinton foreign-policy team, Khatami seemed the best hope for moving toward a normalization of relations between the two countries, and it soon became apparent that the Khobar Towers investigation was not going to get in the way of that.

The FBI didn't report to the State Department, but we needed its authorization to send our agents there. Suddenly, authorizations became far harder to secure. State was after us on another front as well. We had begun fingerprinting and making photos of all the athletes that Iran sent to the U.S. Our reasoning was simple: intelligence officers were almost always embedded in the teams. They would come here, make contacts, run a few sources, and head back home to Tehran with some friendly State Department liaison waving good-bye at the airport. We thought the fingerprints and photos would discourage the practice, and indeed it did, but it also raised the Iranians' ire, and finally that ire bubbled all the way up to the White House, which ordered us to stop the practice.

Not a good idea, I told Madeleine Albright, who had succeeded Warren Christopher as secretary of state.

"The Iranians are complaining," she responded.

"Of course, they are," I told her. "That's the point." But to no avail. Later, her assistant secretary for the Middle East, Martin Indyk, would tell us that the president was, in fact, furious. By then, I was used to it.

This is not to say that many great and dedicated people in Washington did not offer their much-needed support on Khobar. Porter Goss and Arlen Specter, most notably, never wavered in their help and encouraged me to follow through with our investigation at whatever political cost. But that was coming from Capitol Hill. We needed the Executive Branch on our side, too.

The State Department, at least, was transparent in trying to thwart our dealings with the Saudis over Khobar Towers. The White House was far more opaque and, thus, more maddening. We would get word that the president or Al Gore was about to meet with Crown Prince Abdullah or one of the other very senior members of the royal family. Forewarned, we would put together a list of talking points leading up to a request for greater cooperation with our investigation and take them to Sandy Berger, by then the national security adviser and our designated point man on such matters, and Sandy would assure us that gaining access to the Saudi witnesses was one of the president's (or vice president's) highest priorities and that he was sure to bring it up. Then we would wait. And wait. And nothing would happen.

"Didn't the matter come up?" I would ask Sandy.

"Oh, it came up," he would assure me, "but in another context." Whatever that meant. Meanwhile, Prince Bandar, whom I had begun to alert about these talking-point opportunities, would shake his head the next time I saw him and wonder why Clinton or Gore had failed to raise the matter in anything like an urgent way.

Then, in September 1997, the Justice Department, my employer, moved to dismiss the indictment we had obtained against Hani al-Sayegh, who had been nabbed in Canada. The reasons are complicated. Al-Sayegh was a pain in the neck. He suffered frequent changes of heart. Because we were being frustrated in our attempts to interview the cell members being held in Saudi Arabia, we had no corroborating witnesses for al-Sayegh even if we could have gotten him to talk. As a lawyer, I understood all that. But al-Sayegh had been our foot in the door, and what I saw as the almost celebratory attitude at the White House in getting rid of him sat poorly with me. Three months later almost to the day, on December 11, 1997, I met at the FBI's training academy in Quantico, Virginia, with the families of those who had been killed at Khobar Towers.

The impetus behind the Quantico assembly was simple. Nearly a year and a half had passed since the attack at Dhahran, and neither the State Department nor the Department of Defense had spent any real time briefing the families of the Khobar victims. Understandably, the families were very upset. We couldn't bring back their loved ones, but we could let the mothers and fathers, the wives and husbands and brothers and sisters, the fiancées and the children know that their dead hadn't been forgotten. I invited Sandy Berger to join us and add his perspective from the National Security Council. He declined. So did all the major White House figures. Janet Reno was there from Justice. Bill Cohen, the former Republican senator from Maine who had replaced Les Aspin as secretary of defense, showed up too. I'm still grateful to both of them. They were supportive and honest, and their presence was greatly appreciated.

The meetings lasted three days, and I was there for every moment of them and every meal: morning, noon, and night. We had a scale model of Building 131 and its crater to explain the explosion, and a slide show of the suspects we had so far identified. I didn't have to tell these people that the Saudis had been slow to provide information or that the Clinton administration had been reluctant to press the Saudis harder. They already knew.

When the families asked me to promise that the FBI would continue its investigation and do everything we could to see justice done, I vowed that we would do that. As I wrote earlier, that was always the prize in front of us. When one woman, the mother of a thirty-five-year-old master sergeant who had died in the attack, asked why we let the Saudis get away with withholding information and access, I told her that I was a policeman, not a politician. I meant both things, but I empathized deeply with her sense of being let down by her own country after her son had given his life for America.

The White House had never pulled us off the case, never told us that the administration was pursuing other avenues or policies that served other ends, never said stop. Until they did, we would not rest or turn away. I had cut my teeth as an FBI agent working to bring down some of the biggest organized crime families in America. Later, as an assistant and deputy U.S. attorney, I had prosecuted mafiosi who killed people almost casually. As a federal judge, I'd seen what happens when the government fails to be honest with the people it governs. We might bargain away a sentence for testimony to land a bigger fish, but we didn't walk away from murder. And we didn't close the books on nineteen dead just because it suddenly became inconvenient to pursue the matter. Yet all the evidence I could see suggested that's exactly what we were doing.

As 1998 wore on, Bill Clinton was pursuing rapprochement with the Iranians and finding himself in increasingly hot water domestically. Ken Starr was dogging the president; Monica Lewinsky had become maybe the best-known White House intern in history. Meanwhile, Khobar Towers was sliding further and further toward the back burner. By summer, the number of our agents stationed in Saudi Arabia had sunk from several dozen to a lone legal attaché. At one meeting, I can't remember exactly when, Sandy Berger made mention of the seventeen people who had been killed in the attack.

"Look," I said, "there were nineteen killed, not seventeen." I tried to say it as an aside, without putting the full weight behind it of the incredible frustration I was feeling, and I must have succeeded because my little correction slid right by everyone present. It was just Louie being a pain in the ass again about Khobar as far as they were concerned.

I should say here, since Sandy Berger has been fairly prominent in this story so far, that I had absolutely nothing against him personally. He was always a gentleman, always respectful of the Bureau and of me. Unlike a lot of people in the White House, he was punctual, too: If Sandy called a meeting for 10 A.M., you could pretty much count on it starting at 10 A.M. That's worth gold in Washington as far as I'm concerned.

But Sandy had come out of the political side of the Clinton machine. He'd been part of the campaign. Even when he was deputy national security adviser, he sat in on the once-a-week political meetings at the White House, and they weren't discussing foreign policy. Unlike his predecessor, Tony Lake, who had a long academic and professional background in foreign affairs, Sandy had been a trade lawyer with the Washington mega-firm of Hogan and Hartson.

Don't get me wrong: Sandy did have a very sincere interest in foreign policy—of that I'm certain—but the lens through which he seemed to view everything was the politics of getting Bill Clinton reelected and, later, of preserving Clinton's legacy and the Democratic party's hold on the presidency. Among other things, that meant shortchanging the needs of the Khobar Tower families. Or so I read the situation. But I wasn't out of resources.

That September, Crown Prince Abdullah and his entourage took over the entire 143-room Hay-Adams Hotel, just across Lafayette Park from the White House, for six days. The visit, I figured, was pretty much our last chance.

Again, we prepared talking points for the president. Again, I contacted Prince Bandar and asked him to soften up the crown prince for the moment when Clinton—or Al Gore, I didn't care who—would raise the matter and start to exert the necessary pressure. And again, nothing happened. Sandy Berger would later insist that Clinton had leaned hard on Abdullah for cooperation, but that's not the way I heard it. The story that came back to me, from "usually reliable sources," as they say in Washington, was that Bill Clinton briefly raised the subject only to tell the crown prince that he certainly understood the Saudis' reluctance to cooperate. Then, according to my sources, he hit Abdullah up for a contribution to the still-to-be-built Clinton presidential library. Gore, who was supposed to press hardest of all in his meeting with the crown prince, barely mentioned the matter, I was told.

In testimony before the Joint Intelligence Committees on October 8, 2002, I described for members of Congress the many difficult matters that had to be overcome in order that the Bureau might gain access to the Saudi nationals who were being held in the kingdom and who had already admitted to taking part in the Khobar bombing. We didn't want to taint the suspects' prosecution under Islamic law. We understood, too, what an ugly can of worms we would be opening, in Washington and Riyadh, if we could show that senior Iranian officials had been behind the Khobar attack. History was against us also: No FBI agent there had ever been given direct access to a detained Saudi national.

"Despite these extremely sensitive and complex issues," I told the committees, "the Saudis put their own interests aside to aid the FBI and the United States. Supported by Prince Bandar, Prince Nayef, and the Saudi Mubahith, Crown Prince Abdullah decided to grant the FBI's request to interview the detainees."

That's part of the story, but it's not the whole story. I was guilty of a sin of omission before the committee members. A president was instrumental in our gaining access to the Saudi detainees, but it wasn't President Bill Clinton.

The debacle of the meetings during the Hay-Adams Hotel stay had convinced me that we were never going to be able to achieve justice for the Khobar victims, or closure for their families and loved ones, by sticking with the status quo. The job wasn't getting done. From the administration's point of view, the case was a diminishing asset. Nor could I appeal directly to the Oval Office for a change of heart. By the fall of 1998 I had been Bill Clinton's top cop for half a decade, but he hadn't spoken to me in two years.

I did, however, know another president. George H. W. Bush and I had had a casual and friendly relationship ever since he had made me a federal district judge during the third year of his administration. Sometimes I would call the first President Bush for advice; other times he would simply phone to chat. It was during one of those conversations, in late September 1998, that the former president happened to mention that he was going to see Crown Prince Abdullah that Saturday.

"If you don't mind my asking," I said, "what are you going to talk about?"

It was a personal visit, Bush told me. Over many years, he and the crown prince had gotten to know each other very well. Abdullah was passing through Washington again, this time on his way to Hawaii. They were meeting at Prince Bandar's mansion in McLean.

"Well," I said, "would you mind making a request on our behalf?"

"Sure."

"We're trying to get FBI agents to see the detainees in the Khobar Towers bombing. If the crown prince heard the request from you, I think it would be very effective."

I made sure I was up-front with George Bush. I had no intention of using him to do an end run around his successor without his being in on the plan. We're at an impasse, I told him. We've been trying to get our position to the Saudis at a high enough level to make a difference, but every time I seem to have assurances from on high in our administration that the matter will be brought up with the right people at the right time, it never is. Your help could go a long way to resolving this, I told the former president, but I don't want to put you in an uncomfortable position. I wasn't exaggerating on that last point. I didn't, but I felt as if I had run out of other alternatives for fulfilling the promise that had been made twenty-seven months earlier when the dust was still settling over the ruins of Building 131.

When the ex-president agreed, to my great delight, I wrote out talking points and faxed them to him. Then I sat back and waited, but not for long.

"I raised it," Bush said when he called me that Saturday afternoon. "They seem interested. I think you'll be hearing from them."

I did, on Monday morning, from Prince Bandar.

"Louie," he said, "can you come out here and talk with the crown prince?"

A few hours later, on September 29, 1998, I was being waved through Bandar's gates again, this time along with Dale Watson, the FBI antiterrorism chief, and Wyche Fowler, the ambassador to Saudi Arabia, who happened to be back in the States at the time. Straight and dedicated, Fowler was putting himself at risk by challenging the White House to do the right thing on this case. Dale ran our counterterrorism (or CT) section and later the newly formed CT Division, and was my right hand in the most important FBI cases of the decade, the single best–qualified and knowledgeable CT leader and expert we had. None of the FBI's progress in this area would have happened without him.

"Tell me what you need," the crown prince said after he had received us.

"We need Your Highness to get our agents into the facility where the Khobar detainees are being held so we can interview them and come back to our courts and make the case against them."

I assured him that we, the United States and the FBI, respected the Sharia and promised we would do all in our power not to corrupt the Saudi investigation or prosecution. But the gist of my statement was exactly what I had been trying to get someone at the top of the food chain to say to Crown Prince Abdullah all along: we need access.

The crown prince proposed a compromise. Our agents could submit questions to be put to the suspects by Saudi officials, and we could monitor the answers directly. When I agreed, he turned to Bandar and told him to call Prince Nayef with instructions that our agents could have access to the detainees as outlined above. After all the waiting, all the runaround, all the frustration, that was it.

I have no doubt that, but for President Bush's personal intervention, we would never have gotten access to those critical witnesses. When I was finally able to tell the Khobar families about "41's" role, they were extraordinarily grateful. I am also certain that "41"—war hero, model public servant, and one of the primary architects of the Soviet Empire's collapse during his presidency—will be long regarded for his integrity, leadership, and historic accomplishments.

(I should add that when I first prepared to tell this story, in an article for the *Wall Street Journal,* I checked with former president Bush to see if he minded being named in print as the key intermediary. "Fire away!" he said, consistent to the end. I also got Prince Bandar's permission to tell the story.)

Six weeks later, on November 9, FBI agents sat behind a one-way mirror at a Riyadh detention center while Mubahith officials asked 212 questions of eight separate detainees. In the new spirit of cooperation, the Saudis also gave us access to transcripts from other detainees as well as physical evidence they had collected for their own prosecution. The answers, along with the new materials and information we had previously uncovered or been handed by the Saudis, showed almost beyond a doubt that the Khobar Tower attacks had been sanctioned, funded, and directed by senior officials of the government of Iran. The Ministry of Intelligence and Security and the Iranian Revolutionary Guard had both been in on the planning and execution. The bombers had been trained by Iranians in the Bekaa Valley of Lebanon, where the Iranian-backed Hezbollah is based. They had been issued passports by the Iranian embassy in Damascus, Syria, that allowed them to cross the border into Saudi Arabia.

To me, it was a devastating indictment. I went to Janet Reno with the news, once the picture had become clear, and told her we had to brief Sandy Berger. We immediately briefed Sandy in his corner office in the White House's fabled West Wing. His incredible response: "Who knows about this?" Sandy then opined that this was all hearsay. That was nonsense. Our sources were part of the conspiracy.

Later on, Sandy convened another meeting in the West Wing's Situation Room. Bill Cohen was there; army general Henry Shelton, the rock-solid Chairman of the Joint Chiefs of Staff; CIA director George Tenet—all the principals, the usual suspects. I thought that we were meeting to discuss what our next move would be, given the fact that we now had solid evidence that Iranians, with involvement at the highest official levels, had blown up nineteen Americans. But I was wrong. The meeting started with how to deal with the press and with Congress, should news of the Iranian involvement in the Khobar murders leak outside of the room.

Remarkably (although that's an insufficient word), Sandy's people had prepared a script A and script B for spinning the story once it did become public: script A for Republicans on the Hill, script B for those nosy reporters from *The Washington Post* and *The New York Times,* etc. Clearly, someone had been having a nightmare that featured a headline along the lines of "FBI Investigation Determines Iran Responsible for Khobar Attack."

"Wait a minute," I finally said, "are we going to talk about the fact that Iranians killed nineteen Americans?"

I wasn't the only person in the room who wanted to do that: General Shelton did. Others did. But it was Sandy's meeting, not ours, and the national security adviser had other things on his mind. It seemed we were here to *manage* the issue, not do a damn thing about it.

At some point, I tried to catch George Tenet's eye to give him one of those "What the hell is going on?" looks. Instead, I had to wait to buttonhole him as we were walking out of the meeting.

"Do you believe that?" I asked.

"We have a lot of meetings like that around here," George answered.

George, General Shelton, and the Joint Chiefs were my staunchest allies. Once the Iranian sponsorship was clear, General Shelton invited me over to the storied "tank" at the Pentagon to give him a briefing. There, the Marine Corps commandant, Chuck Krulak, known for his candor and integrity, committed himself to doing whatever was necessary to bring the Khobar bombers to justice, even if that meant taking on the White House.

In the eight years I was to spend as FBI director, there was nothing to match that moment in the Situation Room for sheer disappointment. It's a terrible story, but there's a better postscript.

Thanks to our continuing—and continually improving— relationship with the Saudis and the Mubahith, we did finally get direct access to the Saudi detainees, and not just to those we had already seen from behind the one-way mirror. In the year 2000, we were able to question for the first time a Saudi Shi-ite named Mustafa al-Qassab. In the late 1980s, al-Qassab had traveled from Saudi Arabia to Iran to meet with Ahmed al-Mughassil, the commander of the military wing of the Saudi Hezbollah. Now, a decade later, al-Qassab laid out for us in detail the planning and logistics that had gone into the Khobar attack, traced the lineage irrefutably back to Tehran, and as far as I was concerned tied the whole package together for good. We still had to work our way around a wrong opinion from a prosecutor in the U.S. Attorney's Office for the District of Columbia, a civil lawyer who had little knowledge of criminal law. But she, too, passed, as did the Clinton-Gore administration and its apparent indifference to Khobar Towers.

In my first postinauguration meeting with George W. Bush, I raised the issue of the ongoing investigation into the bombing and told him and Vice President Cheney about my frustrations. The president quickly assessed the situation and understood completely the implications of Iranian involvement. He suggested I talk to Condoleezza Rice, which I did that afternoon. Condi was a breath of fresh air, as she too sized up the situation and told me to pursue the indictment, letting the chips fall where they may. (We are fortunate to have her now as our secretary of state.) She sent me on to the new attorney general, and John Ashcroft let me have my new prosecutor of choice, James B. Comey Jr. John's complete support and decisiveness in this important case was greatly appreciated and allowed us to get an indictment, and Jim Comey was just the guy to handle the matter.

I'd come to know Jim in New York when he was a young assistant U.S. attorney there. Later, he had gotten himself assigned to the office in Richmond, in his native Virginia, where he was doing a bang-up job of prosecuting federal gun crimes and sending a lot of very dangerous people to jail. (Jim would go on to become U.S. attorney in my old stomping grounds, the Southern District of New York, and later became the deputy attorney general of the United States. At six feet ten inches, he's hard to miss in a crowd.) Within forty-five days, Jim Comey had accomplished what an entire administration had failed to do over the course of four and a half years. I will always be grateful for his leadership and pursuit of justice. On June 21, 2001, a federal grand jury in Alexandria, Virginia, returned a forty-six-count indictment against fourteen defendants charged with bombing the Khobar Towers housing complex and murdering nineteen Americans.

The timing of the indictment was not by chance. Had we failed to bring the charges by June 26, a number of the counts would have been barred by the five-year statute of limitations. There was a second reason, though, why June 21 was important. Many of the family members of those killed at Khobar Towers had gathered in Washington that day for a fifth-anniversary commemoration at Arlington National Cemetery, where a number of the murdered airmen were buried. I couldn't tell them in advance that the indictment was pending: grand jury proceedings are secret. Nor could I promise the families that, even with the indictment, anyone would ever come to trial. As I write, the case is still open and pending. Warrants have been issued for the fourteen defendants and lodged with Interpol, but these are not people who are going to rush to turn themselves in to the nearest federal marshal or U.S. embassy. No grand jury indictment is ever anything more than just a piece of paper, but to these families, this particular one meant an enormous amount. It said that the government had followed up; that despite all the roadblocks and detours, we had remained committed to doing justice; that we were finally as good as our word.

(In his autobiography, *My Life,* Bill Clinton misstates not only the number of injured at Khobar Towers—"almost 300" in his account, as opposed to the 372 actually wounded—but the facts of the attack. He also appears to have somehow conflated the resolution of Khobar with that of the earlier attack on the Saudi National Guard building in Riyadh. "Eventually," Clinton writes, "Saudi Arabia would execute the people it determined to be responsible for the attack." Not so. Whether Clinton's mistakes resulted from speed of composition or indifference to the fate of those killed at Khobar and their survivors, I'm not prepared to say.)

For me, too, the Arlington ceremony was a form of closure. I had informed President Bush on May 1 that I would be resigning as director of the FBI by the end of June; now I was literally on my way out the door. Chairs had been set up on a green rug at the cemetery. Sitting there, waiting my turn to address the families, I was reminded of another outdoor rug, this one in the desert under a relentless sun. In my mind's eye, I could see the debris, the body parts outlined with red paint. Khobar Towers had been, I think, the biggest test for me, the case I felt the deepest about during my eight years as director of the Bureau. Now I had delivered on my own promise—something to feel good about in the storm of emotion that overwhelmed me at that moment.

Afterward, the families came back to my office for lunch. The place was a mess—boxes stacked on boxes—but my wonderful secretary, Noreen Gawley, who had been with me ever since my days as a judge and is with me still, managed to clear some space and provide us with a meal, even some beer to share if memory serves. We had a wonderful time talking, especially now that the indictments had been brought in, but my guests had an ulterior motive. They had pooled together and had two commemorative plaques made up for me. Two of the mothers, Fran Heiser and Catherine Adams, rose as we were finishing lunch to present them.

For any director of the FBI plaques are almost a plague. They come from every angle: the Boy Scouts of America, the State Police of Mongolia. At the end of your tour of duty, the government boxes them up and mails them to you, and then mails you a bill for the postage. I've got plaques I have probably never seen, dozens of them I've long since forgotten about. But not these. Not ever. One had been signed by all the survivors, children included, and decorated with nineteen purple hearts. At the center was this inscription: "To Louis Freeh, the Most Honest Man in Washington." I don't believe that for a second, but I know the depth of feeling out of which they composed that message, the despair that nothing might ever get done, that their dead might simply be forgotten. I'm proud that didn't happen.

June 21, 2001, was my last official day as director of the FBI, the final curtain on twenty-six years of public service. Two years remained on my statutory ten-year term, but I'd finished most of what I wanted to do in Washington.

CHAPTER 2

"Only If I Yell 'Duck!'"

Noon was my jogging time, a chance to escape the pressures of being a federal judge. My route was always the same—through East River Park and back again—and so regular was my regimen that the guards at the U.S. Courthouse on Foley Square in lower Manhattan had long ago stopped gawking when one of their distinguished jurists showed up at the door dressed like a gym rat. Today, though, I was wearing a suit when I came down the granite steps, not running gear. The date was Friday, July 16, 1993, and I was headed to Washington, D.C., to meet with Bill Clinton at the White House. If the president liked what he heard, he was going to offer me the position of director of the Federal Bureau of Investigation. If I liked what I heard, I was going to accept.

If only it had been that simple, but in Washington almost nothing is.

The fact that I was being considered at all by the White House for the job was a classic happenstance of politics. Ever since he'd taken office, Bill Clinton had been determined to get rid of the FBI director he inherited from the first President Bush: Judge William S.

Sessions, then less than five years through his statutory ten-year term. Clinton had cover for the move. Outgoing Republican attorney general Bill Barr had recommended it. The judge had thrown his own fuel on the fire, too. The bill of particulars against him included numerous incidents that could be interpreted as using his office for personal gain: business trips to San Francisco, where his daughter danced in the ballet; a security fence around his house that Sessions's wife insisted be more aesthetically appealing than the usual government issue. Bill Sessions is an honorable man and I still think the case against him was mostly bunk, but blood was in the water, and the capital was buzzing that the new administration was trying to politicize the Bureau.

The president had wanted to replace Sessions with his old Oxford pal, Richard Stearns, an able lawyer who later became a very respected district judge in Boston. Before he could do so, though, the first of many Clinton scandals bubbled up from far down in the bureaucracy. What became known inevitably as Travelgate was basically a patronage dust-up. Opponents in and out of government claimed that the Clintons and others were using the FBI to house-clean the White House Travel Office to make way for cousin Cornelia. It all blew over quickly enough, but the public already had early doubts about the president's allegiance to strict ethical standards. Add Travelgate to that mix, and it became politically difficult, if not impossible, for the president to put a friend into the sensitive job of FBI director.

Thus it was that the administration decided to find a "stranger" to run the FBI. Not so strangely, maybe, I involuntarily became the one under consideration. I had, after all, spent six years as an FBI agent in New York City and another ten years there with the U.S. Attorney's Office, winning convictions in some of the office's highest-profile cases, in the nation's highest-profile venue. Like Sessions and his predecessor, William Webster, I also had experience as a U.S. district judge. I'd even put in some time in Washington at what was then the new, massive J. Edgar Hoover Building on Pennsylvania Avenue Northwest.

In 1980, after completing one of the Bureau's first organized crime–labor racketeering cases, I was ordered to headquarters to set up a labor racketeering program in the Organized Crime Section. I can't claim the ten months I spent in the capital were the happiest time of my life professionally. The transition from fast-moving investigations, informants, and wise-guy subjects to a windowless room deep in the bowels of the Hoover Building left me feeling suffocated, and I jumped at the chance to get back to the streets of New York via the U.S. Attorney's Office for the Southern District of New York. Personally, though, Washington proved a bonanza. Not only did I get the chance to work with the legendary agent Jules Bonavolonta—my mentor and close friend—I also met a gorgeous redhead from Pittsburgh named Marilyn Coyle, an exceptional paralegal in the Bureau's Civil Rights Unit whom I would have the undeserved good fortune to marry.

Politically, too, I wasn't a bad match for what the Clinton people seemed to be seeking. When I was first old enough to vote, I registered as a Democrat, but that was mainly in deference to my dad, a part-time ward worker for the party in Hudson County, New Jersey. In the years since, both the Hatch Act and my own lack of interest in partisan politics had kept me from associating closely with either party. Senator Alphonse D'Amato had recommended me and Sterling Johnson for judgeships in Manhattan and Brooklyn, respectively, and introduced us to the press at his New York City office. (I later recommended Sterling to replace me as director. A former New York City police officer, federal and state prosecutor, and navy veteran, Sterling was an excellent judge, with the experience, credibility, and—most important—independence to be a great FBI director.) D'Amato, of course, was a Republican, but when a reporter asked him about my party affiliation, the senator, for one of the few times in his life, I'm sure, had no idea what to say. "You know," he finally blurted out, "that's a good question and I don't know." In fact, at no time during the nominating process did D'Amato or anyone in authority ask me what party I belonged to. If someone had, I'm not sure what I would have answered. I always respected D'Amato after that, and our New York City and Italo-American roots led us to be friends.

Finally, and President Clinton would come to regret this, I'd never been anyone's water carrier. Integrity and independence make or break an FBI director. The incumbent has to be able to say no to the attorney general or even the president if no is the right answer. Functioning as merely another direct report and saluting the "General" in all matters was not the role envisioned by Congress when it gave the director a ten-year term, removable only for cause, not disagreement with an improper or unlawful command.

Once, the secretary of state and attorney general asked me to deploy our Hostage Rescue Team (HRT), the FBI's most elite special operations group, to Bosnia in order to find and arrest fugitives wanted by the United Nations tribunal for Balkan War Crimes. I considered the matter but then I said no—the mission was too dangerous for our agents and could not be logistically supported by military or intelligence operations. I later found out that the secretary of defense had declined to send special operations military personnel for the same assignment after he determined it was too dangerous.

Examples of this are endless. Once, early in the new Bush administration, the acting deputy attorney general told me that the "Department's" priorities would be guns, drugs, and juvenile crimes. My response was that terrorism, complex economic crimes, and just about everything else we were doing domestically and internationally was of more import. The response I got was "Those are our marching orders," to which I said, "Those aren't my marching orders." Lockstep, blind obedience by the director to an attorney general without questioning potentially unlawful or even dumb orders is a formula for disaster—both for the FBI and the nation.

So, looking back, I can see why I might have made someone's shortlist for the director's job, but the first indication that I actually was on the list came from another of my mentors, John S. Martin. John had been the one who hired me for the U.S. Attorney's Office back in the early 1980s, a risky move given my lack of experience. More to the point for this purpose, John was an old friend of new White House counsel Bernard Nussbaum, and Bernie, it seemed, had called him to feel out my suitability for the director's job. After my shock wore off, John and I had a good laugh at the irony that he might be a conduit for forcing me back to the Hoover Building after rescuing me from the place only a decade earlier.

I told John what I deeply believed: that I wasn't the least bit tempted. He was quick to agree that I would be crazy to forgo the lifetime tenure of a federal judge for a political post that had all the tranquility of a lightning rod in a thunderstorm. Still, John said, I should at least talk to Nussbaum and tell him myself that I wasn't a candidate.

Every lawyer in New York worth the title knew and respected Bernie Nussbaum. He'd come up through the same U. S. Attorney's Office where I had cut my teeth, and he'd gone on to earn a well-deserved reputation as both a brash and brilliant litigator and a man of the highest integrity. Bernie was thick with the Clintons, too. Back in the mid-1970s, he had hired a new Yale Law School graduate named Hillary Rodham to assist him when he was serving as congressional counsel for the impeachment of Richard Nixon. Bernie liked to tell people that when Hillary introduced him to her boyfriend, Bill Clinton, in the late '70s, she nonchalantly described him as a future president of the United States. No sooner had that prediction come true than Bernie's New York friends began making book on whether he would choose to be White House counsel or U.S. attorney for the Southern District of New York. Bernie had chosen to be Mr. Inside, and that had led him to me.

In our first telephone conversation, I politely told Bernie that I was honored to be considered but that I had no interest in leaving my job to become director. He was charming and pleasant as he persuaded me that I should at least come to Washington to talk to him about the post. Even if I had no desire to be a candidate, we agreed, I could shed some light on whom the White House should be looking for to replace Judge Sessions, once they officially got rid of him. How could I say no? We set the get-together for late April.

On that early visit, Bernie, his deputy, Vince Foster, and I talked for maybe an hour in Bernie's West Wing office about the FBI and the issues we thought were important in selecting the next director. Then Bernie took me to meet Attorney General Janet Reno at the Department of Justice Building, on Pennsylvania and Constitution Avenues, between Ninth and Tenth Streets. Completed in 1934 at a cost of $10 million, Justice was built on a monumental scale, and the massive fifth-floor conference room next to Janet's office is no exception.

I could remember being sent there in January 1981 by then FBI director Bill Webster to argue that Democratic senator Howard Cannon of Nevada should be included in a public corruption indictment as had been recommended by the Bureau's Organized Crime Strike Force. To me, the case was obvious. Cannon had clearly gone along with efforts by the Teamsters Union to defeat a trucking deregulation bill introduced by Ted Kennedy. Deputy Attorney General Charles Renfrew, to whom I made my case, agreed in principle but declined to include Cannon because Justice had already told the Senate Ethics Committee that he would not be part of the indictment. After the jury convicted Cannon's coconspirators of bribery, jury members asked—reasonably enough—why the senator had been left out. Still later, on January 20, 1983, one of those convicted, Allen Dorfman, was gunned down in Chicago while awaiting sentencing.

The attorney general's office is large enough to house a small dining area and a lounge up a small flight of stairs, where Bobby Kennedy liked to take naps, but compared to the conference room next door, the office seemed cozy, even intimate. Janet Reno herself was perfectly delightful. By the end of our brief meeting, though, I found myself wondering exactly why I had been summoned to Washington. Janet and Bernie seemed to be going out of their way not to mention any of the controversy that had swirled around the Bureau, Justice, or the White House in the few months since Bill Clinton had been inaugurated. As I recall, no one mentioned Travelgate or the fact that Judge Sessions had dug his heels in and seemed to have no intention of leaving of his own volition. Given the "Nanny" turmoil that engulfed the administration's first two choices for attorney general—another "-gate" that ultimately had landed Janet Reno in the job—I was also surprised that no one wanted to know if I had a similar skeleton in my closet.

The biggest silence in the room that day was Waco, Texas. The bloody end of the Branch Davidian standoff there was less than two weeks old. More than seventy people had died inside the compound. The TV footage of the fires that had engulfed the place were still red-hot in the public memory. In their aftermath, the attorney general and the Bureau had both come under withering criticism, some of it from people who seemed to forget that the entire sequence had been set in motion nearly two months earlier when four Alcohol, Tobacco, and Firearms agents were gunned down by cult members. I feel fairly certain we mentioned the matter, but only in passing. It was clear to me that no one wanted to get into the nitty-gritty of that.

Pondering my meetings as I headed back to New York that evening, two interpretations seemed possible to me. Either I was the only candidate for the job, so that substantive discussion about the serious issues facing the Bureau was unnecessary, or I was not a very serious candidate at all. It didn't take me long to come down in my own mind on the latter side, which was just fine with me. I'd had an affable day with pleasant people, April was maybe the prettiest time of the year to visit the capital, and now I could go back to a job I loved, surrounded by dear colleagues and friends and plenty of challenges.

When July rolled around and two months had passed quietly, I was sure I was right. Bernie seemed to have taken my word that I wasn't interested. Even better, no one had floated my name for the post to see what kind of flak it might draw—an old Washington practice that can leave plenty of scars. Only Marilyn, Bob Bucknam, John Martin, a few other close friends, and the inside-the-loop crew in Washington even knew I had been approached. Like everyone else with a vested interest in the Bureau, I was curious what the administration was going to do, but I also thought I had a good candidate to replace Judge Sessions. My old boss Floyd Clarke, the Bureau's number-two man, had all the skills necessary to make an excellent director. If anyone in D.C. had asked my opinion, I would have recommended Floyd for the permanent job.

I also was on the verge of solving a time crunch that was leaving me too little space for what I care most about: my family. In 1981, shortly after we were married, Marilyn and I had bought a home in North Bergen, New Jersey, only a few blocks from where I had grown up and within fairly easy commuting distance—by Gotham standards—from my office in lower Manhattan. By rising before dawn, I could generally get in a good run, leave home by 6:15 or so, and be at work no more than thirty to forty-five minutes later. Then, in 1991, just as the first President Bush was about to nominate me for the federal judgeship, I got a call from someone in the White House Counsel's Office who wanted to vet a few final details. Was

I, for example, a resident of the Southern District of New York, on which bench I would be serving?

No, I said, we live in New Jersey. Was that going to be a problem? (Somewhere in the back of my mind, I think, I was aware of this, but I had been going full bore on a case that involved lots of travel back and forth to Georgia.)

Oh, no, my caller assured me, just buy a little condo or apartment in Manhattan. That'll take care of it.

"You probably haven't looked at my financial statement," I shot back, stunned at the prospect.

Marilyn and I solved that dilemma by quickly buying a house in Katonah at the northern extreme of Westchester County. Our new home was affordable, barely, and large enough for a family that had grown to include three sons, but it left me with a grinding sixty-mile, ninety-minute commute to work. (And incidentally forced me to switch my jogging schedule to midday.) I wasn't about to give up my job—or so I thought—but when the call went out for judges willing to transfer to a soon-to-be-opened auxiliary courthouse being built in White Plains, only half an hour from Katonah, I jumped at the chance. The great chief judge and all-around great guy Charlie Brieant and I had all but sealed the deal down to my courtroom and chambers, even my new furniture, when Bernie Nussbaum called again.

Just as I had two months earlier, I told Bernie that I wasn't interested, but this time he was raising the stakes. My prior FBI experience and the recent tradition of selecting sitting federal judges for the director's post made me the ideal candidate, he said. Then he cut to the chase: What would I say if the president offered me the job? Since I honestly didn't know the answer and had convinced myself that the matter would never be raised, I countered with a question of my own: Why doesn't the president ask me and we'll both see what I say? That, Bernie informed me, was unacceptable. The president of the United States was not going to make such an offer unless he knew that I would say yes.

Round and round we went until I finally agreed to meet with the president. After we had interviewed each other, we would see if we could come to an agreement. That way, no one would have to lose face, but I had one stipulation that I insisted on in advance. If I read my name in the newspapers in connection with the director's job, it was all over. Bernie agreed and promised to personally handle all arrangements for the visit in order to avoid any publicity.

It wasn't until after I hung up that I realized why I had been able to dictate the conditions for my meeting with Bill Clinton. Whatever had occurred during the intervening two months had taken the selection to me. I was the only one being considered. The fact that I really didn't care about being picked for the post—that I hadn't done one thing or asked one person to help me lobby for the job—put me in the best position, I figured, and not just for the president's and my head-to-head. It had to be obvious to the White House now that, if nominated and confirmed, I would be a completely apolitical and independent director—exactly the kind of person the country needs in an office of such immense importance.

In its own way, the U.S. Courthouse at Foley Square is as impressive as the Justice Department building itself. One of the last designs by the famous architect Cass Gilbert, the courthouse was finished two years after Justice, in 1936. Both were part of the massive public building projects meant to help pull the country out of the Great Depression. Both are done in the neoclassical style, although the courthouse has a thirty-one-story office tower jutting out of its top. (The tower is meant to suggest the Campanile in Venice's St. Mark's Square.) Both dominate their settings. Most important to me, both are powerful three-dimensional statements of the nation's commitment to the rule of law and to blind justice.

Leaving the courthouse this time for Washington, I felt as if I were walking away not just from my job or my place of work but from a good portion of my own history as well. I remembered how nervous I had been back in August 1975 when, as a raw twenty-five-year-old FBI special agent, I had first testified in one of the building's magnificent courtrooms. Later as a prosecutor, I would try dozens of criminal cases here over a ten-year period, always in awe that I was representing the United States of America in a two-hundred-year-old legacy. My home back then, the U.S. Attorney's Office for the Southern District of New York, was housed in the modern annex next door. Chinatown, Tribeca, Little Italy—they were all around me. The World Trade Center, which earlier that year had been attacked for the first time, was a dozen blocks away. From its upper floors, I could look down on Jersey City across the Hudson, where I was born. I had done some of my earliest undercover work as an FBI agent across the other river in the Red Hook section of Brooklyn, where my dad had been raised, only a stone's throw to the south; North Bergen was maybe six miles north as the crow flies. Some of my fondest memories and closest friends bind me to that courthouse and to courageous judges like Mike Mukasey, Kevin Duffy, Pierre Leval, John Keenan, Milton Pollack, Dick Casey, Barbara Jones, and Ed Palmieri, just to mention a few.

All that was on my mind as I took the subway to Penn Station, a crowded and noisy trip at that hour of the day, and boarded the 1:00 P.M. Metroliner for the trip to D.C. The contrast couldn't have been greater. My car was half-empty; the ride, whisper-smooth. But as we surfaced from under the Hudson and I saw the familiar grimy railscape of my homeland, I distinctly remember wondering if I was riding Amtrak in the wrong direction.

———

Washington was its usual midsummer self: hot, suffocating, and sticky. (Until the malarial swamps along the Potomac River were filled in to lengthen the National Mall, the British considered the American capital a diplomatic hardship post.) Whatever the weather, though, Union Station remains one of the premier urban gateways in existence. When the station opened in 1908 (the same year the FBI was founded), it was the largest train depot in the world. The Washington Monument could be laid on its side in the concourse with room to spare. Seventy years later, when I first started riding the train to D.C., the building was a mess. Part of the great barrel roof had collapsed, and rain damage had sent the place on a downward spiral. By 1981, Congress had to choose between razing the station or rehabbing it. The second option won out, and five years and $160 million later, Union Station reopened as a vibrant travel and commercial hub. Inaugural balls have twice been staged there, in 1997 and again in 2001. Both galas would have been unthinkable two decades earlier.

The heat and humidity were waiting out front at the cab line, but even there the view of the Capitol dome and all it means to so many people around the world never fails to inspire me. This time, too, there was some cloak-and-dagger intrigue to spice the mix.

Speculation on who would replace the FBI director had naturally risen to a fever pitch. The post had been in turmoil for months, and the journalists who cover such matters abhor a vacuum just as much as I hated the prospect of finding my name in some gossip sheet. To avoid any publicity for my visit with the president, Bernie Nussbaum had instructed me to meet him at his apartment at, of all places, the infamous Watergate complex. From that ironic staging ground, he was going to somehow sneak me into the White House. This was the early '90s, not the early '70s. Still, I couldn't help but sense the ghosts of Richard Nixon, G. Gordon Liddy, and all the rest as my cabbie drove past 1600 Pennsylvania Avenue.

Bernie's apartment turned out to be a very pleasant, two-bedroom affair with a nice view over the city. He was waiting there with his wife, Toby, who I would later learn was one of nature's great hostesses but who would be serving this afternoon as our wheelwoman. Also on hand was Deputy Attorney General Philip Heymann. Traditionally, FBI directors have reported to both the attorney general and her deputy—thus this get-together. I can't say that Phil and I did much more than meet and greet, but I'd come across him once before, back in the Carter years, and I knew his reputation as a fine lawyer who understood the department and its intricate relationship with the FBI. Brief as our conversation was, I felt confident at the end that we could work well together.

After about an hour, Nussbaum announced that it was time to go see the president. Heymann took his leave, wished me good luck, and without missing a beat, Toby swung into her new duties. Bernie's plan was simple enough. Toby would drive their car through the West Gate with Bernie in the front passenger seat and me in the back. As we were nearing the White House, I jokingly asked Bernie if I should hunker down on the floorboards. "Only if I yell 'duck!' he shouted back. That broke the tension I was beginning to feel, but as we stopped at the heavily reinforced steel gate, I was far from relaxed. I needn't have worrried, though. The uniformed Secret Service officer immediately recognized the White House counsel and his wife, quickly opened the gate, and waved us in. I'd go through that gate over the next eight years so often that I came to know the names and faces of practically all the guards there, but this time I might as well have been chopped liver for all the attention I drew in the backseat.

Toby pulled up to the West Wing so expertly, with such savoir faire, that I told her she could work the New York City streets with me anytime. Then Bernie ushered me through the West Wing to the elevator that would take us up to the First Family's private residence. Along the way, we said hello to George Stephanopoulos, a fellow

New Yorker with whom I would come to feel a kinship even though our paths crossed only rarely.

"Do you think the president is going to ask who I voted for?" I said only half jokingly to Bernie as we waited for the elevator.

"We think we know who you voted for," came the answer, "but the president wants to speak to you anyway."

We were just filling the time with the usual back-and-forth banter, but Bernie's passing comment would have a profound effect on my decision making.

Strange as it was getting to the moment, my meeting with the president was about as relaxed as such events can be. From the elevator on the second floor, it was only a short walk down an empty hallway to the library, where Bill Clinton and his chief of staff Mack McLarty were already in conversation. Bernie made the introductions. Then he and Mack stuck around just long enough to be polite before leaving me alone with the commander in chief. With Bill Clinton, there's no need to break the ice. He's as engaging and welcoming as anyone could be—a man who could not only sell air conditioners to Eskimos in the dead of winter but also convince them they were suffering from prickly heat rash.

Clinton had done his homework, too. Whoever wrote the briefing memo on me had done a first-rate job, and the president seemed to have absorbed every detail of it. My family, New York City, my few years on the bench, my longer stints with the U.S. Attorney's Office and the Bureau: he had it all down, and he wasn't just racing through some memorized list of talking points.

The president was interested in the organized crime cases I had worked on and wanted to know if the succession of major prosecutions under Rudy Giuliani had broken the decades-long power of the so-called five families. I explained that the cases had been done on a coordinated basis by prosecutors in New York and Italy, and because of that, they had been remarkably effective in undermining the leadership and operations of both our own Cosa Nostra and the Mafia in Sicily. He moved on from there to the string of highly publicized Wall Street cases that the office had undertaken during the late 1980s. Did I think that going after Michael Milken, Ivan Boesky, the Drexel Burnham Lambert Group, and others had had an equal deterrent effect within the corporate community? No, I told him, I thought any deterrent effect on business ethics was only temporary. Sadly, Enron, WorldCom, and too many other examples would prove me right a decade later.

The "library" is that in name only. It's more a sitting room with three or four big armchairs, some shelves of books, end tables, and the like. The president was having one of his beloved Diet Cokes when I arrived. Soon a butler arrived, asked what I wanted, and was back in a flash with my iced tea. I was just settling into it when the president got more directly to the business at hand.

We'd finished a brief discussion of J. Edgar Hoover and his forty-eight-year tenure at the FBI when Clinton said that the current ten-year term for directors made a lot of sense to him. I was quick to agree. The whole idea behind the unique provision was to prevent another interminable reign while also providing some political insulation, since a director would necessarily have to begin and end his tenure under different presidents. Neither of us added that none of the three directors since Hoover had completed a full term. Only William Webster, the best FBI director in my view, had come close at nine years. Nor did we have any exchange about Judge Sessions's departure in particular, but at least I felt that the president and I were singing in the same choir loft.

I was also impressed and heartened by the fact that Clinton asked so many questions about how the FBI operated and about the interplay between agents, the U.S. Attorney Offices, and state and local law enforcement authorities. As a former governor and state attorney general, he was quite familiar with the state and local side of the equation, but he seemed a little surprised when I told him that a fairly skeletal force of ten thousand FBI agents was responsible for enforcing hundreds upon hundreds of federal laws. That's why expanded interplay is so important, I told him; there simply aren't enough agents to do the job on their own.

Every case I worked on as an agent and as an assistant U.S. attorney had been a "task force" arrangement: men and women from many law enforcement agencies working together in a unified effort. That was the model I wanted to pursue, I said—one that would enhance cooperation between the Bureau and the nation's 17,000-plus state and local police departments, which represent over 750,000 sworn officers. Because the FBI had an unfortunate history of limiting its interaction with the larger law enforcement community, we had a great opportunity to make an important change for the better.

The president seemed so receptive to that idea that I jumped our discussion to the larger and equally critical need to expand the FBI's mission overseas. Most Americans don't realize it, but the Bureau had been there before: When World War II broke out, the nation had no external security service except for the military branches that collected what was known as war-fighter intelligence. The FBI was thrown into the breach, charged with setting up a network of foreign-based agents who would collect information and conduct operations against German and other Axis targets. By 1945, the Bureau had dozens of its own agents working throughout South America, Europe, and the Middle East. After the surrenders in Europe and Japan, those agents were gradually recalled with most of the Bureau's overseas offices shut down, only to have the cold war break out.

President Clinton knew all this, and he knew about the power struggle that ensued between J. Edgar Hoover and Allen Dulles for control over America's war against international communism. That battle had been settled by the brokered peace of the National Security Act of 1946, which created the Central Intelligence Agency as America's external security service while giving the FBI exclusive counterintelligence jurisdiction at home. All that was fine then, I told Clinton, but the global nature of crime and terrorism now required the FBI to reestablish itself internationally both to protect America and to bring democratic policing to countries where the rule of law was still tenuous. To me, this was an absolutely critical issue: Elliot Ness might have been able to fight the bad guys from an office in Chicago, but today's criminals were increasingly stateless and borderless. The fact that the president agreed so readily with me said volumes as far as I was concerned.

At one point he leaned back in his chair, yet another Diet Coke in hand, and asked me what I thought about Waco. At long last, I thought: the eight-hundred-pound gorilla is out of the closet. I paused for a few seconds, then said that the critical point about Waco was that David Koresh and his followers had murdered four Alcohol, Tobacco, and Firearms agents while in the performance of their duties and thus declared war against the United States. Everything afterward had to be weighed in the light of that single, controlling fact.

What would I have done, the president wanted to know? I started my answer by acknowledging the luxury of hindsight. No one was better at civilian crisis intervention than the FBI's Hostage Rescue Team, which had been thrown into the middle of a very dangerous situation after the failed action by the ATF agents. As for the attorney general, she had struck me as a smart and decent person in our brief meeting; my assumption was that she basically had followed the advice of the FBI. All that said, I told the president, my decision would have been to wait. During the siege at Waco I had become convinced that Koresh and his principal followers hoped to engage the federal government in a biblical duel of Armageddon. Not only were they ready to perish in the process along with their wives and children, they actually looked forward to the moment.

Waco wasn't a classic hostage situation, I contended. For the most part, the Branch Davidians inside the compound were willing adherents of a fanatical vision. Just as important, so long as the Texas standoff continued, nobody was getting hurt; nor was there any hard information, at least that I picked up on, that anyone was about to get hurt on either side. Public opinion can never be the final determinant in cases like this, I added, but until the FBI launched its armored assault, the public had clearly been on the government's side. And public opinion can never be ignored altogether. Events such as Waco take place on a huge public stage. Mismanage the moment, and other potentially dangerous actors can be adversely affected by media images of what can seem an oppressive government. (None of us at that point had ever heard of Timothy McVeigh, but the Oklahoma City bombing was being born in Waco's ashes.)

Why launch an attack on a fortified compound, I went on, unless circumstances had changed dramatically for the worse? Until then, I would have continued negotiating, erected a perimeter fence around the encampment, and waited for fatigue and boredom to come to our aid. David Koresh wasn't capable of riding this stalemate out. His dementia was such that he would have either lit the fires himself or begun to kill his own followers to jump-start the final battle. That's when the FBI could have responded to Koresh's action by mounting the same attack it did. Yes, the ending might have been no different, no less tragic, but the difference, I told the president, was that the subsequent barrage of criticism against the FBI and Janet Reno—most of it unjustified—would have been muted, perhaps even nonexistent. The Bureau would have been acting to save lives because an insane leader left it no other choice. That's the difference. When I had finished, the president looked at me and nodded his head in apparent agreement, and with that, another load of doubt lifted from my shoulders.

When Clinton asked me if I had ever visited the White House

before, I saw a chance to address my final concern about the director's job. No, I told him, not only had I never visited the First Family's private quarters, I'd never been in any part of the executive mansion, but I had attended a ceremony in the Rose Garden. I went on to describe how, in 1991, just after my appointment to the federal bench, President Bush had given me an award there for prosecuting the mail bomber who murdered a federal judge in Alabama and an NAACP lawyer in Savannah. The president had also used the occasion to announce that he was nominating Bill Barr—then the acting attorney general—for the permanent post. The event wasn't a big deal, and, of course, Bill Barr's tenure was cut abruptly short by Bush's loss in the general election, but I was watching Clinton's reaction closely. Would he flinch at the mention of this obviously partisan occasion? When he didn't, I assumed that at least tacitly we had agreed that the director's job wasn't about politics, and I was glad that I had raised the matter, even if obliquely.

I finished my part of the interview by posing two questions for which Clinton had the right answers. We had spent at least an hour together by then, and although we had exhausted the FBI as a topic of conversation, Clinton was in no hurry to pull the plug. It seemed odd to me that the president of the free world would have so little to do, but I had heard that Hillary and Chelsea were going to spend the night in Hawaii, on their way back from a trip to Asia. Maybe I was the evening entertainment!

As if in confirmation, Bill Clinton graciously offered to give me a tour of the residence. Room to room we went with the president providing the running commentary about former occupants, their favorite books and furnishings, and other arcane details you might expect to hear from some longtime White House docent. Outside on the Truman Balcony, the president pointed to an unrepaired bullet hole and launched into the story of how the British army had fired muskets at the White House during the War of 1812. Inside, he would lay a hand on my shoulder as he gave the history of a paint-ing, a clock, some piece of ormolu. After maybe ninety minutes of this, I couldn't resist asking whether he had known these details be-fore becoming president or had learned them since moving in. Completely matter-of-factly, without a trace of embarrassment, he answered that he had been studying these things since he was very young. I realized at that moment that Hillary wasn't the only Clin-ton who had expected him to be living here someday.

As we passed the kitchen, I asked the president if he happened to have on hand any of the various fast foods he was known to favor. The question wasn't entirely academic. It was now nearly eight in the evening, and my stomach was starting to growl. Yes, the presi-dent assured me, fast food was easy to come by in the White House, but he didn't offer me any. Fortunately, it was just about at that point that Bernie Nussbaum came to the rescue.

"Judge," he called down to the hall to me, in his best New York City street accent, "what are ya doing? I'm down to one client, my *last* one, and you're trying to steal him?"

I took that as my signal to say good-bye and thanked the president for his time and courtesy. Today, I told him, was my son Brendan's seventh birthday. I couldn't be there for the little family party, but I wanted to be waiting for him when he woke tomorrow morning.

Again without missing a beat, the president sat down at a desk, pulled out a piece of his stationery, and began to write. When he was finished, he handed the note to me, and said, "Please give this to him for me."

"Dear Brendan," he had written, "Happy Birthday from Bill Clinton."

If I hadn't thought so before, I knew at that moment that this was the best politician of his generation.

What the hell were you talking about for all that time?" Bernie asked as he ushered me through the West Wing.

I gave him a quick synopsis. The president was impressive, I told him, on numerous fronts, so much so that I now felt persuaded I could serve as FBI director in this administration.

Bernie wanted to know what the tipping point had been. Had it been one of those long discussions about the fine points of policy for which Clinton had already become so famous? (After all, we'd spent hours together.) No, I told him, what really made the difference for me was a very brief exchange when the president asked me if I had any questions about the job. I had two, I answered. My wife and I had four young sons, and I considered it just as important that I serve them well as that I serve the FBI well. I was offended just about every time some government official justified his (or her) departure by saying he needed to spend more time with the family. To me, that cliché indicated that the person had probably done both jobs poorly, and I didn't intend to find myself in a position where I had to choose between the two. In response, the president said that he agreed completely and took pride in the fact that his administration was very family oriented. He encouraged people to spend time at home, he said, even when they had important official responsibilities.

"What's the second thing you want to know?" he asked after a brief pause.

Unlike the first item, which came from the heart, I had spent a bit of time thinking this one out because it was essential for me at a more intellectual level.

"If I'm going to be director," I said, "it's critical that there's no political interference with the Bureau's work." I looked the president directly in the eye as I spoke, just as he had been looking at me the entire time we were together. "The Bureau's investigations must be conducted fairly and vigorously without any political pressure or impermissible attempts to influence how they come out. It's also critical that I make all my own appointments without any interference of a political nature." I firmly believe that absent an act of Congress, the FBI director should fiercely protect the Bureau's independence and not permit anyone to interfere with his or her personnel appointments.

It wasn't particularly articulate, but this was the bottom line with me. I'd hinted at it earlier in our discussions. Now I had said it outright, and the president responded in kind.

"This is exactly what I expect in my administration."

Bernie assured me the president meant every word of it, and then, as if reading my mind, he addressed in particular the departure of the last director. Yes, from the outside, Judge Sessions's departure could appear to have political overtones, Bernie acknowledged, but he and Clinton had tried in every way they could to get the judge to leave the director's job voluntarily, even to the point of indicating he might return to the federal bench if he left on his own. Ultimately, Sessions had balked, which was why his removal was proving so messy, but that—and the media dust-up that followed—was the judge's choice, not the administration's. Bernie was going to be my immediate contact at the White House, and it was clear to me that he was a straight shooter through and through. On that matter at least, nothing in the years since has caused me to change my opinion one iota. I've always been thankful to Bernie for his trust in me and for his oft-repeated remark that he's most proud of the two presidential appointments he worked on simultaneously: my own and that of Supreme Court Justice Ruth Bader Ginsberg.

No one had ever asked me directly if I would accept the director's job. Nor, of course, had I officially said yes. But as I walked by myself down the path to the West Gate, I knew the job was mine and felt I could do it well. Now I had to find a way home. I passed through the gate, stepped out on Pennsylvania Avenue, and threw my hand up for a cab. Hobnobbing with the president at the epicenter of power didn't count for much when it came to public transportation.

Three days later, on July 19, 1993, Bill Clinton fired Judge Sessions. The next day, July 20, I was back at the White House with my entire family, this time to be nominated as the fifth director in the post-Hoover history of the Federal Bureau of Investigation. Thanks to Bernie's clandestine operation, the announcement had been kept secret nearly to the last moment.

In 1991, when I appeared before the Senate Judiciary Committee hearing on my nomination to become a federal judge, Marilyn and I had balked at bringing our then three sons along. Finally, we had caved in, at the insistence of my Justice Department "handler," but with the oldest then only seven, the potential for disaster seemed enormous. This time, of course, there was no question about not including the four boys at the Rose Garden ceremony. What's more, they were all two years older. Justin had almost hit double digits, Brendan was now seven and Sean three. To be sure, Connor was only a year old, but with my parents, brothers, and other family members on hand, along with some dear friends from New York (including Bob Fiske, an extraordinary lawyer and distinguished Southern District U.S. attorney and later the first Whitewater prosecutor), we had all the backup we needed. Surely they couldn't get in that much trouble!

The boys, in fact, looked like angels as we walked into the West Wing that morning. Janet Reno and Floyd Clarke were there to greet us with smiles and plenty of warmth. Bernie Nussbaum was no less welcoming when we stopped in to his corner office. So was Vince Foster, who was waiting on Bernie's couch and who later would sit just behind Bernie and my family.

Marilyn had taken the boys outside, leaving the president and me alone in the Oval Office just before the nominating ceremony was to get under way. We were standing by the famous *Resolute* desk that had been a gift from Queen Victoria. (The desk is made from the timbers of a British vessel of that name aided by American sailors when it became lost in Arctic waters back in 1855. In one of the most famous of all White House photos, John-John Kennedy is curled up in its kneehole, peering out from a secret door.) I was silently rehearsing my remarks when I detected out the window one of those slight shifts of field that happen when a crowd starts doing some serious rubbernecking. I had no idea what might have caused the disruption, but some combination of parental instinct and detective hunch told me that one or more of my sons was at the center of it. Before I had time to give the matter any more thought, an aide signaled that it was time, and I followed the president into the Rose Garden as the press cameras exploded and the television cameras began to roll.

The president gave me one of those flattering introductions that I knew my fellow FBI agents wouldn't soon let me forget. I was just wondering how I would ever escape being called a "law enforcement legend" when I looked at Brendan sitting in the first row in his best church suit and realized he was soaking wet—not perspiration wet, although it was another hot July day, but swimming-pool wet, through and through. The president had also noticed my son's condition and leaned over to ask if he was okay. By then, I had made eye contact with Marilyn, and she had silently informed me that, yes, the boys had not behaved themselves, that we should have left them in the hotel, and that Brendan's wetness was not weather related. I was struck even in that instant with the calm and studied pique that a mother of four boys can communicate so professionally without uttering a single word. Brendan was fine, I assured the president . . . but I wasn't so sure about my wife.

I didn't get the back story until the ceremony was almost at an end and Marilyn and the boys had joined us on the podium. Marilyn, it seemed, had just about managed to herd the boys to their seats when a flurry of music announced that the proceedings were about to get under way. At that moment, Brendan broke ranks and ran over to a little pool that sits in the Rose Garden. He was peering curiously into its shallow depth, leaning forward just enough to be a bit off balance, when three-year-old Sean noticed the target-rich environment, went barreling off in Brendan's direction, and before anyone could intervene, launched his brother into the water. Marilyn and a bevy of shocked aides had just managed to pull Brendan out of the drink and get both boys to their seats when Clinton and I made our appearance.

Marilyn was just finishing a hurried recitation of this sad tale when the president picked up Connor, our one-year-old, and held him up for the cameras. Thank God, I remember thinking, at least *he* was dry, or dry for all anyone could see. Even my parents, who like me didn't want to be asked that morning which box they had checked for president ten months earlier, became instant Clinton supporters as they watched the forty-second president hoisting up their number-four grandson.

The Rose Garden incident, by the way, didn't end in the Rose Garden. Back in the Oval Office, after Marilyn had filled Clinton in on the details, he asked that Sean be brought before him for questioning. As the White House photographer clicked off a series of memorable stills, the tall and handsome president stood over a remarkably calm Sean and asked: "Did you push your brother into the pond?" Without betraying any evidence of guilt, Sean looked up at the president and shook his head no. Although I was now in the uncomfortable position of observing my three-year-old son lying to the chief law enforcement officer of the United States—and my soon-to-be boss—I couldn't help but feel as a lawyer that Sean was simply stating what's known in the trade as an exculpatory no. After all, according to Title 18, Section 1001 of the U.S. Code, a simple denial of guilt doesn't constitute a "false statement."

The president seemed to realize something of the same because he improved his prosecutor's technique considerably with the next question: "Were you happy when your brother went into the water?" An ever-so-slight smile started to curl the end of Sean's mouth and the crowd began to sense that he was breaking! Finally, and to my professional admiration, the president took one last run at it. "Did you feel good when you pushed your brother into the pond?" At that point Sean gave it up and, smiling broadly, silently nodded his head yes as we all breathed a happy sigh of relief. Sweet as the day's outcome was, though, the event could not have had a more bitter ending.

The two-and-a-half-column photo that appeared upper left on page one of *The Washington Post* the next day shows me giving a thumbs-up sign and holding Connor as a beaming president bends over to greet Marilyn. "Federal Judge Nominated as New FBI Head," the headline reads. A third of the way down the front page on the right-hand side is a headline of a much different order: "Clinton Aide Vincent Foster Dies in an Apparent Suicide."

Marilyn and I were at the Key Bridge Marriott across the Potomac from Georgetown when I got the news, sometime after 10:00 that evening. Floyd Clarke, who had been made acting director of the FBI the day before, called to say that Vince had driven to Fort Marcy Park off the George Washington Parkway in Virginia and there, overlooking the Potomac, had killed himself. The body had been positively identified and the White House notified about 9:55, Floyd said. I was stunned as he gave me the details.

Vince Foster was forty-eight years old, the father of three, one of the golden boys from Hope, Arkansas. A photo of the three of them was on prominent display in his office: Bill Clinton, Mack McLarty, and Foster, taken at some birthday party back in Hope when they were all just kids. Like Hillary Clinton, he had been part of the Rose law firm before joining his old friends in Washington. I could still see Vince's face from the ceremony, sitting behind Marilyn and the kids, circulating around the crowd afterward. Bernie Nussbaum said later that he and Vince had gone back to Bernie's office once the festivities broke up. Bernie was in high spirits, not just about my nomination but about the ease with which Ruth Bader Ginsberg's nomination was moving through the Senate Judiciary Committee. "We hit two home runs!" Bernie crowed. Vince, he said, just smiled and said, "I'll see you later." He didn't.

For the already growing legion of Clinton haters and conspiracy theorists, Foster's death was, of course, a huge chunk of red meat thrown into the cage. They would feed off it for years to come. To me, whatever Vince's motivation or demons, his death was simply the horrible end to a life that deserved so much better.

Six weeks later, on September 1, 1993, I was officially sworn in as director at FBI headquarters and began my almost eight-year tenure in office, the second longest of any director in the post-Hoover era. Marilyn held the Bible that day, while Frank Johnson, the courageous federal judge from Alabama, administered the oath.

I'd known Frank personally for only a few years by then, but he had been a hero to me ever since my law school days. Frank was once ostracized by much of the society he lived in. He'd had a cross burned on his lawn, and his own mother's house had been fire-bombed. But none of it deterred him. In the dark days of the civil-rights struggle, no jurist in America did more to break down the barriers of segregation in the Deep South. George Wallace, Alabama's black-baiting governor, once proposed giving Frank a "barbed-wire enema." Martin Luther King Jr. called him a man who gave "true meaning to the word justice." Wallace's enmity and King's praise both speak volumes about the man, but I wanted Frank there with me for another reason. He himself had been nominated to be FBI director in 1977 by Jimmy Carter and almost certainly would have been confirmed by the Senate, but a previously undetected heart condition caused him to withdraw his name.

In my own way, I thought that having Frank swear me in might close the circle, for him and for me, but I was far from alone in revering Judge Johnson deeply. Janet Reno and Bill Clinton were both thrilled to have him on hand. His participation gave the event a historical resonance that had everything to do with him and very little to do with me. Goodwill filled the FBI courtyard that day.

After I had resigned as FBI director and many years after Bernie Nussbaum had stepped down as White House counsel, we ran into each other at an event sponsored by the Federal Bar Council.

"I spoke to your friend today," Bernie said with a laugh.

"I've got lots of friends, Bernie," I told him, already suspicious. "Which one?"

"President Clinton," he answered, now in full good humor.

Bernie went on to tell me that Bill Clinton had told him: "The best piece of advice you gave me that I didn't follow was to oppose a special prosecutor for Whitewater, and the worst piece of advice you gave me that I did follow was to appoint Freeh as FBI director."

"It'll probably be in his book," Bernie added.

I'll leave the special prosecutor comment for legal scholars. As for the president's comment on me, I wear it as a badge of honor. All the agreements Bill Clinton and I had come to on the day I interviewed for the director's job, everything that I thought had been made clear between the two of us, I finally came to realize, was clear only to me.

CHAPTER 3

"You're Not Really College Material"

Even if Bill Clinton hadn't given me the answers I wanted to hear, I'm not sure I could have said no when he asked me to take the director's job. By then, my parents had gotten involved, and for them, answering the call to duty was not an optional activity.

As I wrote earlier, part of that was politics. My mom and dad were old-school Democrats, from a time when the party's patriotism was never questioned. The former Arkansas governor might not have been their ideal president, but to them, the Democrats represented the working stiffs; the Republicans, the bosses in silk hats, and there was never any question which side of that divide they stood on. They did more than talk politics, too. Both had worked for the party in Hudson County, New Jersey, where I was born, knocking on doors, walking the wards to get out the vote and make sure the election went the right way.

But the call to duty went deeper than politics. My father, William Freeh, is a World War II veteran, and he always told my two brothers and me that we were to serve our nation no matter how difficult or inconvenient or even dangerous the task. When I visited my parents the day before I went down to Washington to interview with Clinton, Dad informed me in no uncertain terms that I was to do whatever the president asked of me.

My parents were still close enough to their own hardscrabble roots and immigrant histories to remember just how much America had done for them, and for all of us. Back when I was a kid in grade school, the history books would always describe the nation as a melting pot, a place where people from different backgrounds blended together in search of a better life. I never had any trouble understanding that because my family was practically a trans-European melting pot all of its own. But it was as Americans and loving parents that they gave us their most precious gifts: reverence for God and country, the difference between right and wrong, and kindness.

My paternal great-grandfather, Frederich Fruh, emigrated to America from Sasbaach, in the far west of Germany, in the very early 1870s. Why he left his homeland is lost to family history, but geopolitics is a safe bet. Sasbaach lies in Alsace-Lorraine, not far from Strasbourg and the famous spa at Baden-Baden in the Rhine Valley, an area of almost constant tension between the Germans and the French. In 1675, the Viscount of Turenne, among the most famous of all French military leaders, drove the Germans from the region only to be killed by a cannonball at the Battle of Sasbaach. Another two centuries on, in 1871, the French capitulated to end the Franco-German War, and all of Alsace along with the better part of Lorraine became part of the newly formed German empire. That's just about when Fred took off for the New World, which must have seemed a haven of stability even with the Civil War still fresh in America memory.

The one marketable skill my great-grandfather seems to have brought with him from Germany was music. He settled in New York and got a part-time job with a U.S. Army band that had him playing in Brooklyn, Manhattan, Governor's Island, and elsewhere. Between that and other odd jobs, he managed to marry and raise a family in the Red Hook section of Brooklyn, a round bulge of land that sticks out under lower Manhattan, across the Hudson River from the Statue of Liberty.

One of his sons—my grandfather, William Freeh—landed a job with the New York City Department of Sanitation, and at last someone in the family had a steady income, at least until the Great Depression intervened. On the side, he also held a part-time job that might be the most enviable position any Freeh has ever laid claim to: an usher at Ebbett's Field, erstwhile home of the late, great Brooklyn Dodgers.

If William Freeh couldn't have told you precisely why his ancestors emigrated to America, his wife, Jenny McGee, knew beyond a shadow of a doubt why hers had crossed the Atlantic. The McGees were living in County Cork, in the southeast of Ireland, when the potato blight first struck in 1846. For the impoverished Irish—and that included just about everyone—potatoes were the absolutely essential crop. Without them, the Great Famine followed, aided by typhus and other diseases. To escape death, the people fled in almost unbelievable numbers. By 1851, Ireland's population had collapsed by 25 percent, to about 6.5 million. To achieve a population shift of similar proportion, the United States of today would have to lose on the order of 70 million people in a scant half decade.

Like so many other Irish immigrants, my paternal grandmother's forebears washed up in New York City, where several generations later, Jenny McGee met and married William Freeh. I had never given a moment's thought to how they might have met until I visited Sasbaach for the first time, back in 1991. My position as a federal judge must have impressed the locals because the mayor turned out and introduced me to a very distant cousin named

Ernst Fruh, while the police pitched in by making photocopies of some old family birth and marriage records that had been stored in the local church. What really struck me, though, was the church itself—St. Bridgette's, founded by an order of Irish nuns in this little town right in the middle of Alsace-Lorraine. That's when I knew: fate had brought the German Freehs and Irish McGees together.

I doubt that my grandmother finished more than sixth grade, and my grandfather certainly didn't go a lot higher, but they had the immigrant's determination to succeed. The two of them settled in an apartment on Baltic Street in Red Hook, just like the cheap street in the Monopoly game; and there they had two sons—my father the oldest, born in 1916, and his younger brother, Edward. Both boys not only attended but graduated from St. Francis High School, another big step up the ladder of social mobility.

Dad was working for a Brooklyn trucking company, loading and unloading at the dock, when World War II broke out. He joined the army almost immediately after Pearl Harbor and eventually ended up a combat engineer in England, helping to lengthen runways so American bombers could use them. Once or twice a day for many months, German planes would come droning over the English Channel, spotting and reconnoitering. At the first sound of their engines, Dad says, all the men would drop whatever they were doing and rush off to the parade ground, where they would drill furiously with make-believe rifles—in some cases, nothing more than crooked sticks—until the Luftwaffe had flown by. Dad says the men in his unit laughed uproariously every time they staged their charade.

It wasn't all good times. Dad's combat engineering unit went ashore at Normandy on June 7, 1944—day two of the invasion—and stayed in Europe through the Battle of the Bulge, Bastogne, and more, until Allied troops finally entered Germany en masse in the early spring of 1945. He was still there in August of that year, three months after the German surrender, when his unit was ordered to Hamburg, to join a force that would soon embark for the Pacific to begin preparing for the invasion of Japan. After three and a half years away, Dad was convinced he had another three or four years to go; but the ship sailed west across the Atlantic instead. The bombings of Hiroshima and Nagasaki had finally sealed the war in the Pacific, and a good thing, too, because my German-Irish father had a nice Italian girl waiting back home to marry him.

Bernice, my mother, was first-generation Italian-American all the way. Her father, Luigi Chinciola, for whom I'm named, was raised in the little hill town of Mirabella Eclano, in Avellino Province, east of Naples. He was in his teens when his family emigrated to America near the turn of the century. Josephine Murano, my maternal grandmother and another name source (I'm Louis *Joseph* Freeh), was born no more than fifty miles from Luigi, in Ruoti, near Potenza, but in the Italy of a century and more ago they might as well have lived on different continents. Josephine came to the U.S. at about age seven with her parents and essentially grew up in New York. Still, like Luigi, she barely spoke a word of English when the two of them met and married around 1915. Luigi Chinciola, though, was not a man to let a mysterious foreign language get in his way.

Luigi set himself the goal of landing a job with the federal government, the steadiest employer he could think of; then he knocked on doors and stood in lines until he found one. The job wasn't much—he was a mail sorter deep in the bowels of the cavernous General Post Office at Eighth Avenue and Thirty-third Street, near Pennsylvania Station and Madison Square Garden—but the job was only phase one of the plan. Day after day as he was leaving the GPO, he would stop by the vast bin of undeliverable mail and pull out old magazines, comic books, anything with pictures that could be associated with words. Then in the evening, at their apartment in the Grand Concourse area of the Bronx, he and Josephine would pore over the reading matter until the words started making sense and, in time, they learned enough English to get by in the New World.

I never knew my grandfather; he died before I was born. But I've always had a soft spot in my heart for the U.S. Postal Service thanks to him. As an assistant U.S. attorney, one of the first cases I ever got handed involved some guy who had pilfered a couple of Social Security checks out of delivered mail. The U.S. Postal Service agent who handed me the case was apologetic. Rookie prosecutors like to make a mark for themselves, he knew, and this little theft charge would never be noticed. "It's a 'two-check case,' " he said, in that beautiful prosecutorial shorthand that I would soon come to know and love, "but we got to take it to court." Little did the agent know that one of the worst things you could do in my book was mess with the USPS.

Whenever I'm over in that part of Manhattan, I make it a point to stop and admire Luigi's old workplace. The GPO was practically new when he started there. Opened in 1913, the building was designed by McKim, Mead, and White, maybe the most famous architectural firm of its day. The row of Corinthian columns that fronts the post office is a New York landmark, but what I really admire and always repeat to myself is the motto inscribed above the columns: "Neither snow, nor rain, nor heat, nor gloom of night shall stay these couriers from the swift completion of their appointed rounds."

To me, those twenty-two famous words are more than a reminder of my grandfather's perseverance and determination; they also capture eloquently what I consider to be the first principle of public service: fidelity, courage, and sacrifice. Government doesn't always achieve those goals—and the FBI didn't always get there under my watch—but we never stopped trying.

To a lesser woman, being widowed in the Bronx with two daughters to raise, thousands of miles from her homeland and much of her family, might have been a crushing blow. My mother, Bernice, had just become a teenager (a term only then coming into existence); her sister, Lydia, was younger still. Together, they must have been a handful to ride herd on, but like her late husband, Josephine Chinciola was no pushover. She had worked all along as a freelance seamstress, making and selling dresses, and between that and Luigi's pension, she made ends meet. She didn't stint, either, in the attention she paid to the young men who came calling on her daughters.

Mom and Dad were both fond of ballroom dancing. They'd met at Roseland, the famous dance floor on West Fifty-second Street. Back in the Roaring Twenties, ballroom dancing was king and Roseland was the place to be. The hall made a comeback in the 1940s when it was a must-stop for Duke Ellington, Tommy Dorsey, Benny Goodman, and many other of the biggest bands of the day. In between, in the cash-strapped '30s, Roseland hung on as a dime-a-dance joint, but for poor people like my parents-to-be, it was affordable entertainment, a place to meet someone new.

It wasn't long before Dad was interested in seeing Bernice Chinciola off the dance floor, but before a date could commence, he had to pass muster with my grandmother Josephine. Dad recalls the moment vividly. He drove the family car practically the length of the city, from Red Hook in Brooklyn all the way up to the Bronx, a measure of how different New York City was in those days. He was just parking out front of Bernice's apartment building when his future mother-in-law exited the front door, heading in his direction. They met halfway, exchanged brief greetings, and then as Dad watched in wonder, Josephine marched down to the curb, notepad in hand, and proceeded to copy down his license plate number. A mother of such attractive daughters could not be too careful.

My father survived the inspection, but the war came along before they were ready to marry. Mom wrote him every single day he was in the army. He wrote her almost as often, and she kept every one of his letters. He was barely off the ship back from Europe before they were married. Financially strapped, they moved in with grandmother Josephine, where they would stay for the next four years under her close inspection.

Dad kicked around a number of jobs after the war. The best one might have been as a dispatcher for a Brooklyn trucking company—the business he'd been in before Pearl Harbor—but that job came to an abrupt close when he got involved in trying to organize a union. Turns out, the wise guys who controlled that part of Brooklyn wanted nothing to do with unions in general, and with the International Brotherhood of Teamsters least of all, which meant they wanted nothing to do with my dad either. A dozen years later, when I was a kid and Dad would tell the story of his brief career as a labor agitator, I would always be amazed. Why wouldn't workers want a union to represent them and fight for better pay and conditions? But that was before my work as an FBI agent and as an assistant U.S. attorney had given me a Ph.D.-level education in wise guys and the Teamsters.

Maybe it was his experience with the trucking company or the fact that my older brother, Bill, had just been born the year before. Maybe he was just sick of being cooped up in a small apartment with his mother-in-law. Whatever the reason (and it was probably some combination of all three factors), Dad announced one day in

1949 that it was time to move to New Jersey so the one kid already born and the others sure to come could grow up in the "country."

Only people used to Brooklyn and the Bronx would ever consider the part of New Jersey my parents settled on—North Bergen, in Hudson County—"country." North Bergen did have trees, there was even some undeveloped land back then more than half a century ago, but Seventy-fourth Street was more city than suburb. Our new home was surrounded by two- and three-family houses: horizontally divided duplexes and triplexes. Our tiny frame place had been a boardinghouse, and it stayed that way. The boarders got the bedrooms on the second and third floors. The four of us—once I had come along—crowded into four or five rooms on the first floor (it depended on what you counted as a room), and we all slept in the same bedroom. My grandmother Josephine had been left behind in the Bronx, but it didn't take long for her to join us. As the matriarch, she got her own "bedroom," not a whole lot bigger than a closet.

Maybe most important, moving to New Jersey gave my dad a lifetime career. A natural salesman, he opened up a small real-estate office not far from our house, and he stayed at the business for the next forty-six years, until he finally retired just about the time of his eightieth birthday. Mom worked beside him for most of those years as his secretary. My brother Bill and I used to marvel that two people could spend so much time together and still love each other. Bill and I joined the act, too. Both of us got real-estate licenses as soon as we were out of high school so we could help Dad with the business during the summers.

In their own very different ways, my brothers provided me with valuable lessons. Bill, older than me by a year, not only got us out of the Bronx by agreeing to be born, he also set a standard of academic and behavioral excellence for me to follow. He was the first in the family ever to go to college—the University of Detroit Mercy, founded by the Jesuits in 1877—and he didn't stop there. His senior year in high school, Bill landed a job as a page at the NBC headquarters at Rockefeller Center in Manhattan. At college, he majored in communications, but he kept up his NBC job, mostly leading tour groups through the studios, during summer vacations. When he graduated, he put the two experiences together, became a soundman with one of the NBC News camera crews, and kept at it for more than three decades, traveling the globe, wherever news was being made.

I'd like to write that what I learned from Bill was academic diligence and impeccable deportment. Certainly, those were the expectations he passed down to me, and in my own way, I tried to live up to them, but "try" is the key word there. At the start of every school year in our rigorously Catholic educations, some nun or brother would say to me, "I hope you're like Bill." But alas, at the end of the year, the same nun or brother would usually amend that to: "I wish you had been like Bill."

Strangely, maybe, what Bill really taught me was fearlessness. News crews go where the news is, and the news is often blood soaked. It's the soundman who makes sure you hear the shells exploding in the background, the roar of the rioting crowd, the hurricane-force winds bearing in on some terrified coastal hamlet. Bill ended up in a lot of places most of us would pay money to avoid, but he never complained, and maybe because he didn't, my mother never quite understood just what her oldest offspring was up to. Mom was a little naive about some things. She needed hands-on physical evidence of danger, and she thought she'd had her fill of that at my graduation in 1975 from the FBI Academy at Quantico, Virginia.

In what was then not much of a ceremony, new agents were handed their badges, then headed straight for the gun vault, where they were issued a revolver—in my class's case, a Smith & Wesson 2.5-inch .38—and six rounds in a plastic envelope. (The thrill of the moment is such that I never stopped to wonder what would happen if and when the six bullets ran out.) Mom watched this ritual in utter confusion as long as she could, then asked the parents of one of my roommates, Dan Jablonski, what was happening.

"They're getting guns," Mrs. Jablonski explained matter-of-factly. The Jablonskis were from rural Nebraska. Guns were part of their everyday lives.

"They have guns?" Mom replied in horror.

For her, that was all the evidence needed that I, not Bill, was the one in mortal peril. No matter where Bill happened to be—in Nicaragua, in the middle of a civil war; or in some hotel in Beirut with rocket-propelled grenades whizzing through his windows—Mom would always tell her friends: "My poor Louie is out there in great danger!"

Like Bill, my younger brother, John, shook the family up just by coming into existence. For seven years, my parents had somehow made do in the same bedroom with their two sons, but the thought of adding a third child to the mix was apparently just too much for Dad. Out went the boarders, including the mysterious "Mr. Nickel," so named because every now and again, without ever saying a word, he would press a nickel into Bill's hand or mine. Once Mr. Nickel and the rest were gone, Dad and his brother, Ed, took sledgehammers and knocked down the long wall that separated our living quarters from the stairwell used by the boarders, and suddenly all of us boys had bedrooms of our own with space to spare.

A year or two after that, once John was old enough to be looked after by someone else, Mom went to work permanently as Dad's secretary, and Grandmother Josephine became our permanent baby-sitter. It wasn't as if our parents were far away: we could easily bicycle to the real-estate office, and Dad was often in the neighborhood, selling houses. Still, in Grandma's hands, our lives took on a slightly eccentric quality. Good Italian that she was, Josephine loved opera. Other kids in the early 1960s would come home, flip on their radios, and lose themselves in Elvis, the Drifters, or the Shirelles. We would come home to hear Enrico Caruso singing *"La donna è mobile,"* on Grandma's scratchy recording of Verdi's *Rigoletto.* The experience never quite left me. Later, when I was in college or law school, I would hear some aria drifting out a window, and off I'd go—as powerless to resist as the Manchurian Candidate—to the old Met to purchase standing-room tickets for whatever opera was on the bill that evening.

Maybe because he was so much younger than the rest of us, John became the family rebel. Bill and I attended parochial schools. John wouldn't hear of it, especially when Robert Fulton Elementary was right across the street from our home. Neither Bill nor I would have dared play hooky. John barely went to school at all. At North Bergen High School, he used his considerable intellect to figure out the absolute minimum number of days he needed to attend in order to pass up to the next grade. Then he spent every unneeded day in the park or at the local public library. We older brothers had been trustworthy altar boys. In grammar school, I must have served at least twice a week. John practically had to be dragged inside the church door.

My parents, needless to say, were apoplectic. I can hear Dad to this day: "This is terrible. All John's doing is cutting school. He's an agnostic. He'll never get into college, never amount to anything, never get a government job!" (Note the last item: Having seen his own father out of work in the Depression, Dad also considered a stable government job the highest aspiration of a working man.

Even after I had become FBI director, he would go into a panic whenever I mentioned that I might take a post in the private sector.)

None of it swayed John. He hated school; it didn't challenge him. He saw no point in going to church if he wasn't a believer. After squeaking his way through twelfth grade, John left home and traveled around Europe for six months. My parents figured they might not ever see or hear from him again. But John was listening to his own drum beat. He came back from Europe on time, enrolled the following fall in Fairleigh Dickinson University just up the road in Teaneck, New Jersey, and did well enough there to transfer to Georgetown University the next fall. Three years later, John graduated from Georgetown with highest honors, and then he really hit his stride. Not only did this high school rebel go on to earn his doctorate in Shakespeare and Milton from Oxford University, he also became a teacher, first at the Franciscan-run University, of Steubenville in Ohio; then at Gonzaga University in Spokane, Washington, where he ran the campus ministry; and at Seton Hall University, back in New Jersey.

As that lineup of colleges and universities suggests, John long ago got over his discomfort with the Catholic Church. Far from the agnostic our dad feared he was becoming, my younger brother joined Opus Dei, the devout conservative lay group that Dan Brown managed to paint as some demonic fifth column of Catholicism in his best-seller, *The Da Vinci Code*. When it emerged that Robert Hanssen, the former FBI agent who pled guilty to spying for the Soviets, was also a member of Opus Dei, a number of fringe news organizations and crackpot Internet sites speculated that my own supposed membership in the group had blinded me to Hanssen's malfeasance or, worse, led me to fly cover for him. Sorry, I'm not the family member who belongs to Opus Dei. That's not what Opus Dei is about. And even if it was and I was, it wouldn't have changed my opinion about Robert Hanssen or my approach to his case, but more about that later.

In some ways, John has become a priest without a portfolio. (Like my brother Bill, he's a confirmed bachelor.) Because of John, I'm less quick to judge people, more inclined to wait for the potential in them to surface.

O ther lessons and influences on my life I had to pick up on my own, sometimes the hard way. I remember to this day the officer from the West New York police force who showed up at our grammar school as part of some community relations program. (Despite its name, West New York is in New Jersey, just across from Midtown Manhattan and right next door to North Bergen.) Standing in front of the class in his uniform and badge, he told us that his job was to protect us. I was impressed by both things—the uniform and the job description—and I could see his face clear as a bell years later when word passed up to me in the FBI director's office that eleven West New York policemen were about to be indicted on corruption charges. But I suspect I'll remember to my dying day my first encounter with a policeman whose job was to protect the community from *me*.

Our house was five blocks from Braddock Park, named for James J. Braddock, a local luminary and the heavyweight champion of the world in the mid-1930s. My good friend and schoolmate John and I went up there all the time after school, to hike or walk around, or sometimes just to throw rocks from the palisades, the steep cliffs cut eons ago by the Hudson River. We were practicing our rock hurling one afternoon when this guy came charging at us, yelling that we'd broken his window. (There were some houses down below the cliffs, but like most eight-year-olds, we weren't too concerned with where our rocks landed.) The guy grabbed John, but I managed to elude him and take off for home. I did double back by John's house, a block from my own, to see if somehow, magically, he had been released and gotten there ahead of me. He hadn't, of course, and since in our house we weren't allowed to use the phone to call other kids, all I could do was sit quietly and wait to see if the other shoe would drop. It did, right in the middle of dinner. The state trooper who rang our doorbell looked to be about eight feet tall, and as I rose from my chair and walked forward to meet him, I knew I was as finished as finished could be. My specific sin, the trooper let me know, was leaving the scene of a crime, but it was the punishment my dad dealt out after he was gone that left the greater impression.

Now that so many children spend all their spare time indoors, in front of the TV or with computer games, I wonder if they ever learn the practical knowledge that all of us neighborhood kids picked up in Braddock Park. I'm thinking in particular of a guy maybe in his thirties whom we called Cut Off because he was always chasing after us, yelling "I'll cut off your fingers!" Cut Off did have a penknife he would flourish, and he was certainly our worst nightmare. But if his knife had a blade at all, it couldn't have been more than an inch long and too dull to cut butter. Today's parents would have hounded the local police chief until Cut Off was hauled away and thrown in the slammer, but our parents could never get too excited when we ran to them in panic after another of Cut Off's sorties. They knew, I'm sure, that he lived in the park because he had no other home and that, for all his shouting, he was harmless as a teddy bear. Live and let live, they figured; and all of us, I think, finally came to understand that.

———

The Immaculate Heart of Mary Grammar School, which I attended through sixth grade, was one of the stranger such facilities known to man. The school had taken over a little urban commercial strip. What had once been a vaudeville theater—and still had makeup and prop rooms from its old days—was converted into the chapel. For classrooms, we used the former storefronts. Instead of being promoted from first to second to third grade, we always said that we were graduating from the butcher shop to the candy store, or the candy store to the tailor's shop.

Our teachers were all nuns as far as I can recall, and since I was born left-handed and there was almost no greater challenge on earth for a grammar-school nun than making left-handed boys write right-handed, I came in for some special attention. ("Sinister," recall, derives from a Latin adjective meaning on or toward the left hand.) Going on half a century later, whenever I pick up a pencil in my left hand, I still half expect to hear the swoosh of a nun's ruler heading toward my knuckles!

Our grammar school class consisted of thirty kids at most, small enough that everyone seemed to take on a specific role. Mine turned out to be some of the best early training you can get for running a huge bureaucracy. I proved to be a good broker, a deft intermediary who could get along with the good students and the good athletes, the class stars and the class wallflowers. When a bully was picking on someone, I was usually able to find some middle ground between them, some way both of them could save face. Usually, that is; not always. Once, frustrated by a sixth-grader who kept beating up on one of my second-grade classmates despite my intervention, I hauled off and punched the kid in the nose hard enough that he bled all over the place. That occasioned another visit to our household by someone demanding justice: the sixth-grader's father, apparently not embarrassed that his son had been bested by someone almost half his age. (My father's punishment, by the way, didn't take that into account either, or the facts of the case: another good lesson in practical justice.)

Junior high opened our eyes considerably. We moved on to a school next to the parish's main church, St. Joseph of the Palisades, in West New York, just as the city and the parish were starting to undergo a sea change. Six new students were waiting in our classroom, and not one of them spoke more than a few words of English. They were all the children of refugees from Castro's Cuba, the first wave of an influx that would transform large sections of West New York and nearby Union City into Little Havanas, just as an equal influx was upending Miami, 1,300 miles south of us. Today, St. Joseph's—where my brothers and I were baptized and had our first communions—is largely a Cuban-American parish.

All that was for later, though. After seven years of fairly predictable schooling, we junior highers had been handed something exotic, and most of us tried to take advantage of it. We taught our new classmates English; they taught us Spanish; and before long, we were all getting along just fine. I kept up the Spanish study in high school, and by the time I graduated and got my real-estate license, I was probably the only Spanish-speaking house peddler in all of Hudson County, a nice boon to the family business for a few summers, before the new Cuban-Americans could get into the real-estate business themselves.

At the end of eighth grade, the nuns turned us over to the Christian Brothers who ran St. Joseph's High School, a shock to the system that took some getting used to. A lot of the brothers had trained at Lincoln Hall, a fortresslike facility up in northern Westchester County, New York, where the order had been trying to reclaim delinquent and troubled boys since the mid-nineteenth century. We didn't count many hardened cases among the ninety or so of us in my high school class, but some of the brothers still tended to treat us as if any moment we might slip out the door and steal a car or break into the locker room of the separate girl's high school housed in our same building.

When they weren't on the prowl for incipient criminals or trying to drum Latin through our thick skulls, the brothers made a serious effort to involve us in good works. In that, they were generally successful—in my case, with spectacular results.

The summer after my junior year, I went down to eastern Kentucky with a school community-service group called Young Christian Students. It was my first trip any distance away from northern New Jersey, and it landed us in a place that at first introduction seemed to be on the far side of the moon. This was right in the heart of Appalachia, a land of sandstone ridges and small hollows, tiny towns that looked to be half-abandoned, cold-water shacks, and small tobacco fields wherever the sun shone and the soil was up to the challenge. Our St. Joseph's High School had aligned itself with a local parish whose mission was to educate the people and help them find jobs. As part of that goal, we YCS volunteers were sent out to do a census of the people of the region. Some of those we talked with didn't know what state they lived in or who the president was. ("Roosevelt" was a frequent answer.) Many had never traveled more than two towns away from where they had been born and raised. Ancient cars sat rusted out beside their porches. Televisions were virtually nonexistent.

It was all a tremendous culture shock, and yet the more I talked to the people out there, and especially the ones my age, the more I learned. I could tell my new teenage friends about the Statue of Liberty, the Empire State Building, and *Gunsmoke*. They could tell me about alcoholic fathers, about leaving school at age seven to do what little paying work could be found, about their own run-ins with the law. One friend I made that summer told me about a little town called Sandcastle. The place was so tough, he claimed, that every evening when it got dark, the sheriff just up and left the place to the shooters. All I could do was look at him with my jaw hanging open. How could you have a town without a policeman to keep order?

Sometimes my ignorance was just plain comical. As part of broadening the employment base of the region, we worked part-time on an experimental farm that was trying to encourage locals to plant cucumbers that could then be sold at farm stands and to grocery chains. We would even take people out into the fields to show them how to pick cucumbers . . . except that I kept calling them "pickles."

"You wait until the pickle is about this long," I'd explain, "and this green, then you grab it by—"

"Cucumber!" someone would call across to me. "It's called a cucumber."

"Well, it looks like a pickle to me."

At least I didn't call it a kosher dill.

The program worked, though, even in spite of know-nothing summer farmers like me, and it wasn't just some Save Appalachia flash in the pan, either. Father Henry Beiting, the local priest who ran it, stuck with the project until it was one of the largest employers in that part of the state, and he remembered just about everyone who had passed through his door. I'd been FBI director for maybe a year when I got a note from Father Beiting congratulating me and asking if he could come by for a visit for old time's sake. As he was getting ready to leave, I asked where he was headed next.

"Oh," he said, "I'm off to the Capitol to see one of my good friends, Hal Rodgers. Do you know him?"

Know him? Not only did Hal Rodgers represent the Fifth District of Kentucky, where I had once grown pickles, but he was also chairman of the Appropriations Committee that oversaw the FBI.

Every high school career should have at least one moment when all the self-consciousness of being a teenager falls away and you see the world clearly for what it is. For me, that trip to Kentucky was such a time. Everything I had been told about the joys of serving and helping came together in that experience. I got far more out of those seven weeks than I ever could have given back to the people down there. In a way, though, I was even luckier because I had two such experiences in high school, the second far more negative.

I hadn't given a lot of thought to college by the time my senior year rolled around, but to the extent that I had a fantasy school I wanted to attend, it was the United States Military Academy at West Point. My dad had shown me the campus during a trip to Bear Mountain, and I'd loved everything about it: the uniforms, the way the place sits on a bluff overlooking the Hudson, the crispness of everything. "Duty, Honor, Country" seemed to speak personally to me. Dad was an army guy himself, a big influence, but West Point was also free if you could get in. The real-estate business limped along from year to year, but there was very little margin in the family budget, and my brother Bill's tuition at his private university had taken care of just about all the excess.

In truth, I also thought I might have a fair crack at getting into West Point. My grades weren't as good as Bill's and I was no star athlete, but I'd had my share of A's and B's, and I'd played a lot of intramurals. My classmates had also elected me head of the student disciplinary board. In effect, I was the presiding judge whenever the Christian Brothers would recommend some miscreant to us. Outside of school, I'd made Eagle scout, and I faithfully delivered the *Hudson Dispatch*. Several times a month, I also resumed my old altar-boy duties, and I had my Young Christian Student activities to bolster my résumé, including the time I spent in the evening reading to kids at St. Joseph's School for the Blind, down in Jersey City. I had no idea what the academy was really looking for, but I figured I was at least in the same solar system as its applicant pool.

Before any St. Joseph's student could even think about applying to college, though, he had to go through the oldest brother in the school, and that was a challenge. This brother hadn't risen to his college counselor's post, he'd sunk to it. Not only could he not cut it in the classroom anymore, rumor also had it that the brother had a drinking problem. As near as I could tell, he was stone sober when I showed up for my session.

"What do you want to do?" he asked as I was settling uncomfortably into my seat.

"Gee," I said, "I'd love to go to the U.S. Military Academy."

Why not give it my best shot?

The brother harrumphed a little, picked up my file, had a look at it, then turned back to me.

"You're not really college material," he finally said. "Go to trade school. Plumbers do very well these days."

I felt as if someone had driven a stake through my heart. *I'm finished,* I told myself as I left that meeting. *I'll never get into West Point. There's no sense even applying.* I didn't, either, and I was too dumb back then to get a second opinion. But somewhere in the back of my brain someone wiser than I was must have been monitoring all this because I never, ever again let anyone convince me that I couldn't achieve a goal if I set my heart on it.

Coincidentally, years later I was asked to join a Bronx-based Army JAG unit and was often a weekend warrior assigned to West Point.

CHAPTER 4

"The FBI? You're Crazy!"

Despite Brother Counselor's best efforts to discourage me, I did go to college—at Rutgers, the State University of New Jersey, in New Brunswick—and even got some scholarship aid to attend. As the crow flies, Rutgers is hardly any distance away from North Bergen, all of thirty miles down the New Jersey Turnpike, but in some ways it might as well have been on the other side of the continent.

Most overwhelming, at least initially, was the sheer scale of the place. I'd had ninety kids, all boys, in my high school graduating class, fewer than four hundred of us in the whole school. The first class I attended at Rutgers was Biology 101, held in what is now the old gymnasium on George Street. There must have been a thousand of us enrolled in that section. The teacher lectured from a TV monitor. Somewhere on the screen was posted the telephone number you could call if you had any questions, and the limited hours the teacher was available. Suddenly, Brother Counselor seemed almost warm and cuddly.

Appropriately enough, given the trajectory of my future life, my roommate freshman year was from Arkansas. Even more appropriately, we had trouble communicating. I spoke a New Jersey slang that must have sounded to him like I'd stepped out of some Edward G. Robinson gangster film of the 1930s. He favored homespun colloquialisms and spoke in a soft drawl far different from the twangy Kentucky accents that had been my only other exposure to dialects outside the greater New York City area. We got along just fine as things turned out, but I think we were both a little shocked at first to find ourselves in each other's company.

The biggest shock of all, though, was the Vietnam War. By the time I got to New Brunswick in the fall of 1967, the antiwar movement had begun to seep into the classroom and color student activities. When I finished my undergraduate degree four years later, there were almost daily demonstrations against the war. Often the campus was simply shut down; when it wasn't, there didn't seem to be a teacher of any subject who couldn't turn the classroom discussion to the war. In my two years as an American Studies major, I probably heard more about Ho Chi Minh than I did about Herman Melville, more about the Gulf of Tonkin Resolution than about the Federalist Papers. For a while during the fall of my sophomore year, the so-called Fort Dix 38—thirty-eight mostly African-American soldiers thrown in the slammer at nearby Fort Dix for protesting the Vietnam War—were almost more popular than the Rutgers Scarlet Knights varsity football team; and remember, college football *began* at Rutgers. The first intercollegiate game ever was played on a field along College Avenue: Rutgers topped Princeton 6–4. The year was 1869.

To be honest, I stayed mostly on the sidelines through it all. I was a straitlaced Catholic kid, raised to respect authority. I suppose I had more of a consumer's attitude toward college than many of my fellow students: except for the scholarship aid I was getting, I was mostly paying for all those course hours myself.

That's another factor that kept me from getting deeply involved with the social activism of the times: I was working almost half of every day, month in and month out. Summers, I kept up my real-estate work with Dad and sweated on a truck dock in North Bergen, New Jersey, unloading eighteen-wheelers and restacking the goods into smaller trucks. In New Brunswick, I got most of my jobs through Manpower, Inc., then the nation's leading temp-worker agency. Some nights, I'd be the hired hand on a beer truck; other nights, I'd be mixing and serving drinks at some rich guy's home. (Mixing and serving, I should add, with no training whatsoever. I can't imagine what I poured into the glass when I got my first order for a Manhattan.)

I was straitlaced in other ways, too. Beginning my sophomore year, I rented an apartment over a jeweler's on George Street and began subletting out the bedrooms to other students. I'd grown up in a boardinghouse; this stuff was second nature to me. But this was no Animal House. The third floor of the building was Varsity Sports Central: a constant parade of women up and down the steps, parties all night long. Our apartment, by contrast, was as quiet as a church-yard. Most of us ate in the university dining hall and spent our evenings either working or in the library. Everyone who wasn't holding down a night job was generally in bed by midnight.

Yet I did manage to get outside my little circle, and the circle wasn't quite so small as it often seemed. I got to know one of the football players upstairs, a wonderful young man named Jed, maybe a foot taller and a hundred pounds heavier than me. Like just about all his fellow football players, Jed was very upset by all the antiwar activity on campus. Coaches demand that their players submit to authority, and Jed was a natural patriot. But he was also a deep thinker, and none of the party animals on the third floor had any desire to discuss the war with him, so the two of us talked often about the pros and cons of what was happening all around us and across the Pacific. There were legitimate issues being raised, I told him, and between us we tried to understand what they were and figure out how we felt about them. Whatever doubts we might have raised in each other's minds, Jed joined the marines after college, and he was killed in Vietnam. His death shook me badly.

I found one of my richest undergraduate experiences lying right in my doorway, literally. I came home late one night from working on the beer truck to find an old man sleeping in the alcove of our apartment building. This was winter, about two in the morning. By the looks of him, the guy was homeless. He was certainly disheveled. I can't remember anymore if he was still cradling a bottle, but he reeked of booze. I thought about calling the police and asking them to take him to a shelter, but he looked so forlorn that I carried him up the stairs to our apartment, laid him down on a sofa in the living room, and covered him up as best I could. In the morning, I got him some coffee, and we began talking, and that's when my education began.

He told me his name was Flaherty, and he'd been one of three brothers who had gone through Colby College in Maine in the mid-1930s before heading off to Spain to fight General Franco and his fascists. I'm not sure I had ever heard of the Abraham Lincoln Brigade before then, but the Flaherty brothers had all joined up, part of an unlikely army of almost three thousand Americans drawn from all social castes and walks of life. Undertrained and facing Franco's superior firepower, the brigade suffered terrible losses throughout 1937 and '38 before the Spanish prime minister decreed that all foreign fighters were to leave the country.

I can remember asking why he and his brothers had gone, what was the lure that got them there. I was still trying to understand what was happening in Southeast Asia and the fracturing of my own country and campus.

"We were fighting fascism," he answered, "and if we didn't fight it in Spain, we knew we would have to fight it elsewhere in Europe. We were young. We were idealistic. We felt we needed to go over there and join the battle."

For a while after he returned to the States, Flaherty claimed, he became almost famous. He wrote articles about his experiences, even a book; and Hitler proved his fears about fascism correct. But the road would soon turn rough. Among the anti-Franco forces in Spain, the brigade members remained heroes for decades to come. In the United States, though, many people regarded them as communist agitators, and in fact, many of them had belonged to the communist or socialist-aligned organizations that flourished in America during the dark days of the Great Depression.

To J. Edgar Hoover, for one, the Spanish Civil War was less about defeating fascism than about the Soviets using social upheaval to establish a foothold on the Iberian Peninsula, and as FBI director, Hoover had the wherewithal to make life difficult for those who had joined the fight. Flaherty told me that he had been investigated by the Bureau and subsequently blackballed by it. He would show up at some job he was supposed to get, he said, but FBI agents would have gotten there first and made certain the job disappeared. Before long, he was hitting the bottle, and the bottle led him to skid row. He stuck around our apartment for a day; then I gave him a few bucks and off he went, presumably back to the vagrant's life he had been living for years.

I never saw him again, and I've never known exactly how much of his story to believe. But enough of it was true to give me a deep appreciation for the idealism of young men and women, however it's expressed, and for the potential of government to abuse and mis-use its awesome power. Flaherty might have been hooked on the sauce long before his career collapsed, but without lifting an official finger against him, the Bureau I was to eventually head had set out to undermine his work and ruin his life. No classroom could have taught me that lesson as well.

I had pretty much decided I wanted to be an attorney before I ever got to Rutgers, and I didn't see any reason to change uni-versities for my graduate education. I also knew Newark, where the law school was located, and would be able to live at home, where the price was right. Since I was an in-state student, the tuition was as right as it could get. Problem was, the war protests were still going on, and now they were interfering with my professional training, the real thing.

Early on, I made friends with Hubert Williams. Hubert would go on to become chief of police in Newark, New Jersey, and later head the Police Foundation in Washington, D.C., but back then he was just a Newark police lieutenant trying to slog his way through law school on the side and as frustrated as I was by all the class days lost to the Vietnam upheaval. Finally, the two of us made a sort of bargain. One day, he'd go to school, and if classes were being held, he'd call me and tell me to get myself over there. Another day, I'd reconnoiter and make the calls. The relay system saved us both a lot of time.

Hubert was helpful in another way, too. In that "Up the Estab-lishment" era, he was just about the only fellow student I dared tell that I was thinking about signing on with what the Left considered one of the biggest pigs going: the Federal Bureau of Investigation. In fact, I'll never forget Hubert's response when I first tried the idea out on him: "That's good, but don't tell *anyone!*" I did, though.

Arthur Kinoy was still in his early fifties when I was at Rutgers, but he was already a living legend among constitutional and civil-rights lawyers. He started his career in the late 1940s as a lawyer for the United Electrical Workers Union. Soon he found himself on the wrong side of the House Un-American Activities Committee and its powerful chairman, Joe Pool. (There's a famous photo of the diminutive Kinoy being dragged out of a HUAC hearing by three beefy federal marshals, one of whom has Arthur in a headlock.) He was part of the legal team that unsuccessfully tried to stop the execution of Julius and Ethel Rosenberg. From there, he moved on to participation in numerous landmark civil rights cases of the 1950s and '60s. In 1966, he founded the Center for Constitutional Rights. A few years later, he wrote a famous appeal brief of more than five hundred pages in the case of the Chicago Seven, lambasting Judge Julius Hoffman for presiding over a mockery of justice. Not long before I met him, Arthur had won a landmark Supreme Court decision holding that Richard Nixon could not, in effect, suspend the Constitution in the name of "national security."

Why did I choose Arthur Kinoy of all people to try out my career aspirations on? Probably because, whatever his politics, I admired him so much—his energy, his activism, his dynamic classroom manner, his piercing intellect. Besides all that, we had developed a good relationship. We liked each other. Nothing, though, quite prepared me for Arthur's response when I confided in him that I was thinking of joining the FBI.

"What are you going to do," he said, shaking his head, "go undercover and infiltrate them for us? Why would you want to do that?"

"I just think I could serve my country and do some good," I told him.

He delivered his final verdict with another shake of the head: "You're crazy."

But Arthur didn't despair for me entirely. Years later he told me that another of his students had come to him only a few months earlier and said that he was interested in becoming a federal judge. What should he do?

"I was thinking of you," Arthur told me. "I told him to join the FBI."

As to the "why" of the FBI, I think I had never quite gotten over that West New York policeman who showed up at our elementary school one day on community-service duty. It's amazing how little classroom moments like that can color our whole lives. Hudson County, where I'd grown up, and the jobs I'd held along the way also had given me a pretty fair introduction to the underside of American life and particularly to organized crime. It was hard to walk around the block in places like Jersey City and Union City back then without rubbing shoulders with a bookie or minor capo or some other made guy, or so it seemed. What better place to pursue an interest in organized crime than with the FBI? Assuming, that is, I didn't want to join the Bonanno family.

I realize now as I didn't then the role that religion also played in pushing me toward the FBI. Anyone who has read this far knows I was raised in a seriously Catholic family and educated in Catholic schools. My parents, the nuns who taught me in elementary school, the Christian Brothers we were turned over to for high school, practiced a very activist faith. It wasn't just what you believed and what you said; it was what you did that mattered. That's what I learned during my summer mission work in Kentucky when I was a teenager; it's what I felt reading to those kids at St. Joseph's School for the Blind. To me, government service was a place where I could take my American values and put them into practice.

It wasn't a crusade; I was and continue to be very conscious and very respectful of the primacy of law. The FBI wasn't a platform for me. It was more like a calling. Given who I was and what I believed and practiced, the place just felt right to me.

What really cemented my determination to join the Bureau, though, was a job I took at the start of my second year at Rutgers Law. I'd seen the position posted on one of the bulletin boards at school: the Newark office of U.S. Sen. Clifford P. Case was looking for a part-time clerk. The salary wasn't much, but I already held down plenty of better-paying jobs. The clerk's position, I thought, might give me some practical exposure to the law at the same time as it filled the gaps in my schedule caused by all the school closings and disruptions. So I applied, and Ruby Marshall, the lovely woman who ran Case's Newark office, hired me on the spot.

Cliff Case was what was known as a Rockefeller Republican, after New York Governor Nelson Rockefeller, the leader of the more liberal wing of the party; and he proved to be a remarkable person. Case was a man of great character and rock-ribbed virtue. Whenever he took the train up from Washington, he would always insist on walking the half mile or so from the train station to his office in the Federal Building. Then, as now, downtown Newark had some tough neighborhoods, and the senator's route took him right through one of them.

"Why don't I just pick him up?" I once asked Ruby. "I'm not busy right now."

"No," she said, "the senator doesn't like to have a fuss made." And believe me, he didn't.

At first, I just opened mail and wrote correspondence for Senator Case, but I kept getting more responsibilities during the two-plus years I worked in the office until finally I was representing Cliff Case at functions around the Newark area. But as impressive as the senator was and as much as I learned from him, working for Ruby Marshall was a great education, too. I can remember her telling me one day that the senator was a stickler for honesty and integrity. "Be very careful," she said. "If someone sends a gift, return it and make a note. We report everything." This was back in the early '70s, before such reporting was required. A few weeks later I was having lunch in the cafeteria with a guy my age who was holding down a similar position upstairs in the local office of the state's Democratic U.S. senator, Harrison Williams.

"Have you been going to the racetrack?" he asked me.

"The racetrack? Huh?"

"Oh," he said, "we get free passes to it. We get free everything."

I asked Ruby about it when I got back to the office, and she said, "They do get free everything and they take free everything. We don't do that."

Clifford Case would go on to complete four distinguished terms in the U.S. Senate before losing the Republican nomination in 1978 to Jeffrey Bell, who was subsequently defeated by Bill Bradley. Harrison Williams also would have served four terms in the Senate had he not resigned his seat in March of 1982 after being fingered in the Abscam sting operation in which FBI agents posing as Arab businessmen offered bribes to a number of politicians. Williams was subsequently sentenced to three years in prison. Turns out, insisting on high ethical standards does make a difference.

Maybe the greatest contribution Ruby Marshall made to my legal education and future career was a simple suggestion that I take a little time to go downstairs in the Federal Building and meet the U.S. attorney and his staff, maybe even watch them in action at the courthouse across the street.

"If you're interested in being a prosecutor or just a lawyer, this is a very historic time," she told me. "They're doing stuff that hasn't been done in years."

I took her up on that suggestion, too, and doing so clearly helped to set the curve of my life.

For most of the twentieth century, New Jersey wasn't exactly famous for the aggressiveness of its U.S. Attorney's Office. Political bosses ruled the state, corruption and organized crime flourished, and cronyism was the order of the day from top to bottom. Cliff Case helped to change all that. With Richard Nixon in the White House, Case finally got the chance to nominate a new U.S. attorney for the vacant office, and the fine man he chose, Fred Lacey, wanted nothing to do with old ways or old reputations. Lacey threw out of most of the career guys in the office and replaced them with young, tough, go-get-'em types. Once he had his team in place, he swept over the state like some kind of biblical avenging angel. Heads rolled. The political establishment screamed bloody murder. Even hardened Mafia types began to flinch and grouse, but it was all music to Fred Lacey's ears, and the indictments just poured out.

Maybe Lacey's most spectacular catch was the one closest at hand to the Federal Building he worked out of: Newark mayor Hugh Addonizio. A seven-term congressmen from New Jersey's Eleventh District, Addonizio bailed out of the House in 1962 to run for mayor of the state's largest city. In 1970, he was gearing up for a third term in office and a possible future race for governor when Lacey's team came crashing down on him. By the time the dust had cleared, Addonizio and fourteen others had been indicted by a federal grand jury on extortion and conspiracy charges. Even more spectacular, the case tied Addonizio to one Anthony "Tony Boy" Boiardo, an alleged Mafia boss and the son of the infamous gang head "Richie the Boot."

Addonizio subsequently did ten years in a federal prison, but he was far from alone among the New Jersey political elite. Under Fred Lacey and his dedicated successors, Herb Stern and Jonathan Goldstein, the convictions hit record levels, and I got to watch an amazing number of those trials. Sometimes I simply ran over to the courthouse when the Rutgers campus was in turmoil. Other times, I showed up for work across the street, and Ruby would send me straight to the courthouse so I could sit in the back and absorb it all. She knew where the great lessons were being taught.

The local FBI office was in the same federal courthouse where I watched all those trials, and it was there that I finally applied to join the Bureau. I didn't have much choice in the matter: Bureau regulations required applicants to go through the office closest to where they lived. But over the course of the two-plus years I worked for Cliff Case and monitored Fred Lacey's courtroom dramatics, I'd also gotten to know a number of the agents, including the impressive guy in charge of applications, Joe DiLeo, and a good thing it was because I was going to need a big helping hand.

The problem arose maybe halfway through a huge form I was required to fill out. The question looked innocent enough—"Have you ever been a member of a labor organization?"—but to me it sat there on the page like a live grenade. I remember saying to myself, What am I going to do about *this*?

I did, in fact, once belong to a labor organization: Local 560 of the International Brotherhood of Teamsters. I wasn't ashamed of it at all. I'd had to join up provisionally so I could work on the dock, loading and unloading those eighteen-wheelers, and I'd made a lot of money over the years doing that. But Local 560 was the private fiefdom of Tony Provenzano, and Tony, better known as Tony Pro, had a reputation less than savory. He was, for starters, a blood member of the Genovese mob family. Within a year of my applying to the Bureau, Tony Pro would almost certainly play a part in—and perhaps engineer—the disappearance of Jimmy Hoffa, then the head of the Teamsters' Union. Very credible evidence puts him in the car with Hoffa as it took off for the cement factory. Eventually, Tony Pro would be convicted on racketeering and murder charges, though not for the murder of Hoffa.

True to what were then the best Teamster traditions, some of Tony Pro's protégés also shook down their own local members. Every week the shop steward would come strolling along the dock, collecting $25 from each of us for the "lottery."

I was working with another college guy the first time it happened.

"What lottery?" he asked.

I let him know with my eyes that he should pay the money and shut up, but the lesson didn't take well. When the shop steward came back the next week for another lottery contribution, my friend asked who had won last week's lottery. Happily, the steward just kept walking, shaking his head at the ignorance of the educated.

"You got to understand," I told my workmate once we were out of earshot. "There *is* no lottery."

"Well, then I want my fifty bucks back."

"Oh, no," I told him. "You definitely do not want your money back."

Inspired by their boss's example, some of the senior guys on the dock doubled as loan sharks and the like, but no one who worked there could ever forget who sat at the top of the food chain. Along this filthy, barely ventilated, hundred-yard stretch of ugly loading dock hung an oil portrait of Tony Pro all dolled up in a zoot suit. Once or twice a day, some guy would come along with a stepladder, climb up to Tony's image, and give it a good dusting off.

Had the Newark FBI office known before this moment that I labored regularly on Tony Pro's loading dock, they probably would have tried to work me as a 137—FBI-speak for turning me into an informant. Now, though, I was sitting in Joe DiLeo's office, filling out an application so I could join the Bureau's ranks. What to say? And how much? Finally, I couldn't stand the tension.

"Mr. DiLeo," I said, "I did belong to a labor organization that might be some trouble. Teamsters Local Five-sixty."

"Five-sixty?" he said incredulously, peering over his glasses.

That's it, I figured. Game's over, but I wasn't quite ready to give up.

"All I ever did was buy a lottery ticket," I told him. There was no need for further explanation.

"Are you a member of organized crime?" he asked.

"No."

"Well, strictly speaking, we don't keep track of the lottery tickets, so I wouldn't mention it."

I didn't, and I got the job, and in the circular way of so many things in life, I ended up fifteen years later being the deputy in the U.S. Attorney's Office for the Southern District of New York when the Department of Justice basically handed the International Brotherhood of Teamsters to us, not to control it but to clean it up, make it at long last a democratic institution, and assure that all those guys on the loading docks who spent so many years terrified of Tony Pro and his kind didn't have to be afraid anymore.

When as director of the FBI I was asked to recommend someone to head up the independent review board that was eventually appointed to operate the union, I knew exactly who I wanted—the guy I'd spent so many days watching from the back of the courtroom when he was the U.S. attorney in Newark and later a great federal judge there: Fred Lacey. And, of course, just to complete the circle all the way, the president of the Teamsters' Union today is the son of the man Tony Pro probably helped encase in cement: Jimmy Hoffa Jr.

The FBI training facility in Quantico, Virginia, shares a large swath of federal land with the U.S. Marine Corps base of the same name, but the academy is far closer to being like a college campus than a boot camp. The sixteen-week program was divided into three parts. The academic instruction focused on how the Bureau does its communicating (back then, almost entirely by teletype and memo), how to write a report and conduct an interview, and a lot of instruction on the legal elements of investigations and prosecutions. (In those days, only about 5 to 10 percent of recruits had law degrees, so I had a leg up on the legal side.) The physical training included distance running, a gym program that featured rope climbing and shuttle runs, and general fitness. Firearms required us to qualify with a .38-caliber revolver from fifty yards away, no small feat.

The biggest issue for a lot of us, though, wasn't making it through the training program but where we were going to be assigned once we completed it. For me, there was no question. I wanted to go to New York City. My family would be nearby, and I had grown up on the outskirts of the city. Thanks to my Newark experiences and my days as a member in good standing of Local 560, I'd gotten the organized-crime bug, and if you wanted to bring down the wise guys, you had to go where they were most likely to gather. That was New York and environs, for sure.

In theory, bucking for the New York office should have given me a high chance of success. As exciting as the city is, most new agents would rather have gone anywhere else. In any other American city, the FBI is the law-enforcement kingpin, but in the Big Apple, the Bureau has to compete with a local police department of over forty thousand people—including its own organized-crime unit—plus two U.S. Attorney's Offices and the offices of five different district attorneys. Unless you really know what you're doing or, like me, had a free place to stay just across the river, New York is also the most expensive assignment going, and the FBI office there is so large that you can end up in some very specialized niche out of which you can never move.

In practice, landing a New York assignment had been brutally tough for a number of years, not because anyone wanted the jobs but because no one in New York wanted to take on first-year guys. The office had become packed with careerists who didn't want the apple cart upset. But attrition had begun to take a heavy toll, and all of a sudden space had opened up. Nine of the twenty-four of us in my class at the academy were assigned to New York, an almost unheard-of number. One of them was a young lawyer from New York, Lew Schiliro, who would later become the Assistant Director in Charge (ADIC) of our New York office and one of the best agents ever in the FBI. Twenty-six years later we would work together at MBNA.

We graduated in August 1975, were handed our badges, then went to the gun vault, where we were issued our .38s and six rounds of ammunition sealed in a plastic envelope, at which my mother almost fainted dead away for fear that her Louie was about to become a gunfighter. And with that, most of the nine piled in one old car with our small arsenal of unloaded Smith & Wesson 2.5-inch .38 revolvers—we weren't allowed to put the bullets in until we got to our assignment—and set off up Interstate 95 for the big city and our first brush with the bad guys and the real world. Except that it didn't quite work that way.

In New York, we were entrusted to the care of Bob Sweeney, a wonderful agent who opened the first meeting with the news that no one in the office wanted to work with us.

"You need experience," he said. "You can't just hit the street coming out of Quantico."

Then Sweeney asked us all for our guns.

"What?" we said, shocked. We'd just gotten them.

"Your guns—give them to me. I don't want you to shoot anyone by mistake."

"Uh, Mr. Sweeney?" one of my fellow graduates asked as our new supervisor was locking our guns in the office safe.

"Yeah."

"Would you like the bullets, too?"

"Geez," he said, "you're walking around New York with un-loaded guns? That's nuts!"

I'd made no bones about my desire to work in the organized-crime section. I wanted to be out hitting the pavement, doing the things I had been dreaming about doing all through the academy. Someone must have been listening because before long one of the senior agents grabbed a handful of us new guys and asked if we wanted to work the "street."

"The street? Yeah! Sure!" I said. And thus I got the first assignment I was ever to get in the Bureau I would come to lead eighteen years later: parking cars.

The office in those days was located at a fashionable Upper East Side address—201 East Sixty-ninth Street—in a building shared with Hunter College. For subway riders, it was terrific. We were practically on top of the E train. But driving to work was another matter. No one wanted to pay to park, but finding legal spots on the nearby streets could take up hours each week. For long periods, the New York police were happy to accommodate us: the office would bundle up its parking tickets, take them to some precinct house, and the violations would disappear. Sometimes, though, the NYPD got tired of playing footsie, or was mad at us for something, or just wanted the revenue. We were in one of those down periods when I arrived, which is why I was called into action.

I'd wait downstairs behind this little desk. The guys would come in and throw their keys on it, and I'd have to race off and find their cars—some couldn't be bothered to tell me where they'd left them—then circle block after block until I found a legal space. For excitement, I'd listen to the bank robbery squad's channel on the police radio while I worked. My law-school classmates would call and ask how things were going, and I'd say, "Gee, it's really interesting work. I'm out on the street all day, but you know how it is, I can't really talk about it." And I really couldn't. I was too embarrassed to tell them that after three years of law school and sixteen weeks of specialized training, I was a parking valet with no gun.

Then, a *Sports Illustrated* ad salesman named Samuel Bronfman II got himself kidnapped, and the tabloids went nuts. Despite his relatively lowly job, Bronfman was an heir to the Seagram's fortune and lived in a mansion in Purchase, New York, from which he was presumably snatched. That was enough to drive the *New York Post* and *Daily News* into a front-page frenzy, and to drive us into a frenzy, too. For nine days, until Bronfman was released unharmed and his father's $2.3-million ransom payment recovered, the office did almost nothing else. There wasn't a clue to go on, no leads. But that didn't stop us from having twenty guys stationed in cars at the Holland Tunnel just in case something broke. The national security and counterintelligence sections were called to duty. Shifts stretched out to twelve hours at a time. Backup was nonexistent. Everyone was exhausted, which makes it even stranger that none of us new agents were included in the search party. But we weren't. They didn't want us screwing it up. Still, the Bronfman case did create a serious manpower shortage back in the office, and ongoing investigations had to be tended to. Finally, the office got so desperate that Lew Schiliro and I were assigned to a Title 3: a court-authorized wiretap. Action, at last!

First, though, since wiretaps hadn't been a part of our training, we had to learn how to do one. The two of us ran all over the place, grabbing guys who were bleary-eyed over Sam Bronfman and asking them how to work a Title 3. Then we settled down to the particular case at hand. Our subject was a bookie who lived down on Mulberry Street, a part of Little Italy much favored by the mob. (John Gotti, for one, loved to stroll down Mulberry Street like some lord of crime.) As with a lot of bookies, you could set your watch by this guy's schedule. Every Monday through Saturday night at precisely 10:30, he left his apartment, got in his car, and went from wire room to wire room to collect his take. Following him couldn't have been easier, but the equipment we had to work with was another matter.

Someone had hidden a microphone in the guy's glove compartment, but it was a radio-frequency broadcast. To hear what was going on in the car, you practically had to stick on his bumper. Worse, you needed big aerials on your own car to pick up the signal.

"The guy's going to know we're following him," we screamed at our boss once we'd doped out the situation.

"No," he said, "he's old. He's stupid."

"But isn't he organized crime?"

"Oh, yeah," he said, "he's a made guy, but gamblers don't hurt anyone." This was good news since we still didn't have our guns back.

"And no one's going to notice us on Mulberry Street, of all places?"

Apparently not, the silence seemed to say.

So, sure enough, we set out our first night in a government-issue black Ford sedan with huge aerials waving off the back, parked ourselves right in the middle of Gangland Central, and waited for our gambler subject to exit his apartment at precisely 10:30 P.M., which he did. Then we followed him in our anything-but-undercover car as he went from wire room to wire room, sticking hard on his bumper, ready to record any little tidbits, and picking up not a single word of anything. An hour into this, the gambler came out of yet another wire room, waved to us, said, "Hi, guys, how ya doing?" and set off for his next stop. Then it dawned on us. There was no one in the car with him, and this was before cell phones, almost before car phones. Of course, we weren't picking up anything to record.

There *was* nothing! Nor would there be anything for the two weeks or so that we followed our gambler friend. He couldn't have been *that* stupid and still manage to get out of bed in the morning.

It was pure Keystone Kops, to be sure, but it was all experience, all on-the-job training, and far more serious work waited just ahead.

CHAPTER 5

"The Kid's Got Nothing to Do with It"

I f you went solely by the numbers, the FBI I joined in the summer of 1975 had been fighting organized crime to a standstill. Gambling cases, loan sharking, extortion—we were all over them, opening up investigation after investigation, securing wiretaps (a lot of them more effective than the one I had cut my teeth on), filling up the jails with wise guys and assorted thugs. To a congressional oversight committee, the results must have looked very impressive. Arrests were up X percent for the fiscal year; convictions up Y percent. Clearly, the Bureau was giving American taxpayers their money's worth.

In truth, though, the numbers were a lot of sound and fury signifying very little. The cases were overwhelmingly penny ante, the guys we collared nobodies. The bulk of the arrests involved gambling because they were the easiest ones to make and thus the surest way to inflate our numbers, but the people we pulled in on them were almost always associates, guys waiting to be made. They'd be out on bail almost before we got them behind bars. They'd keep their mouths shut because the punishment for ratting was far more swift and certain on the other side of the law than on ours and because they knew that, even without talking, their sentences were going to be next to nothing. Meanwhile, the enterprise behind the gambling or loan sharking or extortion—the five New York families of La Cosa Nostra, or the other mob families around the nation—were supremely unfazed. So what if some punk takes a fall? Punks are never in short supply.

The Omnibus Crime Control and Safe Streets Act of 1968 began, slowly, to change all that. Organized-crime strike forces, set up under the bill, brought together the FBI, local law enforcement officials, and strike-force leaders from the U.S. Attorneys' Offices, and set them loose on targets that would shake the mob families at their roots, not just out at the extremities. To make it all work, though, the Bureau had to lose its old show-me-the-numbers mentality, and for that Tom Emery gets huge credit.

Tom was running the organized-crime division at the FBI's New York office when I first got there. A brilliant and iconoclastic guy, he was near the end of a long career with the Bureau, and perhaps because he wasn't worried by then about incurring the wrath of anyone at headquarters—or maybe simply because he had seen how much wasted motion and energy went into hauling in small-time hoods—Tom set off on a crusade.

Unlike the average gambling collar, the International Longshoremen's Association was a worthy target. The union was monstrously corrupt, and the corruption spread into the shipping industry itself. What's more, what with hijacking, cargo theft, insurance fraud, and extortion fattening the kitty, controlling the docks was so profitable that, at least in the New York area, all five families had a piece of the action. Bring the mobbed-up union leadership down, go after the rotten managers in the shipping industry, and you'd hit the Mafia where it counts, but you couldn't do that on the cheap, Tom argued, and you couldn't do it if you were looking over your shoulder at statistics the whole time. Running the ILA to ground would take time, and it would take resources. At the end of the day there was also no guarantee you would net a single conviction, but the convictions you did get would count. We wouldn't just be treading water against the mob any longer.

For a conservative bureaucracy like the FBI, it was a radical proposition, but Tom found a champion at headquarters in the person of Sean McWeeney, who had once worked Organized Crime in New York and was now section chief of Organized Crime down in Washington. And in Bob Fiske, of the U.S. Attorney's Office for the Southern District of New York, the UNIRAC case, as it became known—for Union Racketeering—found a leader worthy of the challenge. Among the young strike-force attorneys assigned to the case was Barbara Jones, a brilliant lawyer and now federal judge who continues to add to her impressive résumé. (Barbara presided with distinction over the trial of former WorldCom CEO Bernard Ebbers.)

I was still learning my way around the New York office when I was added to the strike force, along with Bob Cassidy, a former CIA officer and a terrific investigator. Part of my job, going back to my legal training, was to put together a memo of all the various violations and federal statutes that might apply both to labor racketeering and management corruption—a handbook of sorts for the agents involved in the UNIRAC case. Many of the violations were obvious; any second-year law student or even talented paralegal could have done the work. But I found myself thinking as I pored over the possibly relevant statutes that with racketeering small can be beautiful. Take the Taft-Hartley Act, for example. It makes it a misdemeanor for a labor official to take a gift. The Labor Department maintains a small office to enforce the provision, but the misdemeanor is so commonplace and the penalty so minimal—a maximum one year in prison—that no one worries much about it. I discovered, though, that that little, puny misdemeanor had hidden strengths. For one thing, it was what's known as a "predicate offense" for a racketeering case: you could use this relatively tiny infraction to build something far larger. Even more important, taking a gift in violation of the Taft-Hartley Act gave us standing to pursue a federal wiretap on the individual involved. And the gift misdemeanor wasn't flying solo. Plenty of other small statutes gave us entry through the back door to big-time malfeasance.

At first, FBI headquarters was a little dumbstruck by what we were proposing. We've never really done anything like this, I can remember Barbara Jones saying; we've never used misdemeanors to build a racketeering case. But it didn't take her long to see the advantages and to begin to apply them. When I'd started on UNIRAC, Bob Cassidy and I accounted for at least 20 percent of all the New York "OC" (organized crime) agents assigned to the case. Soon, we had thirty or forty agents—at least a third of the Organized Crime Division—working full-time on it, maybe the most intense and sustained street work the division had ever known. Wiretaps were everywhere: in cars; in phones; in offices; hidden on bodies, some of them suspects we had managed to flip, some of them our own people.

Given the relatively primitive technology of a quarter century and more ago, any wiretap was a constant source of tension. Would it work? Would it be discovered? If it was on some informant, would we ever see him again? Inevitably, a few wiretaps also provided us with some of the greatest comic relief of the whole investigation. Thank God wise guys aren't necessarily the smartest people in the world.

Take George Barone. George was a member of the Genovese family and an ILA official, but he lived and worked out of a Florida address so that's where we went to run the wiretap. We once equipped our witness with a simple pocket transmitter and sent him off to a "meet" with George and the results were great. George knew and trusted our guy, and he talked his head off. After the meet, they were both in the bathroom when somehow, in the process of pulling his trousers up, our informant managed to let the transmitter slip out of his pocket. When we heard it go *clang* on the tile floor, we were ready to race in and rescue our guy, but he calmly says to George, "Oh, don't worry. It's just my pacemaker." And George, bless him, says, "Gee, I'm sorry," and keeps right on yakking away.

Then there was the case of the two supposedly very smart street guys who were always extremely careful about where and how they communicated. We got a wiretap order, at any rate, figuring they had to talk to each other over the phone now and again, but we didn't have much hope for it, especially after the informant we had working on them assured us that if they said anything at all, it would be very cryptic. No sooner do we turn the wiretap on than they're on the phone to each other, talking not in code but in whispers, as if the bug were somewhere else in the room, not in the phone wires themselves.

Sometimes, too, the guys doing the monitoring provided our own comic relief. One of the people we wiretapped in the UNIRAC case was Sal—or Salmonella, as we always referred to him. We put a tap on Sal's phone at his house in the Bensonhurst section of Brooklyn, but because of the technology on this particular device, we could receive the signal only from a high point somewhere above it. The only place high enough and accessible enough was the local VA hospital, so we arranged with the security chief there to let us have a room on one of the top floors of the building. To provide cover, he issued us security cards, complete with photos.

"What kind of doctor do you want to be?" he asked me.

"Neurosurgeon," I said, and bingo, I was one, a twenty-seven-year-old wonder boy, at least on my plastic ID card.

My partner opted for being a "transplant doctor," which the security chief amended to cardiologist.

Every day, we would show up in our doctor uniforms, flash our doctor IDs, then take the elevator up to the top floor and spend the day waiting for Sal to call someone or receive a call. That was our routine—until, that is, my partner began hitting on one of the nurses in the hospital library during his breaks.

"You can't do that," I told him. "We've got work to do, and you'll blow our cover."

"Aw," he said, "don't worry. I told her I'm sort of a new doctor. She's giving me cardiology books to read. I'm helping her study."

For a while, it seemed he was right. The romance blossomed. Our work went along unimpeded. Then one morning we were reporting for duty when the nurse burst out of an operating room with a panicked look, spotted us, and yelled, "Doctors! Doctors! We need you in here now. It's an emergency!" At which point, my partner and I looked at each other and took off running. We weren't going in there on a bet!

Maybe my favorite of all the UNIRAC wiretap tales involved another witness who agreed to meet a wise guy in one of the Italian-American social clubs that the New York mobs love. We fitted our guy with a tape recorder—not so miniature back then—which we strapped into his groin. (He was sure to be frisked when he walked in, but delicacy generally didn't permit a pat in the crotch.) Sure enough, the recorder works fine, and we're getting terrific stuff. Since the two of them have moved out front, we can even see the meeting going down. Then, lo and behold, an old mangy dog that looked as if it hadn't moved off its spot on the social club floor for a decade staggers to its feet, sets its sights on our guy, walks over, and buries its nose between his legs. Old, the dog was; but it could still hear the sound of the tape whirling on its reel. Knowing the gig is up, our guy turns and runs down the street, where we grab him and whisk him away, eventually to a federal witness protection program. Maybe an hour after all this happened, we drove by the club again and found a street celebration going on. They must have bought a case of steaks for that old dog—the Canine Hero of the Hour.

They were all dangerous people, all people who had stolen at will, extorted money from innocents, in some cases killed and maimed their fellow citizens. But sometimes all you could do was laugh. The investigation, though, was no laughing matter. The prestige of our New York office, the reputations of Tom Emery, Sean McWeeney, Barbara Jones, and the rest of us who had signed on to the crusade were all on the line. If we had nothing to show after two years of turning normal protocols on their head, we all knew that the Bureau and our office were headed back to trying to humble the mob and appease our congressional masters with an abundance of almost meaningless nickel-and-dime gambling arrests. But damned if it didn't work, and big-time.

UNIRAC led to the indictment and conviction of the senior-most officials of the Longshoremen's Union in New York, but we didn't stop there. Lead led to lead, thread to thread. Soon we were rolling up union officials and shipping-company executives in Newark, Norfolk, New Orleans, Miami, and other port towns. We didn't go after the shippers who paid out money to the union basically because they were being shaken down—they were victims, not criminals—but plenty of other shippers were paying for a competitive advantage, and we swept them up right along with the mob whenever and wherever we found them.

To the five mob families of New York City, UNIRAC was a devastating blow and a clear signal that the rules had changed. After decades of playing cat-and-mouse with their petty minions, we finally got their attention. Anthony Scotto made sure we did.

In the ILA, Anthony Scotto was Mr. Big. His dad had been a longshoreman in Brooklyn, and Tony had grown up on the docks, but a life of heavy lifting wasn't for him. Tony went into management, heading up Local 1814, which ran the Brooklyn docks, and serving also as a vice president of the national union. Tony also rose up handsomely in the Mafia, eventually becoming a captain in the Gambino family. In honor of his dual but closely related professions, he kept an office on Court Street in Brooklyn to see to his local duties, and in lower Manhattan where he became a mover and shaker among New York's elite.

He was from the very beginning one of our prime targets, and we worked him hard. A wiretap in his Manhattan office picked up all sorts of incriminating evidence, but we dogged him by foot, too. I was part of a small team following him one day in 1976 when we got word that a big political rally on behalf of then presidential candidate Jimmy Carter was going to take place on Court Street, in front of the union local. We sent word to the Secret Service that we would be in the crowd. When the rally got under way, we were there, dressed down, and thus got to witness the future president of the United States receiving a golden grappling hook from Scotto, whom we were closing in on arresting, and from his local vice president, Anthony Anastasia, nephew of Albert "the Mad Hatter" Anastasia, who had been blown away in the barbershop of the Park Sheraton Hotel in Manhattan nineteen years earlier.

Carter, of course, didn't know about any of this. He was just campaigning, but I can remember all of us who were there undercover shaking our heads as we walked away and saying this is going to be an interesting prosecution. And was it ever.

Two other things Tony Scotto was: a political power broker and a kind of Mafia-chic socialite. Tony's union voted the way Tony told it to vote, and there were enough members that Tony was courted and feted by politicians throughout the city and state. Hugh Carey, then the sitting governor of New York, appeared as a character witness at the sentencing phase of Tony's trial, after he had been convicted of racketeering, in large part by playing back his own words for the jury as captured on the wiretap. Former New York City mayors Abe Beame and Robert Wagner, and onetime mayor and "Silk Stocking" district representative John Lindsay joined the parade to the character witness stand. It was as if the guy had won the Nobel Peace Prize, not been exposed as a bullying, lawless, Gambino family capo, and an unrepentant one at that. When Scotto emerged from prison three years later, the pols flocked to his gala welcome-home dinner.

All that was a lesson for me, too, this one in how politics can sometimes destroy judgment and corrupt moral sense.

I spent four of the most intense years of my life working on the UNIRAC case, and my reward at the end, in 1980, was to be summoned to headquarters in Washington and handed a sterile office deep in the heart of a massive, layered, classical bureaucracy. The street, it was not. The wise guys weren't the same either.

My job was twofold. The first part was to set up a nationwide labor-racketeering program, not geared just to the usual suspects— the ILA and the Teamsters foremost among them—but also reaching out to include a broad cross-section of unions. We worked with the Bureau's various division offices to establish labor-racketeering coordinators, many of whom went on to set up racketeering squads of their own. All bureaucracies resist change, and the FBI was and still is no exception. But then-director William Webster was a big supporter of what we were trying to do. He knew what a blow UNIRAC had dealt the mob and wanted to keep the momentum going. Still, the work was slow and tedious, especially by comparison to what I had been doing.

Fortunately, the other half of my job—working with the Permanent Senate Subcommittee on Investigations, what had once been known as the McClellan Committee—was just the opposite. Sam

Nunn, the Georgia Democrat, and Warren Rudman, newly elected to the Senate as a New Hampshire Republican, were chairman and cochair at the time, and both were looking for a splashy target. They decided to hold hearings on organized crime's penetration of the labor unions, and I set about preparing committee members and staff for the hearings. Both Nunn and Rudman were not only excellent investigators, they were wonderful public servants from whom I learned a great deal.

Teddy Gleason, the president of the International Longshoremen's Association, had come out of the UNIRAC investigation unscathed. We were never able to get enough goods on him to send him to the slammer, but at the least, he would have had to be blind, deaf, and dumb not to realize what was going on inside his union. None of that, though, discouraged Teddy. He showed up at the Senate hearings, promised that the ILA was free of organized crime and corruption, and generally gave out the impression that no one in the union movement was more for truth, justice, and the American way than Thomas W. "Teddy" Gleason.

Warren Rudman, who had spent six years as attorney general of New Hampshire, listened to this as long as he could, then broke in to Teddy's paean to his presidency.

"Well," he said, "I understand that when you were asked to testify in the New York [UNIRAC] case, you took the fifth before the grand jury."

Teddy went berserk as soon as Rudman spoke. You could just see the huge balloon of his ego collapsing in front of the committee members. Every time I read that the ILA has presented its annual Teddy Gleason Scholarships to deserving college aspirants, I think of that moment and recall the person whom the scholarships memorialize. Sometimes good things can come of bad people.

The Senate hearings also gave me a chance to have a minireunion with one of the most colorful characters I had run across in

(left to right)
Louie Freeh, a cousin,
William Freeh (brother),
and two cousins. Jersey
City, N.J., circa 1955.
Personal photo

FBI Girls Basketball Team,
New York, circa 1975–76
Personal photo

Louie and Marilyn
on their wedding day.
Washington, D.C.,
April 16, 1983.
Personal photo

Giudice Giovanni Falcone, Italy. Assassinated at Palermo with his wife, Francesca, and two police officers on May 23, 1992.

Photo courtesy of the Falcone Foundation

Their destroyed car

Associated Press

Family meeting with John Cardinal O'Connor, Archbishop of New York, July 1993   *Personal photo*

Swearing-In Ceremony, FBI Headquarters, September 1, 1993. Receiving FBI Director credentials from Attorney General Janet Reno.

Photo courtesy of the FBI

Swearing-In Ceremony, FBI Headquarters, September 1, 1993.
(left to right) Louie and Marilyn Freeh, President Clinton, Attorney General Janet Reno, and Judge Frank Johnson.

Photo courtesy of the FBI

Swearing-In Ceremony, Courtyard of the FBI Headquarters, September 1, 1993. *(left to right)* Judge Frank Johnson, Marilyn, Justin, Brendan, Louie, Sean, President Clinton, Bernice Freeh, Connor, Bill Freeh, and Floyd Clarke.   *Photo courtesy of the FBI*

Dedication of Falcone
Memorial, FBI
Headquarters,
September 22, 1994.
Anna and Maria
Falcone (sisters) next
to bust, and Attorney
General Janet Reno
on stage.
Photo courtesy of the FBI

FBI Badge
Photo courtesy of the FBI

Opening of the FBI Academy in Budapest,
April 22, 1995
Associated Press

Papal Visit, Cardinal's Residence, New York, 1996. *(left to right)* Louie, Brendan, Justin, Marilyn, Bernice Freeh, and Cardinal O'Connor (obstructed) with the pope.

Photo courtesy of papal photographer

Freeh and Elie Wiesel at the Holocaust Memorial Ceremony, FBI Headquarters, January 1998

Photo courtesy of the FBI

East African Embassy Bomb Site, 1998. *(left to right)* Don Kerr, Leo West, Louie Freeh, Jerry Bamel, Jimmy Carter, Dale Watson, and Greg Carl.

Photo courtesy of the FBI

President George Bush Sr. and Louie Freeh
at the FBI's 90th Anniversary Ceremony,
Courtyard of the FBI Headquarters,
September 1999

Photo courtesy of the FBI

President George Bush Sr. and Louie
Freeh at the FBI's 90th Anniversary
Ceremony, September 1999

Photo courtesy of the FBI

Louie's parents, Bernice and
William Freeh, 2000

Personal photo

Pizza Connection agents, Rome, 2000. *(left to right)* Carmine Russo, Louie Freeh, Charlie Rooney, and Pat Luzio. *Personal photo*

Louie Freeh and family with President Bush in the Oval Office, Washington, D.C., April 2001.
(left to right) Chief of Staff Bob Bucknam, Roger Coyle, Sean, Mary Coyle, Marilyn, President Bush, Liam, Sean, Connor, Louie, Brendan, and Justin.
Photo courtesy of the White House

Colin, Sean, Brendan, Marilyn, Louie, Liam, Connor, and Justin. Maine 2001 *Personal photo*

My Office and "The Wall" in FBIHQ, May 2001. Over the years I "exhibited" the boys' drawings on my wall next to my desk. *(left to right)* Roger and Mary Coyle, Brendan, Sean, Colin, Connor, Louie, Marilyn, Liam, and Justin. *Photo courtesy of the FBI*

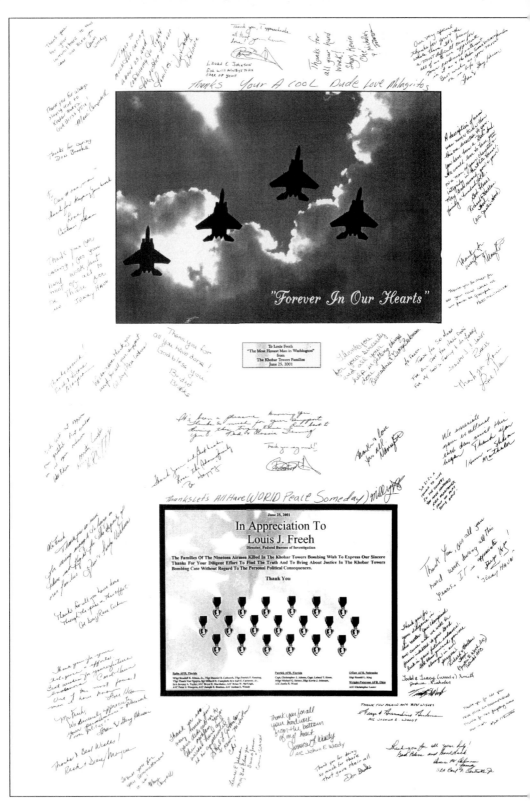

Plaques presented to Director Freeh in June 2001
by the families of the nineteen Khobar Airmen

the four years of UNIRAC. The first time Mike Clemente and I met, I was walking around naked in the locker room of the Shelton Health Club on Schermerhorn Street in Brooklyn Heights. That was my job. I was still a wet-behind-the-ears agent. Mike was a seventy-two-year-old overweight gambler, extorter, and Genovese family captain who liked to do business in the health club sauna. Regular as any mailman, Mike would show up, doff his clothes, and head into the sauna. Once he was settled in, other guys would walk in, strip down, and head in to join him, except many of them would be carrying packages full of cash from different people in the shipping industry. Sometimes, the guy who went in to see Mike would be our own witness, John, who worked for a ship stevedoring company, but John never went in with a wire because there was no place to hide it. That was Mike's genius of using the sauna for an office.

My primary job was to protect John—to be there just in case something went wrong—but I was also there to spot the guys going in with the cash envelopes and let our agents on the street outside know when they were leaving and what they looked like so they could try to identify them from the cars they came and went in. Not surprisingly, after days and days of parading around the locker room in my birthday suit, I drew Mike's attention. He was in the club's rinky-dink café, enjoying his daily apple juice, when he broke the ice.

"How you doing?" he says to me. "You a lawyer?" (The club was just behind the Brooklyn courthouse. Most of its clientele were lawyers, judges, and local politicians.) Amazingly, nobody had said what to do if "Big Mike" spoke to me.

"Yeah," I said.

"Where do you work?"

"Well," I told him, still being honest, "I'm not working as a lawyer right now. I'm not sure if I ever will."

"C'mon," he says, "be a judge. They got all the power; they make

115

all the decisions. I know some. I'll talk to them about you. They'll hire you."

"That's kind—"

"No, I mean it. They're my friends. I'll tell them. They'll see you." And probably they would have.

We kept this banter up for weeks until it became a running joke between us. Then my coveted undercover role ended, and I figured Mike had forgotten me. But he hadn't. A year or so later, I was sitting in the well of the Manhattan federal courtroom with the prosecutor when Mike's UNIRAC arraignment got under way. He spotted me immediately and started giving me one of those thumbs-up, everything's going to be okay signals, and I kept thinking, What is he, nuts? We've got the goods on him! But it was me, not himself, Mike was worried about. Finally, Mike's lawyer came up to me and asked, "Are you an FBI agent?" I said, almost sheepishly, "Yes." "I told Mike that," he said, "but he insisted that I tell the judge, 'Let the kid go. He's got nothing to do with it.'"

Mike was still atoning for his sins in prison when the Senate subcommittee decided to hold its hearings on organized crime, so we had to make special arrangements to bring him down to testify, which was just what Mike wanted. We talked for a while before his appearance, reminiscing about the not-so-good old times. Finally, he got down to business.

"You know, kid," he said, "I'm gonna take the fifth."

"Gee, Mike, I sort of suspected you might do that."

"Careful," he went on, holding up his hand. "Don't tell no one. I've been keeping them up in the air a bit so they'd let me out."

I didn't rat him out in advance, and Mike did take the fifth in front of all those senators and their staffs, and he got two lovely weeks out from behind bars to come to the nation's capital and testify, or not, as things turned out. Payback, I figured, for all his concern for my well-being.

"THE KID'S GOT NOTHING TO DO WITH IT"

That first tour in Washington had too few days filled with Mike Clementes and too many days weighed down with bureaucratic drudgery. I should have been complimented by being summoned to headquarters, and at one level, I was. As I wrote earlier, I also met my wife, Marilyn, while I was in D.C., the biggest and most unintentional reward of all for my UNIRAC service. But at heart, I'd been handed a desk job, and I wasn't ready for one. New York City and all the excitement of the work I had done there kept whispering in my ear, luring me back. The question was how to get there and with whom.

I'd had a feeler from the U.S. Attorney's Office for the Southern District of New York even before coming down to Washington. Bob Fiske, who was then heading up the office, told me that he thought my investigative background could make a big difference for the staff and asked if I was interested in a position. I was, but I thanked Bob and said no, in part because I didn't want to leave the Bureau and in part because I found the prospect intimidating.

No U.S. Attorney's Office has launched more prominent legal careers than the Southern District of New York. Bob would later become famous as the Whitewater special prosecutor during the Clinton administration—a choice, by the way, that I was proud to support. And Bob was just one in a long string of distinguished people to hold the office. Robert Morgenthau, a great prosecutor and still the most powerful of New York City's five district attorneys, served eight years in the office, beginning in 1962. Rudolph Giuliani ran it with great dedication for six years in the 1980s, amassing enough political capital in the post to eventually become a two-term mayor of the city. Rudy was not only a brilliant lawyer and U.S. attorney, but he epitomized for me the highest principles of public service.

Three of the office's very best alumni—Bob Bucknam, Jim Bucknam, his brother, and Howard Shapiro—later worked with me at the FBI as chief of staff, senior adviser, and general counsel, respectively. I could not have done the job without their talent and dedication. Mike Chertoff, now the Secretary of Homeland Security, was one of my closest colleagues in the office. I helped hire and tried cases with Frances Fragos-Townsend, a great lawyer from the Brooklyn DA's office whom FBI agents told me to hire. She was later a key assistant to Janet Reno and Condi Rice, and is now the special assistant to President Bush on homeland security.

Historically, the Southern District has always exercised a strong degree of independence from the federal Department of Justice even though it is officially under Justice's thumb. (At DOJ, it's jokingly known as the U.S. Attorney's Office for the *Sovereign* District of New York.) The office is also the nexus of a network like none other in the U.S. attorneys system. Alumni respect each other and for the most part maintain their friendships and collegiality—a fact I would note two decades later when I appeared before the 9/11 Commission investigating the attacks on the World Trade Center and Pentagon. Some observers expected Richard Ben-Veniste to lead the attack on me. As he showed all the way back at Watergate, he's a relentless and expert prosecutor. But Richard had come through the Southern District of New York, too, and we had known of each other for many years. We chatted amiably before the hearings and he seemed to have confidence in the accuracy of what I was about to say. Afterward, he complimented my testimony as balanced after ripping into so many others. All that, though, and the confidence I felt going into those hearings, is for later.

Inevitably, high-profile offices and high-energy U.S. attorneys attract the best and brightest new lawyers, and that's what really concerned me about the position I had been offered. The office was stuffed with overachievers from law schools such as Harvard, Yale, Stanford, and Michigan. Rutgers was a fine law school, but it just wasn't in that class. To be honest, I told Bob Fiske, I didn't know if I could compete with those guys. I meant what I said, but after a few months crawling around the belly of the J. Edgar Hoover Building, I was willing to give it a try.

Bob had returned to private practice when I called him, but he put me in touch with John Martin, who had replaced him, and John and his staff interviewed me and eventually offered me a position. By then, there was no question that I wanted the job, but meeting Marilyn had me thinking I was on a lucky streak, so I made one last attempt to have things both ways, appealing directly to Bill Webster to grant me a leave of absence to go to New York with the U.S. Attorney's Office. The director wanted to say yes, but there was no precedent for doing so and plenty of reason to worry that others might line up behind me with similar requests if he granted mine. I'd still be working closely with the Bureau and its agents, but when I quit headquarters for New York in the early spring of 1981, I figured I was leaving the FBI for good.

Mob clans are inherently unstable, but as the 1980s broke, the Bonanno family seemed to have arrived at some kind of inner harmony. Carmine Galante, who had headed the family through most of the previous decade, had been gunned down in July 1979. By 1981, Philip "Rusty" Rastelli seemed set to succeed Galante in what for the Mafia was a surprisingly smooth handover. Then just as I was arriving at the U.S. Attorney's Office, three Bonanno captains were gunned down, and the air filled with lead once more. This time, though, we had our own guy right in the middle of the action: Joe Pistone, a.k.a. Donnie Brasco. (It was Brasco that Johnny Depp played in the film of the same name.)

I'd known about Joe back in New York, before I ever went down to Washington. It was an open secret around the Organized Crime Division that he was being put in undercover full-time, although once he was inserted only a very few agents had any idea of his exact whereabouts or even what his cover was. (Joe had taken courses in gemology so he could pose as a jeweler and fencer of precious stones, a calling of considerable interest to men who like to sport large diamond rings and don't expect to pay full retail for them.) By the time I returned to New York as an assistant U.S. attorney, Joe had already become an unsung law-enforcement legend. The Bureau had never before managed anything like this with any agent, never penetrated so deeply into one of organized crime's core groups, but once the new war broke out, Joe's very success became a problem. He was too trusted, too much a Mafia associate on the rise.

Probably to test Joe and maybe also because he was short of guns, Joe's captain, Sonny Black Napolitano, gave him a contract to kill a guy. If he fulfilled it, Joe would be a made man; he'd have his bones, something the Bureau had only in its wildest dreams thought Donnie Brasco might achieve. Joe would be right at the heart of the action, a pipeline to the top of one of the five families. The intelligence he already relayed had been unparalleled; now it would be truly amazing. And that, of course, is when the FBI pulled the plug on the whole operation. Penetrating the mob was one thing, but doing its dirty work, actually whacking somebody, was way beyond the bounds of the possible.

Beware of what you wish for, the old proverb goes, and so it was at that moment with the U.S. Attorney's Office. We had never had such access, and we almost never had to move so quickly. Indictments that had been projected for months down the pipeline were secured in a fraction of that time. Arrest warrants fell like rain. An incredibly complex prosecution had to be fast-forwarded by six to twelve months. And the stakes were huge: more than half a dozen major leaders of the Bonanno family were included in the indictments, along with a dozen-plus lesser soldiers. Bring them down, and we would drive a stake right into the heart of a major organized crime family. But how to do it in the time available? That's where I came in, through the back door.

The case was so big that John Martin wanted to try it. That was his privilege as the U.S. attorney, and no one could have been more up to the task. John would eventually go on to serve thirteen years as a U.S. district judge before joining the litigation department at one of Manhattan's premier law firms, Debevoise & Plimpton. Another very senior attorney in the office, Bruce Baird, signed on as John's number two. (Bruce would gain renown a decade later for his successful securities-crimes prosecutions of Michael Milken and Drexel Burnham Lambert.) In the number-three slot was the original workhorse of the team, Barbara Jones, my old mentor and friend from the UNIRAC investigation. Barbara is the one who secured the indictments on the fly and set up the whole intricate prosecution mechanism. That left room for a number four, a go-fer attorney to feed data, information, precedents, and whatever else was needed to the top three, and because we had worked together in the past and she knew I had experience with complicated gangland cases, Barbara asked me to fill that role. Then things began to unravel.

For a variety of reasons, John Martin decided to take on another case. There were time considerations: U.S. attorneys have a lot of obligations, and this trial looked initially as if it might gobble up half a year or more. (It actually took slightly less than five months to try.) Simultaneously, the office got handed a Bronx public-corruption case that promised to be shorter and that seemed more in keeping with the sort of trials U.S. attorneys commonly take on. Not surprisingly, John jumped on it.

Almost no sooner had that happened than Bruce Baird was reassigned. Within months of launching our prosecution, Barbara Jones was the lead attorney and I had moved up to number two. Thanks to Barbara's trust in me and her generosity, I was a genuine number two, not just some go-fer dressed up in second-banana clothes. This was my first case of any consequence, and I got to put people on the stand, many of them old pals from the Sixty-ninth Street office of the FBI. Barbara let me do the opening statement. After she had done the summation and the defense had summed up its own case, she handed the rebuttal to me. I'm not sure I ever again had as hard a case to prove.

Our secret weapon at the trial was a retired New York City police sergeant named Gene McDonnell, who worked in the U.S. Attorney's Office as a technical expert; his ability to enhance audio tapes and prepare evidence for trail gave us a unique advantage. Gene was also a great investigator and supplied much-needed street smarts to the case. Still, we had no bodies. The three dead capos had gone swimming with the fish, just as the mob prefers. It was not until 2004, when former Bonanno boss Joey Massino decided to cooperate to save himself, that he gave the FBI the long-secret grave of the three Bonanno captains. (The FBI agent who broke the case was Joe Bonavolonta, my friend Jules's son.)

We had no eyewitnesses either, at least none who would come forward or admit to what they had seen. All we had to offer up were discussions on tape, things said to Joe in his guise as Donnie. And we did it. We put together a case on the fly; we ad-libbed as we went along; and in the end, we proved the murder of the three capos, put a lot of very bad wise guys behind bars, and took out a whole tier of leadership of one of America's more evil crime networks. But we weren't through with the Bonannos.

"THE KID'S GOT NOTHING TO DO WITH IT"

We knew even before we went to trial that we had one large, unfinished piece of business waiting for us when it was through, and that's what I turned to next: the Sicilians and what became known in the press as the Pizza Connection case.

The Italian underworld divides into four principal groups: the Sicilian Mafia, based (obviously) in Sicily and the fountainhead of all the other Italian-based Mafias; the Camorra, or Neapolitan Mafia, out of Naples; the 'Ndrangheta, derived from the Greek for "courage" or "loyalty," formed in Calabria in the 1860s by Sicilians banished from their island home; and the Sacra Corona Unita (United Sacred Crown) out of the Puglia region in southeastern Italy. The American Mafia, officially La Cosa Nostra (or, roughly, Our Thing), owes a debt to all four groups; but its greatest ties, far and away, are to the Sicilians.

Historically, the Mafia and the Cosa Nostra kept an ocean between them, but by the late 1970s, the Sicilians were becoming commonplace on Bonanno family turf, particularly the area around Knickerbocker Avenue in Brooklyn. They seemed to own the narcotics trade, or at least they were heavily sharing in it with their American hosts. Some Sicilians could even be found in the Bonanno chain of command, but close as the ties were, the two groups operated in distinctly separate spheres, with radically different styles.

The Cosa Nostra guys were arrogant to the point of recklessness. They would let key bits of information slip while talking on phones that could be easily tapped. Sometimes we wouldn't have to wire the phones at all. One Italian-American gangster we kept close ties on liked to stroll out in front of his social club and do business in the street, standing next to a mailbox. So very late one night we stuffed an FBI agent into the box the goon liked to lean on and let him listen in. Unfortunately, we couldn't retrieve our live microphone until the middle of the next night, but if he got a horrible backache, we got great intelligence.

The Sicilians were just the opposite, more like KGB than Cosa Nostra. They'd use pay phones, and they wouldn't stay on long. What's more, they spoke a language that even native Italians have trouble understanding. The Sicilians trusted no one other than their own, and except for those few who had corporate ties to the Bonanno family, they reported to their own hierarchy back in Sicily. No FBI agent had ever been so embraced by the Cosa Nostra as Joe Pistone, but even "Donnie Brasco" couldn't get beans out of the Sicilians.

"I can't get close to these guys," he kept telling us. "They grunt and walk away because I'm not Sicilian."

Yet something had to be done. The deeper we dug into the Bonannos, the more we could see that the Sicilians were clearing hundreds of millions of dollars in narcotics profits, principally heroin sold by pizza parlor owners in New York City and up and down the East Coast, and into the Midwest as well. (That's where the Pizza Connection moniker came from.) The question was how to get inside the Sicilians, how to bring them down. Then we learned that a courageous judge in Palermo, Sicily, Giovanni Falcone, was doing the same thing at the other end of the pipeline: trying to make a case against the same mob drug lords we were after but at far greater peril than we were facing. In America, it's rare that a Cosa Nostra member even tries to bribe a judge or a prosecutor, and rarer still for a bribe to be taken. At least at the federal level, judges are almost incorruptible. Witnesses in America are often threatened, but they're only seldom assaulted, much less killed. In Sicily, one Mafia investigation after another had come to grief in seas of blood: prosecutors, police, judges, witnesses murdered. The Mafia there even had a term for the government officials it had assassinated: The phrase translates as "excellent cadavers."

Judge Falcone and his staff were people of exceptional bravery and determination, and it wasn't long, I think, before their best qualities began to rub off on us. We didn't have enough corroborating evidence to get permission to put wiretaps on the New York Sicilians—we had no informants, no way to get inside their shell—but we knew from our Bonanno family investigations and from undercover work who some of them were, so we started watching them, maybe as they'd never been watched before, and as we watched, a pattern began to emerge.

The Sicilians we already knew about would regularly drive up to street corners in Manhattan and deliver boxes and bags to men we didn't know, who would then take the parcels into nearby hotels. From the hotels, the parcels went to banks down on Wall Street, where the money they contained was deposited into accounts from which transfers would eventually be made to numbered Swiss bank accounts. Or the money would go to some Wall Street brokerage house for laundering before finding its way to Zurich or Bern or Geneva. Whatever the routing overseas, the transactions involved vast sums of money, all of which started out as fives and tens and twenties. It smelled so much like drug-transaction proceeds that you could practically get a contact high just thinking about it.

Simultaneously, Judge Falcone and his excellent colleague, Liliana Ferraro, were pushing backward from the other end—tracking the money from Sicily, where a lot of it ended up, to Bulgaria, for instance, where it was used to pay transporters who had brought in raw heroin shipments from Turkey and elsewhere, including Iran. It wasn't long before the two sides, by pooling sources and intelligence, could begin to posit a global pattern at work: a drug network that connected the Sicilian Mafia to heroin sales in New York and Philadelphia, Chicago and Cleveland and Detroit. In time, they would limn a global network, operating on parts of four continents, that over the course of almost a decade, beginning in the mid-1970s, imported into the U.S. and distributed almost two tons of heroin and vast amounts of cocaine, netting over $1.6 billion.

Falcone's top investigators—Gianni De Gennaro and Antonino Manganelli, brilliant and fearless anti-Mafia police leaders—gave the FBI and me the blueprint to prosecute the case together with Falcone. Both of them now courageously lead the Italian National Police despite years of threats and efforts to kill them.

As the pattern became clearer and the source of the revenue more definitely illicit drug sales, we had the standing to approach a variety of federal judges and ask for wiretap orders; and as the wiretaps came on line, we were able at last to breach the Sicilians' wall of silence. Not that it was easy to understand a word they were saying.

The greater New York area is full of fluent Italian speakers, even Italian translators. Like me, a lot of New Yorkers and New Jerseyites grew up with grandparents who were far more comfortable with their native tongue than their adopted one. But Sicilian is another matter. We had one and only one FBI agent in the New York office, Joseph Cincotta, who was fluent in the language—more that, really, than an Italian dialect. We quickly put this outstanding agent to work monitoring the phone taps, and because his wife, Rachel, and her brother, Dominick Buda, were fluent, we hired every one of them and handed them headsets.

By 1984, though, even the hardworking Cincotta family couldn't come near keeping up with the need. We had taps everywhere, and monitoring plants all around the city, and to handle them all, we brought in police from Sicily itself and swore them in as deputy U.S. marshals so that they could listen in to ongoing investigations. By any strict-procedure book, it was loosey-goosey at best, an inspiration that could turn south the minute one of our police-translators took it upon him- or herself to tip off the countryman he was listening in on. Just like the Bonanno case, we were making this one up on the fly. But the Sicilians we pressed into service proved as trustworthy as Judge Falcone himself, and those wiretaps were critical to piecing together the puzzle and teasing out of it a dramatis personae to indict.

"THE KID'S GOT NOTHING TO DO WITH IT"

If anything, I was even more focused on this case than I had been on the one that spawned it. For starters, I had more riding on it personally. I was the lead prosecutor this time around. Among the tight community of assistant U.S. attorneys, this was the chance to earn my own bones. Beyond that, the case was just so complicated and fascinating, with a cast of characters—once we had finally assembled it—that Hollywood never could have dreamed up on its own.

At the center of it all, at least initially, was Salvatore "Toto" Catalano. Fittingly, he was a Sicilian-American with a foot in both camps. He was born in Ciminna, Sicily, in 1941, and had come to America at age twenty-five, settled in Queens, where he had opened a bakery, and gone to work for the Bonannos on Knickerbocker Street. With Carmine Galante's murder in 1979, Catalano completed a meteoric rise, emerging as "street boss" of the entire family, but the speed of his ascension was also part of the problem. He'd never really learned much English. That was okay with the Sicilian clans who were supplying the narcotics and pocketing a significant part of the profits, but Toto simply couldn't communicate effectively with the Italian-American crews on this side of the Atlantic. Frustrated, he stepped down voluntarily after less than two years at the helm, ceding total control of the family to Rusty Rastelli, just prior to the outbreak of the warfare that had spurred our previous trial.

Still, if he was no longer street boss when we began our investigation, Catalano was a key nexus, the essential ingredient for the kind of joint venturing the Bonannos and the Sicilians had entered into, and he led us, like a bee to honey, to the guy who would become the central figure in the case.

Gaetano Badalamenti began as a voice somewhere in the ether, at the far end of one of the phone lines we had tapped, but what a voice it was! Whoever was speaking was clearly directing the entire narcotics operation, brokering deal after deal. In time, we traced the calls to, of all places, Brazil, and eventually, we were able to identify the voice as Badalamenti's. (His nephew was plying the family trade in Chicago. We'd bugged his phone there, which helped with the identification.) And in Gaetano Badalamenti, we had the beginning of a very prime catch.

Badalamenti had been born in 1923 in Cinisi, near Palermo in the northwest of Sicily. Like a lot of his fellow Mafiosi, he got involved in a variety of building projects and schemes throughout the island in the years after the war, but Badalamenti thought bigger than most of his contemporaries. In 1957, he took part in what was to become an infamous meeting in Palermo. Joe Bonanno and his capo Carmine Galante came from America. Lucky Luciano, exiled from the United States to Sicily and five years short of his own grave, was on hand to serve as intermediary and mentor. Among the locals present, in addition to Badalamenti, was Tommasso Buscetta, then maybe the most powerful of all the Sicilian dons and later to be one of our star witnesses in a trial that would put Gaetano Badalamenti behind bars for the rest of his life.

The subject that day was narcotics, specifically how to globalize the trade. America had the money and the customer base, and the American Cosa Nostra had the infrastructure to serve it. The Sicilians, meanwhile, had access to the raw goods and a transportation network in place. Cigarette smuggling out of Turkey was the Sicilian mob's growth industry. From tobacco to opium was not a far leap, especially since the smuggling routes out were largely the same, and in clannish, remote Sicily, the Mafia had the perfect place to refine morphine base into user-friendly heroin. An apostle of modern business practices, Luciano convinced everyone that a multinational undertaking just made sense, but even in organized crime, sea changes don't happen overnight. Other, equally infamous, meetings in Sicily and New York would be needed to nail things down. For two decades to come, cigarettes, not narcotics, would continue to be the Sicilian Mafia's main source of income. Still, this was the meeting that began to lay the framework for what would finally become known as the Pizza Connection. I was just seven years old.

Lucky Luciano had a second agenda to press at the Palermo meeting. Now that he had been back in his native island for a number of years, he could see what a mess the mob there was. Mafia clans, named for the towns from which their members had come, were in constant warfare. There was no organization, no superstructure to help settle disputes peacefully. Money was going down the drain; inefficiency was everywhere. What the Sicilians needed, Luciano argued, was what he had done for organized crime in America: a board of governors, of sorts; a grand council. The Sicilians agreed with that, too. They called their new council the Cupola, and one of those to head the Cupola in its early years was none other than Gaetano Badalamenti.

By the mid-1970s, Badalamenti was Sicily's boss of bosses—the most powerful gangster in one of the biggest mob strongholds on earth—but the fragile peace that the Cupola had fostered was beginning to fall apart. Cigarette smuggling was beginning to take a backseat. In its place, the heroin trade had blossomed into a fabulously profitable undertaking, and a particularly lethal Mafioso named Toto Riina of the Corleonesi began to get designs on taking it over. The more he decided he wanted it all, the more people Toto killed or had killed. Finally, in 1979, by which time every Mafia clan on the island was involved to a greater or lesser degree in heroin trafficking, Badalamenti fled the island to Spain and eventually to Brazil, where his old friend Tommasso Buscetta was now living with a new wife.

Undeterred by being run out of the Cupola and off his island—and now, of course, near almost unlimited supplies of cocaine to be added to the mix—Badalamenti set up shop in São Paulo and resumed direction of the Pizza Connection, and that's where we found him at the other end of a phone line. Eventually, he and his son were arrested by Spanish police as they landed in Madrid for a visit, and we were almost ready to begin our prosecution.

The trial itself was an absolute three-ring circus complete with actors, thugs hamming it up, and enough defendants to field two football teams. More than three hundred witnesses took the stand. We introduced 15,000 exhibits, thirteen foreign depositions, and 41,000 pages of transcripts. From stem to stern, the whole thing took seventeen months—from September 30, 1985, to March 2, 1987—the longest criminal jury trial in the history of the U.S. Federal Courthouse where I would later sit as judge. My fellow prosecutors liked to joke that I had a baby conceived and born on the government's direct case alone, eleven months in the presentation. Rudy Giuliani had become U.S. Attorney for the Southern District of New York by then. He supported me every inch of the way and I needed every bit of help I could get. The case was tried by Pierre Leval, one of the finest judges in the storied history of the Southern District bench. His rulings and decisions were as close to flawless as a judge ever gets.

Once again, the government's case was almost entirely circumstantial. The only reason it succeeded was because agents such as Bob Paquette, Charlie Rooney, Carmine Russo, Pat Luzio, Joe Cincotta, and Mike Slattery—as well as customs agents Mike Fahy and Tom Loreto and DEA agents Tony Petruci and Mario Sessa—performed investigative magic every day. Paralegals Afredo Principe and Mary Ellen Luthy also helped us carry the day.

One defendant was murdered during the trial. We didn't know it at the time, and to this day I don't know why, but one day he just didn't show up in the courtroom. We asked the judge to revoke his bail, and he did, and then we found out our defendant had been revoked altogether. Another defendant was shot the evening of his lawyer's summation. His attorney finished up, the two of them went down to the Village for a little dinner, and before he knew it, he had a bullet in him that left him paralyzed. When we next saw him a few days later, he was shackled into a wheelchair. Yet another defendant was so sore at his attorney's summation that he put out a hit contract on him. As the old saying goes, you just can't make this stuff up.

Tommasso Buscetta was our sole cooperating Mafia witness, and he was an impressive one, from the highest ranks of Sicilian crime. Giovanni Falcone had basically talked him into the role: he was the first of the *"pentiti"*—the Italian Mafiosi who chose to repent and cooperate under pressure from Falcone. Since Italy had no equivalent to a federal witness protection program, Buscetta went into our own program for safekeeping while prosecutions were being prepared on both sides of the Atlantic. Whenever Judge Falcone's people needed to interview him, they would fly over here for the meeting. It was an extraordinary act of cooperation between the two judicial systems. But Buscetta was a major narcotics dealer. He'd murdered people, and he had been living in Brazil when a lot of the action in question went down. There are no choirboys in cases like this, and Buscetta was great for identifying people authoritatively as Mafia members—"men of honor" as they're known—but jury members weren't likely to take his word on more refined matters of good and evil.

The wiretap transcripts were the true heart of our case. We had hundreds upon hundreds of hours of wiretaps to introduce. I'd had it all translated, and the translations had been authenticated. But what to do with the results? Wiretaps are only episodically interesting. Guys will talk for fifteen minutes about their dog or their bunions or the problems they're having with the wife before they drop the ten words you've been listening for all along. If jurors had to read through all those pages just to get to the few nuggets buried inside them, they were bound to fall asleep. So I did something never tried before as far as I knew. I hired a troupe of actors—bona fide professionals, equity members—to take the parts of the defendants and other key players, and read their lines to the jury. One actor played Gaetano Badalamenti, another enacted Salvatore Catalano, and on and on.

The defense objected, naturally, and there was no precedent. But the judge ruled that I could present the case any way I wanted to, and the actors proved to be a huge hit. Day after day, they would show up and perform their roles, as if they were in some long-running off-off Broadway show that required new dialogue every day. The witness room became, in effect, the actors' green room. I'd see them in there from time to time, slipping into their roles, putting on the characters. They all had great voices, and over time the jury came to love them, even anticipate their performances. (I kept thinking of my opera-loving grandmother. This was a spectacle she would have appreciated.)

As a delivery mechanism for evidence and general information, I still can't think of a better approach than using those actors, but as always, the moments that really stand out in my memory are the ones with the real players: the defendants, the witnesses, the people who couldn't leave the courtroom at the end of the day and switch back into being someone more normal.

Gaetano Badalamenti was our biggest net and in some ways our most theatrical. Most times in a trial like this, a defendant has to be crazy to take the witness stand. The upsides are minimal, the downsides many. But this case was so circumstantial in nature—built out of phone calls, translations from a language no one on the jury spoke, distant Sicilian connections, testimony from narcotics experts, and the like—that I really couldn't blame Badalamenti for wanting to take the stand. It was the way he played his part that was a little mind-boggling.

At one point, I remember asking him on cross-examination why he felt it necessary to do business on pay phones from Brazil. Surely, there was a more convenient way to have a conversation.

"It's because of the Normans," he answered.

"The Normans?"

"Yes, Mr. Freeh," he explained in effect. "We Sicilians have been conquered by the Normans, occupied by the Germans, and ruled by the French, the Spanish, the Austrians, and the Italians. We're naturally a little suspicious of who might be listening in on our calls. That's why we're reluctant to talk on a regular phone."

In his opening statement, Badalamenti's lawyer had described his client as a member of the Italian partisans during World War II. As Badalamenti sat there smiling and doing his best to look bravely modest, his lawyer went into great detail about his client's fearless exploits against the demonic Nazis. It was ridiculous. I was certain he was no partisan, but I had no proof, so we contacted Judge Falcone's team and asked for their help, and they came through in spades. Turned out, Badalamenti had served in the Italian army and had taken part in several battles against the Allies and specifically American units. Even better, our Italian connection managed to find a photo of Badalamenti in his army uniform. On cross-examination I got a chance to revisit the matter.

"Now, who was it that you were fighting?" I asked him.

"The Germans."

"Were you shooting at Germans?"

"Oh, yes, I was killing them."

We showed him a picture of an American GI then, and I asked if he shot at any of them.

"Oh, no," he protested, "they were our friends."

So I showed him the photo of himself in an Italian army uniform and recited his service record. Even then, he had some crazy explanation—he had an explanation for *everything*—but toward the end of his two days of cross examination, the jury had begun to laugh at him, not with him, and I knew then that Gaetano Badalamenti was toast, or maybe I should write that I knew it as surely as I could know anything in that roaring carnival of a proceeding.

In addition to the twenty-two people on trial at the defendant's table, there were at least twenty-two lawyers. I tried the case with four extraordinary prosecutors: Bob Bucknam—who later became chief of staff at the FBI—Dick Martin, Bob Stewart and Andy McCarthy. Add in our bailiffs, my troupe of actors, a sea of witnesses, an avid press, and plenty of spectators, and you couldn't tell the players without a program. And even then, people sometimes got it wrong. Witnesses would take the stand. I'd say, do you know Mr. Badalamenti or Mr. Catalano, and they'd say, oh, yes. Then I'd invite them to look around the courtroom and pick him out, and they'd examine that sea of faces and point to our own lawyers, FBI agents, you name it. The choices were just too many.

One of my favorite such witnesses was an Italian named Salvatore. He fancied himself a financier, but in fact he was a bagman. His job was to pick up the cash and deliver it—purely a middleman, at least in this operation, but a character through and through. Plump with big bifocals, he wore a seersucker jacket everywhere he went: the same jacket, literally everywhere. We would look at surveillance photo after surveillance photo taken over many months, at all times of the day, and we'd keep saying, "Isn't that the same jacket?" And it was, always.

When we put Sal on the stand, one of the defense lawyers noted that he had a long history of passing bad checks, and Sal was quick to agree.

"Do you think that's a serious offense?" the lawyer pressed him.

"No," Sal answered without missing a beat.

"Why not?"

"Well, I also have received a lot of bad checks."

From my point of view, Sal's main role was to identify a lot of the guys who were on trial. He'd carried cash for many of them. But I wanted to make sure beforehand that he named the right guys.

"If you don't see Mr. X or Mr. Y," I told him, "just don't pick anyone. Say you don't see him."

"Well, Mr. Freeh," he asked, "could you indicate where they are, and then I'll pick them out."

"No," I told him, "I can't do that."

"Just give me a hint."

"No."

So Sal comes into the courtroom, takes the witness stand, and gets sworn in. Then, instead of sitting down, he stands there with his hand over his eyes like a visor, darting glances around the room, trying to pre-identify everyone I'm going to ask him to point out. The defendants meanwhile, in a rare show of unanimity, were all trying to duck their heads under the table. What a scene!

As I wrote earlier, there was a light side in all this. Some of the goons we dealt with were genuinely funny, some of them genuinely warm . . . if you could ignore the fact that they broke kneecaps and shook people down and sometimes sent them to the bottom of the East River for a living. I think most federal prosecutors felt as I did. If you didn't laugh about these guys once in a while, you'd have to cry all day long.

What matters ultimately is that we won convictions on all counts against all the defendants save for four. Three of the twenty-two defendants were acquitted on two of the sixteen counts brought against them. Only Vito Badalamenti, Gaetano's son, got off entirely, acquitted of the sole count he was charged with. Salvatore Catalano was sentenced to a total of forty-five years in prison and required to pay $1.15 million in fines and an additional $1 million to go toward the care and rehabilitation of those who had become addicted to narcotics through his criminal acts. Gaetano Badalamenti was also sentenced to forty-five years in prison, with mandatory release after thirty years—part of the extradition deal we made with the Spanish after he was arrested—and fined $125,000. Badalamenti would die in jail. Two other defendants drew thirty-five-year sentences; one got thirty years; one, twenty-five; three, twenty years; and so on. In all, the sentencing judge imposed almost $6 million in fines and restitutions.

Justice was done; the public interest was served. Just as important in some ways, the case became the template for future international cooperative efforts, especially once I became FBI director. The vital element, though, in the whole package was Giovanni Falcone himself. Over the course of the four years the case stretched on—two years for the investigations, two more years for the indictments and trial—Giovanni became both a dear friend and a hero to me.

Our trial in New York City reached record lengths for the federal courthouse involved, but Giovanni's trials were by Cecil B. DeMille, with a cast of thousands. Ultimately 475 Mafioso were charged, and 338 of them were found guilty and sentenced to a collective 2,665 years in prison. Known appropriately in Italy as the Maxi Trials, the hearings took place in a specially built bunker next to Ucciardone, Palermo's main prison. Security was extraordinary, and still eighteen of the defendants were murdered during the hearings. And the bloodshed wasn't confined to the courtroom or even those directly involved in the trial. The period of and around the trials in Palermo became known as the Years of Lead. In the end, though, Giovanni and his fellow courageous jurists and police—along with Tommasso

Buscetta and other *"pentiti"* they had convinced to talk—tore the veil of secrecy off the Sicilian Mafia and Italian organized crime generally. They shone light where it had never penetrated before, including on the corrupt politicians who made common cause with the gangsters and thugs.

Giovanni had been born in Palermo just before the war. He had been a judge since the mid-1960s, and had spent most of that time focused on organized crime. He knew the danger he faced, both because of his judicial decisions and because of his refusal to back down in the press. Death threats against him were common, yet he forged on. As the trials in Sicily wound down, he and his staff shuttled frequently between Palermo and Rome, where the Italian anti-Mafia task force was headquartered. Then on May 23, 1992, while riding on the autostrada between the Palermo airport and downtown, Falcone and his wife, Francesca Morvilio, a civil judge, were assassinated by explosives packed into a narrow underpass. Three members of their police escort were blown up with them.

I was shattered by the assassinations. I felt as if someone had come after me with a bomb, too. I had every intention of attending Giovanni's funeral, but Gianni De Gennaro, my good friend and one of Giovanni's top investigators, asked me not to come. Protecting the Italian officials at the funeral would be challenge enough, he said. I would be adding to a logistical nightmare and placing myself at great risk. Conditions were simply too dangerous. (And indeed Giovanni's fellow crusading anti-Mafia judge, Paolo Borsellino, would soon be murdered himself.)

I wasn't convinced, though. I admired Giovanni so deeply that I felt I had to be there, whatever the risks involved. Then I had a second conversation on the matter, this one even more emotional, with Liliana Ferraro, a judge who had worked as Falcone's right hand during the Maxi Trials. She, too, told me not to come. They had yet to figure out who had murdered Giovanni and his wife, she said, and I had become so closely identified with him during the Pizza Connection cases that they felt I would be in grave danger. Back at home, Marilyn, who knew my capacity for pigheadedness better than anyone else, was equally opposed to my attending: I was a father, a husband. Finally, I agreed. Instead, a year later, in the fall of 1993, I flew to Italy to attend a memorial service in Giovanni's honor. By then, I was FBI director. I have since gone back every year.

I'm not a big one for office decorations. When I was director, I kept framed artwork from my kids on the wall and not much else, but four photos hung there, where I could see them every day. One was of Frank Johnson, the federal judge and civil-rights hero who swore me in as director. The second photo showed Elie Wiesel, the great humanist and Holocaust survivor. I kept it on the wall as a reminder of what happens when police power is made to serve wholly political ends. (More about Elie in the next chapter.) The third photo showed Teddy Roosevelt in his Rough Rider uniform—he was also New York City police commissioner—and the fourth was of Giovanni Falcone. We can't bring the dead back, but we can remember them and do honor to the causes they died for.

Being an Italian-American and having spent a career prosecuting La Cosa Nostra cases, I became deeply sensitive to the heroism and gifts that countless Americans of Italian heritage have bestowed on our nation. My involvement in the National Italian American Foundation and with its charitable and educational good works is how I try to balance the equation of the cases I prosecuted. Great jurists, warriors, doctors, captains of industry, benefactors, FBI agents, and entertainment pioneers—Antonin Scalia, Anthony Zinni, Tony Fauci, Lee Iacocca, Bill Fugazy, Lew Schiliro, Joseph Guccione, United States Marshal for Manhattan, the Scotti brothers—have more than made up for the misdeeds of a tiny minority of this great heritage.

CHAPTER 6

"That's Moody's Bomb"

When the Pizza Connection case finally wound to a close in 1987, I had been going almost nonstop for eleven years: four on UNIRAC, two on the Bonanno prosecution, and four more on the Sicilians and their drug deals. The only break of any sort I'd had was my eleven-month stint in Washington, and that wasn't exactly R and R. For the most part, the work couldn't have been more exciting—I loved it—but Marilyn and I had two sons by then, and I was determined not to give them or her the short end of the stick.

There was also the practical matter of money. We wanted more kids, but looking down the road at orthodontist bills, camps, clothes, and scariest of all, college tuition, Marilyn and I kept seeing way too many detours ahead. If newspaper clippings were gold, I would have been just fine. The trials had attracted plenty of media attention, but ever since my first day with the FBI, I had been on a government-service salary schedule. Political demagoguery aside, no one gets rich off government-service paychecks.

Unambitious, I was somehow climbing up through the executive

ranks of the U.S. Attorney's Office. As the deputy U.S. attorney and
chief of the Organized Crime Unit for the Southern District of
New York, my principal responsibilities had shifted from the courtroom to managing two hundred or so assistant U.S. attorneys, most
of them from the very law schools that had intimidated me so much
only seven years earlier. Luckily for all of us, Benito Romano was
our U.S. attorney when I became deputy and led the office with
great skill, earning the respect of all. If the day-to-day pressure wasn't
greatly reduced—even Yale Law graduates need lots of watching—
the hours were more regular. The title on the door, though, didn't
solve our future cash-flow concerns. Only the private sector, I came
to believe, could do that.

I'd made a pact with Marilyn that I would leave government service no later than the end of the decade, and by early 1990, I was
ready to honor it. I'd made some inquiries, talked with several law
firms, and now I was just about to join one of the largest and most
successful firms in New York City. Then, as so often seems to happen in my life, I got a phone call that changed everything.

My duties as deputy U.S. attorney for our office had brought
me into frequent contact with the Department of Justice in Washington, including then–attorney general Richard Thornburgh,
the former Pennsylvania governor, and especially one of his aides,
Robert Mueller. A highly decorated Vietnam War veteran—and, of
course, my eventual successor as FBI director—Bob had been an assistant U.S. attorney for the District of Massachusetts before joining Justice and would soon be placed in charge of its Criminal Division, so
we had plenty of common ground. Already we had worked together
on a number of civil matters regarding the Teamsters Union, as well as
on general issues coordinating our two offices. His call this time, I figured, had something to do with one of those issues, but I was wrong.

The attorney general wanted me to take a look at a case down
in Georgia and Alabama, Bob said. Four mail bombs of seemingly

identical make had been mailed in December 1989, with lethal results. One bomb had killed Judge Robert Vance, who sat on the Eleventh Circuit Court of Appeals in Birmingham. Another had murdered Robert Robinson, an African-American lawyer and NAACP leader in Savannah, Georgia. A third sent to the clerk's office of the United States Court of Appeals for the Eleventh Circuit, in Atlanta, had been intercepted by an alert security officer. The fourth bomb, mailed to the Jacksonville, Florida, office of the National Association for the Advancement of Colored People, had also been intercepted and turned over to police by NAACP staff members put on high alert by Robinson's murder. A suspect had been identified, Bob told me, but still it was proving a very, very tough case.

I could appreciate that, I said, and certainly I knew the broad outlines. When a federal judge is murdered, everyone in the federal system pays attention. But this was a difficult time for me, I told him; I was just preparing to leave office. The job, the law firm, Marilyn— they were all spinning through my head when I asked Bob the fatal question:

"Why me?"

"We know you worked on the pizza case," he said. "We know how complicated that was. We think this case right now is in a highly confused state. Three different U.S. Attorney's Offices are working on it—in Atlanta, Birmingham, and Savannah. There's just not much coordination. You've had experience with this kind of situation. We want you to go down there and take charge."

I protested again that the timing was all wrong. Besides, I said, the last thing that the people in Georgia wanted was for some New York lawyer to come barging in the door, telling them how to run the show.

Bob was undeterred.

"We really want you to do this," he said. "The attorney general will call if that makes a difference."

"Okay," I told him finally, "I'll go for sixty days, review the evidence, talk to the witnesses, but that's it. I can't get involved beyond that. I don't have that kind of time frame."

I emphasized the sixty-day limit again, and Bob once again agreed. But even as I spoke, I could see that job with the Manhattan law firm begin to disappear into the mists, along with any financial security it was supposed to bring us. A little over a dozen years later when I resigned from my post as FBI director, newspapers accounts frequently noted that Marilyn, myself, and our by then six children lived in a heavily mortgaged house in Great Falls, Virginia. We did. Second mortgages and credit cards had certainly aided my twenty-six years of public service, but Marilyn's love and sacrifice made it happen.

Bob then told me I would be transferred "on paper" from my current position to a more "generic" trial attorney in the Criminal Division of the Department of Justice. It was a typical Washington apparatchik cover to satisfy the DOJ politics of having a "Southern District" prosecutor taking over another district's most important case. (Sending someone down from Washington bordered on strong-arming; sending someone from New York City was downright insulting.) But I'd been with the Southern District of New York for almost ten years by then and wanted to finish my government career there. Besides, it was only for sixty days, right? I've never done well with form over substance so I simply told Bob no. I would go down south as I was or I wouldn't go at all. The alternative was fine by me since I really didn't want the assignment. Bob said this couldn't be done, but then called the next day and said okay. That's when I told him that I was bringing another prosecutor who was also not going to change his Southern District of New York title or his office for the privilege of leaving his family for the next year.

I won that battle, too. Howard Shapiro and I had been working together for several years by then. We knew each other's minds, and we liked each other, and I thought I would probably need all the friendly faces I could find once the case got going. Howard was also a brilliant lawyer and well liked by the agents, and he would go on to serve as chief FBI counsel during most of my years as director. I asked Bob Mueller if either he or Dick Thornburgh would call the U.S. attorney in Atlanta and pave the way for our arrival, and he assured us that would be no problem. So in April of 1990, Howard and I hopped on a plane and flew south to see what we would find. What we found was, to put it charitably, a mess.

The investigation was in the hands of a multipoint task force that included the FBI; Alcohol, Tobacco, and Firearms agents (because of the bomb); U.S. Marshals (because one federal judge had been murdered and others threatened); U.S. Postal Service Inspectors (the mail had been used to deliver the bombs); the Georgia Bureau of Investigation; and others. That much made sense. The suspect the team had identified, Walter Leroy Moody Jr., made sense as well, for multiple reasons. But when we met with the task force for the first time in the rickety old annex next to the Richard Russell Building where it was headquartered, I could see problems all over the place.

Task forces can be a disaster when no one shares. Information gets hoarded, then traded as if it were gold. This task force had "don't share" stamped all over it. Each component agency was housed in its own room; there was virtually no bullpen area where everyone would come together in the normal course of the day and kick around leads and other information. The three FBI agents who had been assigned to the case were great, but they looked like kids. I asked them how long they'd been with the Bureau. Oh, seven or eight years, they answered. Ever worked a major case? No. Uh-oh, I thought, but I was wrong. The primary case agent, John Behnke, proved to be without exception the very best FBI agent investigator I would ever meet. John's colleagues, Todd Letcher and Tracey North, were an equally pleasant surprise—the top class of agents. All three later came to FBI headquarters to help me out.

Our next stop was the Russell Building, home to the federal courthouse and numerous federal offices, including that of the U.S. attorney for Atlanta. The post was being held down temporarily by Ray Ruckles.

"Hey," he said after Howard and I had introduced ourselves, "how you doing?"

Fine, we assured him, and took a seat, but Ray had already run out of conversation. After an awkward silence, I took the lead.

"Ray," I said, "we're really pleased to come here and work with you on this case."

"What case?"

"No one from Washington called you?"

"No," he said, "I thought you guys were just stopping by to say hello."

"It's not quite that simple, Ray," I told him. "I'm supposed to take over the Moody case."

"What? You can't just come in here and take it over! I haven't heard anything about it. I haven't seen any paper. You guys don't even know what you're doing down here!"

Just to make matters more complicated, the U.S. Attorneys' Offices in Birmingham and Savannah were each doing their own investigations, and all three offices, including Atlanta, had different theories of the case. These were hate crimes, or it was a case of simple extortion, or maybe the bombs were the work of someone who was incredibly angry at the courts themselves. It all depended on whom you last talked with.

Lucky for me, the chief judge of the Eleventh Circuit Court of Appeals, Gerald Bard Tjoflat, who knew the facts of the case as well as anyone in Georgia, briefed me on the case shortly after my arrival and steered me in the right investigative direction. I also got an unexpected call from former attorney general Griffin Bell, who charmingly offered me the use of King & Spalding's law library as well as his considerable Atlanta connections—"a few folks I know around here," as he modestly put it. Both offers were gratefully accepted.

The presumed perpetrator had sent a slew of threatening letters to all the judges in the Eleventh Circuit, including Judge Vance. (The roster included Frank Johnson, who two years later would swear me in as FBI director. I met Frank for the first time when I went to see him about the threatening letter he had received.) The letters, sent in the name of a fictitious racist organization called Americans for a Competent Federal Judicial System, appeared to leave no question as to motive: the judges were going to be killed because they favored African-Americans in their rulings. The murders of Judge Vance, who had courageously taken on racism from his bench in Birmingham, and of Robinson in Savannah certainly supported racial hatred as a motive, as did the attempted bombing of the NAACP office in Florida. To reinforce the point, Americans for a Competent Federal Judicial system followed the assassinations with a letter to an Atlanta television news anchor claiming credit for the murders and threatening further violence.

What's more, the perpetrator appeared to be the same person who in August of 1989 had sent a "Declaration of War" letter to the Eleventh Circuit Court of Appeals and television stations nationwide, accusing the court of "rank bias" and threatening to unleash the deadly war gases tabun and phosgene on "citizens of densely populated cities." Simultaneously, a mail bomb loaded with a tear-gas canister was sent to the NAACP regional office in Atlanta, where it released clouds of choking fumes.

That was where the case began, but the available evidence and leads, such as they were, had sent the various investigative agencies and U.S. Attorneys' Offices chasing off in different, sometimes competing, directions.

A prodigious act of memory had first brought Roy Moody into the picture. A handmade bomb almost always leaves a signature, quirks of materials and fabrication peculiar to the individual that put it together. Once a bomb goes off, the signature is often lost along with its packaging, but half these mail bombs had been intercepted before explosion, and from them and the shreds remaining from the exploded ones, a portrait was quickly assembled. Each device was made of a steel pipe packed with smokeless powder and surrounded on the outside by finishing nails. (Eighty such nails had exploded outward from Judge Vance's package at his home in Mountain Brook, in the suburbs of Birmingham. The best estimates are that the nails traveled at an initial speed of three thousand feet per second. Vance's wife, Helen, who was sitting nearby, was seriously injured in the Saturday morning attack.) For detonators, the bomb maker had used the casing of a ballpoint pen, a flashbulb filament, and a green powder that served as a high-explosive primer. The bomber had placed his devices inside cardboard boxes that had been painted black on the inside, presumably to cover up any lingering traces of a fingerprint. (Opening the hinged lid of the boxes triggered the explosions.) On the outside, he had used plain brown paper and string. Each package had been addressed with a typed red-and-white label and mailed using stamps that showed an American flag flying over Yosemite National Park.

All that was relatively easy to discern for the ATF agents first assigned to the case. The bomb had a highly distinctive signature, but whose was it? Brian Hoback, the outstanding ATF agent on the case, had no idea, but he did have the good sense to phone an ATF forensic chemist named Lloyd Erwin, who happened to be attending a conference when the call came through. Erwin listened for a moment as Hoback described the bomb. Then he grabbed a napkin and began sketching, and as he sketched, he realized that he had seen virtually this same bomb construction more than seventeen years earlier, in May 1972.

"That's Moody's bomb," he said. Erwin's "spontaneous expertise" is the best reason for task forces.

The 1972 bomb, contained inside a package addressed to an auto dealer who had repossessed Roy Moody's car, had exploded prematurely in Moody's home when his wife unwittingly opened the box. Moody contended that the bomb had been made by someone named "Gene Wallace" who was helping him regain his car. Although Wallace appears to be a complete fiction, a jury accepted that explanation. It did, however, convict him of possessing the bomb, and he served three years in federal prison.

Multiple searches of Moody's home failed to turn up any traces of the specific powders used in these new bombs—Red Dot for the smokeless powder and a CCI primer for the detonator—but federal agents did find a prototype for a pipe bomb in the basement of a house in Chamblee, Georgia, where Moody had previously lived.

It wasn't nearly enough to indict him for the bombings, but enough pieces had fallen into place to put Moody under constant and very public surveillance. (He knew from the searches that the task force was after him.) He'd leave his house in the morning, agents would follow, the media trucks would follow the agents, and every now and again, Moody would oblige his entourage by holding an impromptu press conference. The case seemed to be a matter of when Moody would crack or make a fatal mistake, or when the government would find the smoking gun that would bring him down . . . except that while the case against Moody was still developing, other investigators had followed a different trail to a different suspect, and had almost managed to embarrass Attorney General Dick Thornburgh and FBI director Bill Sessions in the process.

For this group, the anonymous threatening letters had become the key to the case. Typewriters, like homemade bombs, have their own distinctive signatures, and these letters, it turned out, had all been pecked out on the same aged Underwood machine. On the theory that whoever was behind this would have a long history of rancorous relationships with the Eleventh Circuit Court of Appeals, one of the agents had gone rooting through piles and piles of the court's old correspondence. There he had found a letter that not only was a perfect match but had also been signed by a junk dealer from Enterprise, Alabama. The letter made clear, he was really, really angry at the Eleventh Circuit.

Calls went up to Washington: Forget Moody, we've the real goods down here. A plane was ready to whisk Thornburgh and Sessions to Alabama so they could announce the arrest on site. (Remember, this was a federal judge who had been murdered—a major case.) Just to put an exclamation mark on the moment, the task force decided to do the arrest in grand style. A couple hundred agents scrambled to Enterprise, a town small and tight enough that a single stranger is noticed. Inevitably, the press got wind of things. A small army descended on the junkyard. The dealer and his wife were interrogated for hours. Other agents were caught on TV, digging their way through the junkyard, and digging, and digging. In the end, the typewriter wasn't there because, after all, the guy is a junk dealer, and junk dealers by definition deal junk. Yes, he had once been in possession of the typewriter; sure, he used it to write the letter in question, but he had sold the machine to some young woman. (She turned out to be Moody's girlfriend, but that gets ahead of the story.)

More calls were made to Washington: things aren't quite matching up; this might not be the best time for the attorney general and the director to board a plane. In Atlanta, Moody held a press conference to once again proclaim his innocence, this time with the added evidence of the Alabama raid. In Enterprise, one very irate junk dealer was holding his own press conferences, saying the government had ruined his reputation and threatening to sue everyone and everything in sight. And that roughly was the state of things when

Howard Shapiro and I arrived in Atlanta to take control of the investigation: a Looney-Tunes scenario.

In the Pizza Connection case, we had managed to get investigators and jurists on two different continents, out of two different legal systems, reading from the same page. Here, three U.S. Attorneys' Offices with contiguous jurisdictions couldn't even agree on what the case was about, and half a dozen or so investigative agencies with a mutual goal were basically not talking with each other.

The first fixes were the easiest. Instead of settling into the cushy Russell Office Building, Howard and I moved into its decrepit annex with the task force and set about rearranging the architecture so people would spend less time isolated in their own rooms and more time interacting across the various agencies. We also let all three U.S. Attorneys' Offices know that while we would be coordinating with them, we would be calling the shots from now on. What's more, we would be empaneling a grand jury in Atlanta—not Birmingham, not Savannah—when we were ready to seek indictments. Not everyone agreed with us. Not everyone even liked us. We were their worst-case scenario: two know-it-all lawyers who had flown in from the Big Apple to rip apart their cozy little world. We didn't even talk right! But for the first time there was someone truly in charge of the investigation.

We also got some vital help from the FBI early in 1990 when Director Sessions wisely sent agent Larry Potts to take command of the task force. Larry's leadership and investigative ability quickly helped organize the vying agencies into a cohesive force.

With a new infrastructure in place, we set out to build the case against Walter Leroy Moody Jr. the way it should have been built all along: meticulously, block upon block, with everyone pooling their various areas of expertise. That's where things really got tricky because Moody, we were to learn, was very much the definition of an evil genius.

Proof of the genius part came in the form of a psychiatrist we hired to evaluate Moody for the government and the defense, once he had finally been indicted. Moody described himself as an inventor, literary consultant, and publisher, but the psychiatrist told us he could have been anything he wanted to be. Moody was brilliant. He could pick up a book on, say, neurosurgery, read it, and probably perform competent basic brain operations on a first try. Half the time during their sessions, the psychiatrist said, it was hard to tell who was interviewing whom.

The deeply evil side of Moody's character emerged more slowly but with even greater power. He was a racist, to be sure, but the August 1989 "Declaration of War" and tear-gas explosion at the Atlanta NAACP office and the later bombs sent to the NAACP in Jacksonville and to Robby Robinson in Savannah had been red herrings. In effect, Robinson died an agonizing death over several hours simply to throw investigators off the trail. Roy Moody was indeed enraged at the Eleventh Circuit, but not because it favored African-Americans. In the mid-1980s, the court had failed to overturn his conviction on the 1972 charge of possessing a bomb: that was Moody's beef. Because he couldn't clear his record, we would finally learn, Moody was unable to achieve his life's ambition: to become a lawyer. And because he couldn't become a lawyer, he had declared war on the court. Irony upon irony.

By bits and pieces, the case began to fall together. I was only just getting settled in Atlanta when ATF agents uncovered a former gun-store clerk named Paul Sartain, who said he had sold a four-pound keg of Red Dot powder and four thousand CCI pistol primers to Moody while working at a store called the Shootin' Iron in

December 1989. Months later, a Florida welder named Ted Banks—Moody's cellmate while the mad genius was imprisoned on the earlier bomb charge—would add another piece to the puzzle. At Moody's behest, Banks had fixed end plates onto three metal pipes, similar to the end plates found on the unexploded bombs. (The pipe and plates used to murder Judge Vance were separately acquired.)

All of it was titillating. Everything seemed to fit into a larger picture. But it was all circumstantial and would remain so right to the end. The person who tied the various elements of the case together was Moody's girlfriend and later wife, Susan McBride. Once she saw the light and began cooperating with us, the noose began to tighten for good around Roy Moody's neck.

"Saw the light" is perhaps too kind. We had prepared a criminal case against Susan for aiding and abetting Moody in the bombings, but her assistance had been almost robotic rather than willing. He was in his fifties by then; she was still in her twenties and obviously greatly under his sway. Almost everything he did, Susan told us, was with an eye to eliminating any evidentiary link to the bombings. He would assemble the bombs in motel rooms, she said, but before he began to do any work, he would remove all this clothes and put on a shower cap. And so it was with every part of the bomb and every step of the procedure. Moody worked meticulously to eliminate forensic evidence, and with very few exceptions, he made Susan his errand girl.

In November 1989, Moody sent Susan McBride from Atlanta to Florence, Kentucky, with instructions to purchase the shipping boxes he would later use to contain the bombs, the aluminum cake pans he employed as part of the electrical triggering mechanisms, and the priority postage packages he used to mail the bombs. As he had with his "Declaration of War" letter, he also gave Susan original documents and instructed her to make numerous copies without reading the papers or even handling them with her bare hands. Off Susan went, as she always did, and performed exactly as instructed, making the purchases and then locating the photocopying store Moody had told her to use and slipping on a pair of gloves before she began to make copies. This time, though, there was a tiny flaw in the execution. A threatening letter enclosed with the Jacksonville bomb had two good, identifiable fingerprints on it. They weren't Moody's or Susan's, but they were prints, and unless we could identify whom they belonged to, Moody's defense was sure to claim we were overlooking the real letter sender and, beyond that, the actual bomber.

Susan couldn't remember the name of the photocopy shop, but we had agents drive her around Florence until she found it. Sure enough, a clerk who worked there recognized the odd woman who had come in months earlier and donned gloves before copying. That gave us a corroborating witness for Susan's story—an important breakthrough—but we took prints from everyone who worked in the shop and none of them matched the one we had. We were back in Atlanta, still sweating the matter, when the Florence, Kentucky, store clerk called with a new piece of intelligence: she had just remembered that a young boy named Gordon Horton was working at the shop at the time Susan had come in. Among Gordon's jobs, she said, was loading paper into the machines. Back the agents went to Florence to take young Gordon's prints, and when they matched, one large concern was lifted off all our shoulders. The critical value of this evidence, corroborating Susan's account, would be devastating to Moody at trial.

Then, at last, we got our first direct proof of actual value from the evil genius himself.

To keep the pressure on Roy Moody while we were building the larger case, we decided to go after him on a lesser charge: suborning perjury by a witness in connection with his appeal in the mid-1980s of his old bombing conviction. That case was pretty much an open-and-shut affair. Moody had clearly recruited and paid a destitute, handicapped young woman to lie on his behalf about the existence of the alleged bomb maker "Gene Wallace." The trial was to be held in Brunswick, Georgia, so in December 1990, I went down there to handle my first case outside of New York City, an education all its own.

I was used to jury pools where half the prospects showed up reluctantly, some with *Daily Racing Forms* sticking out of their back pockets. These potential jurors showed up scrub faced, wearing coats and ties. I was also accustomed to having the full range of legal maneuvering available to me. It still was, of course, so long as the maneuvering didn't involve memos or standing up in the courtroom to object or ask for a recess. Judge Tony Alaimo, his clerk informed me, didn't do memos, and he entertained objections and recesses only if you sent him a note at the bench.

How long would I need to present my case? the judge asked me.

Oh, I told him, four to six weeks.

Fine, he said, we'll do it in a week, and we did. (Apart from running a rocket docket and being a great guy, Tony Alaimo was a B-26 bomber pilot in World War II, helped with the famous "Great Escape" from one German POW camp and later successfully escaped from another.) But as minor as the case was in the larger scheme of things, it did give me a chance to examine Roy Moody close up, and fairly early on in the course of doing that, I discovered a chink in Moody's armor: he talked to himself. No one knew what he said, but the possibility of getting something incriminating from his own mouth was tempting enough that Howard and I had written up an affidavit, asking permission to put a wiretap in Moody's Atlanta jail cell, and sent it to the Justice Department. You're crazy, the answer came back: a tap presumes one person talking to another. But Justice gave me permission to pursue it, so I took the affidavit to a wonderful but crusty old Atlanta judge named Richard Friedman, who had the same first response.

"You're crazy." Then he added, "And you're from New York, too!"

But he gave in as well. So we put the microphone in Moody's cell, and for a solid week agents listened to nothing but gibberish and blather. (By court order, they had to stop listening if they thought Moody was saying something to himself that might pertain to the perjury trial. Our wiretap order didn't cover that.) Then, sometime in week two, one of the agents came racing into my office, saying, "You're not going to believe this." There, clear as a bell as far as we were concerned, was Roy Moody on tape, saying to himself, "Now you've killed two. . . . Now you can't pull another bombin'."

No murder trial is simple, and this one was no exception. Our Atlanta grand jury indicted Moody on more than seventy separate counts in connection with the bombings, but the case clearly couldn't be heard in Atlanta or anywhere else in the Eleventh Circuit's jurisdiction. Moody had sent threatening letters to every judge in the circuit. We couldn't possibly argue that he could get a fair trial. In such instances, it's up to the Supreme Court to find a trial judge. For this one, the chief justice chose the U.S. District Court in Minnesota, presided over by its longtime chief judge, Edward J. Devitt. So off we all went in the spring of 1991 to St. Paul: myself and Howard Shapiro; Susan McBride and a slew of other witnesses; Moody's excellent lawyer, Ed Tolley, with whom I was becoming good friends; Moody himself; and a truckload of evidence.

On its best day, our case was never completely solid. Even Susan couldn't put Moody in a room with a bomb that had been sent to any of the four targets. He was too careful for that. Ed Tolley argued brilliantly on his client's behalf; and Moody, during four days of rambling narrative testimony, lied brilliantly on his own behalf, never more so than when he insisted to the jury that what we caught him saying on our wiretap was not "Now you can't pull another bombin'" but rather "Now you can't pull another farmin'." Susan's testimony, though, carried our circumstantial evidence beyond a reasonable doubt, and in the end, for all his dissembling and Mensa-level intellect, Roy Moody couldn't escape his own words.

After Moody was found guilty on seventy-one separate counts—for which he would ultimately be sentenced to seven life terms plus four hundred years—Ed Devitt asked Tolley and me to accompany him back to the jury room. A big blackboard stood against the wall with a single phrase on it: "Now you can't pull another bombin'/farmin'." Someone had drawn a big chalk mark through "farmin'." Case closed.

Roy Moody would pop back up in the news in 1994 when an FBI crime lab chemist, Frederick Whitehurst, accused several of his fellow employees of withholding evidence and manipulating scientific tests in order to gain convictions, and by extension myself and Howard Shapiro of misconduct by offering their testimony in the case. I didn't believe it at the time, and I don't believe it now. Whitehurst's allegations were more about the validity of competing scientific methods than about anything intentional, and indeed they did lead to changes in some of the Bureau's lab procedures, but for Whitehurst to level such serious charges against his co-workers was way over the top. As for Howard and me, we had no idea the controversy was even simmering below us, and a Justice Department review agreed. But by then, Howard was the Bureau's chief counsel and I was its director, an awkward position for both of us.

The far more pleasant lingering effect of the Moody case was the judge who heard it, Ed Devitt. Among trial lawyers, he had a towering reputation. He'd been a grade school classmate of Warren

Burger and Harry Blackmun, both of whom were destined for the Supreme Court. After serving in the navy in World War II, Ed had briefly been a member of Congress before losing his House seat after a single term to Eugene McCarthy. But it was as a U.S. district judge—for thirty-eight years—that he'd made his true mark. Ed was coauthor of the standard guide to jury instructions in criminal cases. He knew everyone. For nearly a quarter century, the American Judicature Society has been presenting an annual award in his name to outstanding federal judges. He was the perpetual grand marshal of the annual St. Patrick's Day parade in St. Paul, where he was known as the unofficial mayor. Most important to me, Ed Devitt had a heart full of compassion and a great sense of humor.

The U.S. Senate had confirmed my nomination to become a U.S. district judge while the Moody case was going on. The week before the trial was to end, the attorney general called to say he was ready to sign my judicial appointment certificate, the last official act before I could be sworn in, and would be sending it out to me by express mail. I dutifully reported the fact to both Devitt and Ed Tolley, the opposing counsel, just to make sure no one thought my pending status would prejudice the outcome. Neither of them did, but as Ed Tolley and I were packing up our papers in the courtroom after the trial was over that Friday, Ed Devitt's clerk handed me a note from the judge. "Mr. Freeh," it read, "I understand your certificate is about to come in. If you'd like, I'll swear you in myself."

I went back to his chambers and talked with him about it. My soon-to-be colleagues in New York might not like his jumping the gun like this, Ed warned, but he had impressed me so greatly during the four weeks of the trial and he was so genuinely warm that I called Marilyn to get her okay. The next day, a Saturday, Ed Devitt administered the oath of office, and I left St. Paul as a U.S. district court judge, though Ed wasn't through with me yet.

In August 1991, I was more formally sworn in again as a judge, this time at a more appropriate venue, my new courtroom in lower Manhattan. The event, obviously, was strictly ceremonial—a chance for my wife and kids, my parents, and close friends to see me put on the black robe of office and take my place on the bench for the first time. At most courtrooms around the country, it's a very festive time. Friends get to say a few words, as do family members. The ceremony is drawn out a bit, so everyone can savor the moment, but not in the Southern District of New York. The great jurist and Supreme Court justice Learned Hand scripted the rite for the New York court, and he kept it Puritan simple: a stark, emotionless oath-taking that might consume all of 120 seconds. Ed Devitt not only insisted on coming, even knowing the ceremony would be grim, but he had kindly offered his robe maker in Minnesota to make my own first robe, and that's what was put on me after I had signed the oath of office (a second time) and the chief judge instructed U.S. marshal Romolo Imundi, a heroic ex–New York homicide detective and pal, to robe me that I might approach the bench.

I admit that I did notice a slight stirring as I made my way across the courtroom, but it wasn't until I was seated at my spot on the very lowest end of the bench that my new fellow jurist Kevin Duffy leaned over and asked me the question that was on everyone's mind:

"Hey, Louie, what's with the blue robe?"

In the audience, I noted, Ed Devitt was laughing hysterically.

"I just wanted to make your swearing-in distinguished," he told me later. "Those guys on the bench didn't have a smile among them. It'll shake 'em up a little." It happened that when Ed forgot his own robe while riding circuit in Minnesota, he borrowed one from a state judge, who wore blue.

Sadly, Ed fell seriously ill not long afterward. Ed Tolley and I determined to go visit him at his hospital in Minnesota, but before we went, we called his clerk to ask if there was anything we could bring. Yes, we were told, there was, and so it was that two upstanding officers of the court—with the help of New York FBI agent Bob Lennick, a technical wizard on the Moody case—snuck a bottle of Jack Daniels past the nursing station and into Judge Devitt's room so we could all have a last few slugs of bourbon together. Ed Devitt died not long afterward, at age eighty, an inspiration to the very end.

Funny how life works out. I'd gone down to Georgia expecting, at one level, to be there no more than sixty days. That two months grew into more than a year, but I had honored the fiction that I would be leaving any day by putting up the whole time not in an apartment near the Russell Building, which would have been sensible, but in a suite at a Marriott near the airport, which was probably delusional at best. (The Marriott manager was kind enough to dedicate the suite to me when I finally checked out.)

Had I said no to Bob Mueller when he called about Atlanta and left instead for the private sector, I'm sure I would have been better off financially. I might even have still been put up for a seat on the U.S. district court. I had a long relationship with Al D'Amato, the New York senator who recommended me. And if I had never been a federal judge, I feel certain I wouldn't even have been considered for director of the FBI. With good cause, too, because my time as a U.S. district court judge proved to be excellent preparation for the job I was going to tackle in another two years.

When I was going through my confirmation before the Senate Judiciary Committee, Senator Joe Biden had the good sense to ask about the gaping holes in my résumé.

"You have a long background in criminal law," I can remember him saying, "but how are you going to get up to speed on civil practice?"

He was right. I knew criminal courtrooms inside and out, but there were large areas of civil law I had only a nodding acquaintance with. To compensate, I promised Senator Biden—one of the most honorable men in Washington and my own senator now that I live in Delaware—that I would hire smart clerks, and I did just that.

Eileen Minnefor was two years out of Harvard Law School when her application came to my attention. I was clearing out my Atlanta office, getting ready to drive everything back to New York by way of my in-laws' home in Pittsburgh. Eileen was working for a Boston firm. Since time was short, we arranged to meet in the Pittsburgh FBI office. The special agent in charge there, Bob Reutter, had been my supervisor in the UNIRAC case and is a great guy in any event. He was glad to give us the space, and I was immediately wowed by Eileen.

My other clerk, Burke Doar, has the pedigree of a legal thoroughbred. Burke is the son of John Doar, the fabled Justice Department lawyer who had been instrumental in breaking down segregation barriers in Mississippi in the 1960s. (Doar was by James Meredith's side when he became the first black student to register at the University of Mississippi, on October 1, 1962.) Just to make sure Burke's bloodlines stayed strong, he'd been named for his father's close friend and eminent colleague Burke Marshall, assistant attorney general for civil rights in the Kennedy administration. Both were also superb lawyers.

Early on in my judgeship, Eileen and Burke had their hands full keeping me from tripping over my own tongue. I can recall wading into the middle of a raging battle between three or four law firms during a morning conference in my chambers. At issue was some discovery dispute in a civil matter. The lawyers were at each other's throats over getting access to a witness who lived halfway across the country. To me, the matter was simple. Under criminal procedure, which is what I knew, a grand jury can issue a subpoena nationwide. What I didn't know is that under civil rules, subpoenas are good only within a hundred-mile radius.

"This is ridiculous," I finally said after another round of shout-ing. "Get a subpoena!"

The silence that greeted my suggestion was absolute. Off to the side, Eileen was shaking her head, wondering if I was even trainable.

"I just said something really stupid, didn't I?" I told the lawyers. At least I got that part right.

But I was trainable, as things turned out, and in Paul Blumberg I found the perfect court clerk. Paul was a born-and-bred New Yorker: he and his wife had grown up eight blocks from the court-house. They still lived in the neighborhood, and indeed Paul had been a roving clerk in the federal courthouse for a number of years. When I offered him the chance to settle down with one judge for what I thought would be years upon years, Paul jumped at it, and I couldn't have been happier. Short, heavy-set, with a moustache and big, thick glasses, Paul had a New Yorker's natural instinct for cutting to the chase, and I had been handed a docket that needed plenty of cutting and chasing.

Rookie judges are like rookies in any other endeavor. They get dumped on by the old-timers. But the situation in my new court was extreme. One judge had fallen sick, and I got half of his docket. Ten vacancies on our bench had left the other judges with overwhelming caseloads. At the chief judge's decree, all but one of them (Judge Pol-lack, true to his character, offered to take any case I didn't want to keep.) handed me twenty cases, and almost without exception they were the twenty cases the judge most wanted to be rid of: one where a motion had been argued a year ago but no ruling made, or maybe a bench trial complete with transcript to which the judge had never had time to add his findings of fact so I would have to go back and read the entire thing from word one. Eileen, Burke, Paul, and I labeled the docket "the kennel," and believe me, those dogs wouldn't stop yapping.

Just to put a little extra pressure on, someone from the Justice

Department's administrative office called to urge me to attend a two-week training session for new judges.

"Where's it being held?" I asked.

"Atlanta."

"No," I practically shouted. "I just spent a year living in a hotel in Atlanta. I'm not going back."

I phoned Ed Devitt in a panic and asked what to do about my bulging docket. Get an extra courtroom, he advised, and try two cases at once! Then he gave me some more practical advice: put everybody down for a trial, call conferences, and bring the lawyers in. Most will settle. And keep a disciplined time frame, run a tight calendar. If you don't, the cases will get away from you.

Paul Blumberg proved amazingly effective at getting cases settled. I later learned that as he was bringing an attorney in to conference, he would say, "Do you really want to go to trial with this?"

"What's the matter?" the lawyer would say, newly nervous.

"It just doesn't look like much of a case," Paul would answer with a despairing shake of his head. Then he would bring the opposing lawyer in and say exactly the same thing. Suddenly, instead of motivated litigants, we had motivated negotiators—a big change.

To tighten the calendar, I scheduled all my conferences for eight in the morning and promised the lawyers they would be out by nine. And I kept my promise religiously. The hour was early—no other judge in the courthouse was holding conferences then—but at least the attorneys knew they wouldn't be sitting around the courthouse all day while I dawdled my way through a chronically late schedule. Trials started as soon as the conferences ended: promptly at nine. I broke at noon for my jog along the East River, then resumed trials until five sharp. Thanks to Paul, Eileen, and Burke, the place ran with military precision, and the system worked. In two years, we went from having the largest number of active cases in the district to the lowest number.

All the while I was learning and, without realizing it, preparing myself for what waited ahead. Our docket was a mix of criminal and civil cases, and because the Southern District of New York is it-self so incredibly diverse, our cases were diverse, too. One day we'd be handling a maritime case, some dispute about bills of lading. That would be followed by a patent or copyright infringement, an at-tempt to knock off someone's toy or clothing design or to steal an idea for the Next Big Thing, whether it was a movie, a book, a theme restaurant, or some new piece of electronics.

As in most courts in America, our criminal-case docket was clogged with drug trials, but even though I'd spent a good deal of my professional life on such matters, I could still be surprised by some twist in a case, for good or for ill. And of course I was seeing the trials from a whole new perspective.

I remember particularly one case brought by the Department of Justice. The defendants had all been convicted several times before. If they pled guilty this time, they were facing stiff mandatory sen-tences, so they had nothing to lose by putting their fate in a jury's hand. But in truth, they didn't have a chance. An undercover agent had been dealing one-to-one with them. He'd caught them on tape, incriminating themselves all over the place. If that weren't enough, a court-authorized phone wiretap had piled up more self-incrimination, and a search had turned up guns, financial records, and drugs—enough to convince a couple of the dealers to begin cooperating with the government. As a kind of audiovisual guide for the jury, the evidence being displayed on the prosecution table seemed to be growing by several inches an hour, an expanding blob that threatened to engulf the entire courtroom.

I knew several of the defense lawyers. They were very able peo-ple, but even they weren't able to manufacture much conviction. The jury was clearly tired. The marshals had been ready for hours to march the defendants back to the Metropolitan Correction Center, where they were overnighting. More out of a sense of completeness than any real necessity to drive a stake further into the defendants' collective heart, the government called an agent who had participated in some relatively minor act of surveillance, and he added his few cents to the pot. Then, on cross-examination, one of the defense lawyers asked the agent about an inconsistency in his testimony, and the agent lied about it. Not a subtle lie either—one of those lies that sounded like one the minute it left his mouth.

The defense lawyer asked the question again, almost as if he were giving the agent a chance to correct himself, and the agent lied again. And now my sleepy courtroom started perking up. From the bench I could see the demeanor of the jury change almost instantaneously. Instead of concentrating on the witness, the jurors started to look away from him. They were shuffling their feet, twiddling their thumbs, looking both embarrassed and annoyed. The prosecutor got up on redirect exam and tried everything he could to fix the damage, but the agent was by now insistent in his lie, and he was still insistent as four or five of the defense attorneys took turns destroying his credibility even more.

At the end of the session, most of the jurors were looking right at me as they filed out. I could see them rolling their eyes, shaking their heads, and I knew right there and then that the government had lost the case. The trial went on for a few more days, but it was like watching a slow death, and everyone knew it. The evidence was overwhelming. Guilt screamed from the defendants' table. But jurors had lost confidence not just in the case their government was presenting but in the government itself, and in the end they acquitted most of the defendants on the bulk of the charges leveled against them.

As a prosecutor, I had never been able to talk to a jury after a trial. Now I could, so I walked into the jury room to thank them and to take their temperature, and found a very emotional scene.

"Judge, those defendants were drug dealers, weren't they?" one of the jurors asked me, obviously upset.

"That's not for me to say," I told him. "You made the decision."

But he wasn't letting me off the hook with the usual bromides.

"No, no," he went on. "We knew they were, but we couldn't convict them."

I asked him why.

"When we came in here after your charge, I think all of us felt the government had overwhelming evidence," he said. "We started to vote, and it seemed as if everyone was going to vote to convict. We'll be out of here in no time, I thought. Then someone says, 'But what about the agent who lied?' And that turned everything around."

"You could have concluded that the witness lied and still convicted everybody," I told him, but by now the rest of the jurors had joined in.

"Judge," one of them said, "we felt that if an agent would lie about something that unimportant, how could we trust the government on the big issues? We had a terrible time. We felt terrible about it. But we just couldn't convict."

I thought about that case often during my time as a U.S. district judge, and I was still thinking about it early in my tenure as director when I asked about what kind of ethics training we did with new agents at the academy. Oh, came the answer, we do a couple hours in the sixteenth week of the program. That's not good enough, I said. We've got to change that. We revamped the program so that ethics training came in the first week, not the last. We made it two days, not two hours. We also created an Office of Law Enforcement at Quantico to oversee the training, and we started to take the program on the road to our field offices so everyone in the Bureau, not just the new guys, would get the message.

For years, the academy had handed out three awards at graduation: for academics, marksmanship, and physical fitness. I suggested that we add a fourth award to the package—an ethics award for that class member deemed the most reliable, trustworthy, and honest— and it's still being given out. I started a program at Quantico where sitting federal judges came to teach new agents about ethics. Every chance I got, I also carried the message personally to new agents, to police officers, to supervisors, to nearly every crowd I had a chance to address: integrity is the most important asset we have as law enforcement officers—more important than our witnesses, than our evidence, than anything else. If the people we serve don't trust us, if they don't respect us, then we can have the most impressive evidence in the world and still not win a conviction. We're seeking to deprive people of their most precious possession, their liberty. If the people in the jury box don't have confidence in us, they won't let us do that. I'd seen that firsthand from my seat on the bench, I would tell audiences, and it wasn't pretty.

That trial was on my mind, too, when I was invited early in 1994 to give a talk at Jagiellonian University—Copernicus's school— in Krakow, Poland. For all sorts of complicated reasons, our then-ambassador didn't want me to go. But I had read so much about the concentration camps in Poland, and I had been so moved by photos I had seen at the United States Holocaust Memorial Museum in Washington of smiling German police beating Jewish shopkeepers during those horrible days in the spring of 1933. Auschwitz-Birkenau is the largest graveyard in human history: 1.3 million people had been murdered there. I wanted to visit it because Auschwitz was, in one respect, a colossal police failure, and I thought it was important to acknowledge that and learn from it.

I'd also gotten to be friends with Elie Wiesel. I'd read his books and talked with him, and I remembered well the story of the local Hungarian policeman who knocked on the Wiesels' window one night and tried to warn them to flee town because something was about to happen. The family didn't flee. Elie's father couldn't comprehend the evil that was already forming, and they were hauled away the next day to the transports and from the transports to the death camps. But the courage of that single policeman stuck with me, his apparent attempt to do good when so much malevolence was all around him.

To make sure that lesson got through to our new recruits at the FBI, I asked Michael Berenbaum, then the director of the Research Institute at the Holocaust Museum, to put together several hours of instruction on the role of the police in the early years of the Holocaust, and Michael and his staff came up with a powerful presentation: archive photos, first-person accounts of both good and bad police, scenes that you just couldn't turn away from. Then I asked the people at Quantico to include a visit to the museum in their new agents training program. There was some resistance at first. The sixteen weeks are already jam-packed. But I asked them to try it with one class and see what the feedback was, and the reviews were incredible. Not only did we continue it with our training, but the program is now being used by the FBI's National Academy, also based at Quantico, which to date has trained over 39,000 local, state, federal, and foreign police officers in its premier eleven-week program.

To further drive home the point that one man of extraordinary courage and moral character can make a great difference, I also had a memorial garden dedicated at Quantico to honor Giovanni Falcone, near the spot he had visited in 1982 when the groundwork was first being laid for international cooperation on the Pizza Connection cases.

Over the years, the Anti-Defamation League had done training sessions for the Bureau. No one, after all, has a better feel for hate crimes than the ADL. When I learned that the group had a Holocaust exhibition touring its own regional offices, I asked Abe Foxman, the longtime ADL executive director and one of my heroes, if we could tour it through our field offices, too. To kick off the program, we had Elie Wiesel speak at the first Holocaust Remembrance Ceremony at FBI headquarters. Again, the feedback was outstanding.

Ethics were central to what I was trying to instill as director because those drug dealers my anguished jury had set free drove home to me the practical consequences of ethical failures, but beyond that, I wanted to establish a set of core values that would inform everything the Bureau did. I helped write that document—it still hangs in field offices, FBI facilities, and foreign legats from Quantico to Beijing—and I made sure to include not just honesty and integrity but other values not always associated with police forces such as fairness and compassion. Why? Because I had had some experience also in the benefits of treating even hardened criminals as human beings.

Back in my days as an FBI agent, my partner and I had gone out to serve an arrest warrant on an organized-crime guy at his house. The normal drill was to grab the guy in the morning before he was really awake: knock on the door, cuff him if he resisted, the whole nine yards. But we had been watching this guy for a number of days and knew that he had a wife and small kids living at home, and I hated the thought of those little kids seeing their dad hauled away. So I did something I never should have done. On the morning of the collar, I called the guy from a pay phone down the street—this was before cell phones—and told him we had a warrant for him.

"I know," he said. "I've been expecting you."

"Listen," I told him, "I don't want to do this in front of your wife and kids. What I want you to do is walk out of the house in five minutes and come down to the corner. We'll be waiting in our car, and we'll arrest you there."

I recall his response to this day: "Mr. Freeh, thanks, I'll be right with you."

Just to be on the safe side, in case he did decide to run, I told him that we had ten guys around the house. There were only two of us, and fortunately, that's all we needed because within five minutes the guy was heading our way down the street. Three years later, this same guy sent word from a federal prison that he wanted to see me. "I'm paying you back," he told me, "for not arresting me in front of my kids." And then he handed me a big case—against someone he obviously didn't like and under the condition that he wasn't in any way named—but it was all because someone had treated him decently when no rulebook said that had to be the case.

Obviously, we have to treat the victims of crime and their survivors with equal, even greater, compassion, and to me that meant being true to our word when we told those families of the dead at Khobar Towers that we would leave no stone unturned to bring the killers to justice. My distraught jury had taught me that. People who feel they can't trust their leaders to be true to their word will eventually lose faith in government altogether.

Sometimes the cases I was handed touched me in deeply personal ways. One day I was randomly assigned a Title 7 complaint, a woman alleging sexual discrimination by a Wall Street firm. I looked at the firm's name, and all of a sudden my memory went shooting back more than three decades to a story my mother had once told me. She had just left high school and was trying to land her first full-time job in New York when she went down to this Wall Street firm to fill out an application. A friend worked there and thought it would be a good fit, and indeed the interview seemed to go very well. Two or three people were under consideration, her friend told her, but my mother seemed to be the front runner. Finally, after waiting half the afternoon, the personnel head came out and told my mother, "We'd like to employ you, but we don't hire Italians."

Here it was, almost half a century later, and the son of that woman they wouldn't hire had been handed a case with allegations that substituted sex for country of origin. Only in America. I had to recuse myself from the matter, obviously, but it served as a useful reminder that while discrimination can change stripes, it doesn't go away.

There were moments, too, during my two years as a federal judge when history just came rushing at me, in ways that would have foretold my future if I could have read them at the time.

I was sitting in my courtroom on Foley Square in lower Manhattan on February 26, 1993, when the World Trade Center was first struck. Six people died in that attack, but it's worth remembering that if the bomb that exploded in the parking garage beneath the towers had been better configured, one or both buildings might have collapsed then, with a terrible loss of life, eight years before Osama bin Laden's suicide aerial bombers finally succeeded in bringing them down. (Eerily enough, one of the people in the towers at the time of the first attack told a reporter, "It was like an airplane hit the building.")

I'll never forget hurrying down from the courthouse to the site of the bombing. People were mostly fleeing in the other direction. Panic was in the air. I suppose I should have stayed away and let the emergency rescue teams do their job, but that's just not me. Without knowing it, I was looking at the bookends of my tenure as director. Within half a year, I would be leading the FBI. Eight years later, a little over two months after I'd left the job, these towers would be reduced to rubble.

For a lot of lawyers, joining the federal bench is an economic sacrifice. Private-practice attorneys are among the best-paid professionals in the country, especially at the top law firms. Judges do better than most civil servants, but it's still government pay. When I became a federal judge at age forty-three, my colleague, Kevin Duffy, a great and brave jurist, had warned that it was going to be hard for me to stick with the job, particularly with Marilyn's and my growing family. (Kevin knew whereof he spoke. He had joined the bench at age thirty-eight, the youngest federal judge in the Court's history.) But my flirtation with private practice had been broken off by Walter Leroy Moody and his lethal bombs. I'd been surviving for eighteen years on a government salary, and Marilyn and I figured we could survive for eighteen more.

Besides, being a U.S. district court judge is a dream job, the goal of many attorneys, even those pulling down a lot more money annually than I had been. The caseload was staggering, but I closed the court at five every night and headed straight for the subway, Grand Central Station, and Metro North. Soon I would be moving to the new courthouse, far closer to my home. I felt I was being useful, and the cases were a wonderful cross-section of America—its ills, its aspirations, its endless conflicts.

I honestly thought it was a job I could do for the rest of my useful years. It was a job I *expected* to do for all that time. Then the phone rang again, and this time the White House was calling.

CHAPTER 7

"If Anything Happens, You Drive. I'll Shoot"

My first great challenge as FBI director was to get inside the headquarters building for my own swearing-in. Marilyn, I, and the four kids showed up early at the Ninth Street entrance to the underground parking garage, all packed into our Volvo station wagon. Frank Johnson was waiting, the president was coming, and I was anxious to get the formalities over with and start settling into the job. But the uniformed FBI officer on duty at the parking garage entrance had other ideas.

"Do you have identification?" he asked me.

I tried my driver's license on him.

"No," he said, "do you have an FBI badge?"

"Not yet," I told him, "but I expect to soon. Has anyone mentioned that they're swearing in a new director today?"

He knew about that, but he had no guest list to check visitors off against.

"Well, listen," I said, "I'm the guy getting sworn in!"

That, at least, got his attention.

Later that day, as if to make up for the affront to its new boss, the FBI security detail had three cars waiting to tail us when I pulled the Volvo back out onto the street for the thirty-block ride across the Potomac to the Key Bridge Marriott where we were staying. The cars were waiting a few hours later when we drove off to dinner, and waiting when we left the restaurant, and waiting the next morning when we were ready to leave the hotel again.

"You guys are going to be with me a while?" I asked one of the drivers.

"All the time," he said, and he meant it.

We moved immediately into a rental house in Great Falls, Virginia, out toward the suburban edge of the Washington metropolitan area. By sheer luck, we inherited wonderful neighbors in Dick and Patricia Carlson. A former ambassador and media genius, Dick became a mentor to me. Beautiful and brilliant Patricia became Marilyn's dearest friend. Together they taught us how to survive in D.C.

We thought Great Falls would be a nice place to raise the kids, and we wanted to get them started in the schools there while we shopped for a house to buy. A few days later, the head of my security detail came to see me.

"Director, we're thinking of putting a construction trailer outside your house. That way, we could have people there all the time."

"You can't do that," I told him. "We can't have a trailer sitting out there."

"Okay, then," he said, "we'll do it in the backyard."

"No!"

The kids, naturally, loved the attention. We went to weekend soccer games, to the grocery store, to everywhere in convoy. But apart from traveling like a celebrity, the kids had gained a second benefit from my new status.

"This is really cool!" one of my sons said as we were convoying our way to Blockbuster one Saturday early in my tenure.

"C'mon," I told him, "don't you find it annoying to be followed everywhere?"

"No, and you don't yell at us anymore when we're outside the house!"

I realized in that instant that he was absolutely right. The kids had six agents as witnesses everywhere they went. I was on model behavior! That was it, I decided. I needed to be unprotected.

The large security detail favored by my predecessor, William Sessions, had naturally transferred to me. I couldn't just fire them en masse, but over the next several months, I managed to get all of them assigned to someplace they wanted to go or some duty they were hoping to draw. (One member of the security detail, an excellent agent with the captivating name of Icey Jenkins, would eventually head up the FBI investigation in Saudi Arabia, following the Khobar Towers bombing. Despite massive initial skepticism on the Saudis' part about sending a female to take charge in a male-dominated culture, Icey handled her role spectacularly.) Finally, I was left with two drivers as my security detail: one who retired shortly and John Griglione, a onetime varsity football player at the University of Iowa who had been deputized as a U.S. marshal so he could carry a gun.

Out of a sense of duty, John took me down to the bowels of the FBI parking garage once we had worked out our new arrangement to show me the three-ton armored limousine that directors were occasionally expected to ride around in.

"We can't do that," I told him. "It's out of some comic opera."

"Great," he said, "It's a pain in the ass to drive, and you have to change the brakes every couple hundred miles."

Instead, we got a Chevy Suburban to come and go in from Great

Falls. John carried his gun. I carried mine, in the car and pretty much everywhere else. For backup, we had a machine gun stowed in the center console. That was our new security. (Carrying a gun is not traditional with FBI directors although a specific statute permits it. In my case, it was a good substitute for a security detail and I liked qualifying once a quarter with the agents.)

"If anything happens," I told John Griglione, "you drive. I'll shoot."

Almost as hard as adjusting to the security demands was adjusting to the power of my own voice, at least within the walls of the J. Edgar Hoover Building. In my other positions in government, the wheels of the bureaucracy moved very, very slowly. Now, the least request would filter down from the director's office, gaining strength at every new floor it passed through until it came out as a roar at the other end.

I was still in the process of transferring myself and my family to Washington when I called Noreen Gawley, my incredibly organized secretary who had moved down ahead of me to get things in order, and asked her about the few items I wanted to hang on the walls. What were the weight limitations? Did the office have any bearing walls or were they all for show? Noreen transferred my query down to the facilities people, and the next thing she knew, a crew from facilities had come up to office to do a little measuring.

"What are you doing?" she asked.

"We're here to move the wall for the director."

"Why?"

"Someone called down and said he wanted a bigger office."

I already had plenty of room. Noreen had plenty of room. In between us was a conference room so huge I had to shout whenever I wanted to get Noreen's attention. (Although he didn't live long enough to occupy them, the suite of offices had been designed by J. Edgar Hoover himself. He obviously didn't want his secretary listening in on his calls.) I didn't need room. I just wanted to know if I could hang my kids' framed art without pulling down the sheetrock.

Being FBI director meant never being off duty. That's true of a lot of high-pressure jobs, of course, but with this one, the stakes could be so terribly stark. I wrote earlier that my mother was making dinner for us in New Jersey when Khobar Towers was hit. A year and a half earlier, two days before Thanksgiving on November 22, 1994, Marilyn and I and the kids were on the New Jersey Turnpike, again headed to my parents' house, when I got a call informing me that FBI agents Martha Dixon Martinez and Mike Miller and D.C. police officer Hank Daly had been gunned down inside Metropolitan Police Headquarters in Washington. I turned around at the next exit, went straight to my own office, and had one of the agents drive everyone else back to Great Falls.

The facts of the case were almost unbelievable. Martha and Mike were on detail to the D.C. police, helping with "cold cases," homicides in which the leads or witnesses had dried up or momentum was at a standstill. They were in the cold-case room on the third floor, minding their own business, when a D.C. drug gang member, Bennie Lee Lawson, burst in wielding a Cobray M-11 assault pistol. Lawson was looking to take revenge on the narcotics squad but got the wrong room. Never mind. He began firing anyway. When he was through, the three officers were dead and a fourth badly wounded. Before other police in the building could apprehend him, Lawson put the pistol to his own head and ended his life as well.

Martha was newly married to an FBI agent. Mike was the father of two small children. I didn't know either agent before the shootings, but I went to the morgue with Martha's husband when he had to identify her, and I attended both funerals because, to me, being

175

there at the bad moments is even more important for a leader than being there for the good ones.

I'll never forget either the first time I got called in the middle of the night to inform me that an agent had been killed. That was March of 1996. The agent, Charles L. Reed, had been shot in Philadelphia during an undercover drug operation. For the five-plus years I had remaining to me as FBI director, every call after midnight set my heart racing in fear of an agent being hurt.

Part of the pressure of the job was the simple lack of privacy. I could dump the security detail that wanted to surround me everywhere I went, but I couldn't escape the daily and hourly obligations of the post. It must have been the summer of 1998 when Marilyn and I rose well before sunup one morning, packed the kids and mounds of gear into the car, and took off for Cape Cod. Thirteen or so hours later, we finally had unpacked the car and were settled on the beach, surrounded by sand and water with four glorious days ahead. I was just contemplating the sheer joy of doing nothing when a sweet elderly lady tapped me on the shoulder and asked if I was the FBI director. When I said I was, she pointed to the top of the dune behind us. Two agents were standing there in government blue suits and city shoes that wouldn't do in the sand. They had an affidavit with them that needed my signature.

But the largest part of the pressure by far was politics. That was the one thing I wasn't ready for coming into office: navigating through all that. Maybe it was naïveté on my part, or the triumph of hope over experience, but I just wasn't prepared to find the waters so teeming with reefs, dangerous shoals, submerged icebergs, killer sharks, and just about every other form of hazard imaginable.

A ten-year term of office was supposed to help the director ride out political storms. You could never be beholden to just one president, one administration. But the reality of the job is that, as head of the FBI, you have such great power for good or ill. Directors of the

FBI can launch an investigation or stop one, or they can influence the drift of an ongoing one if they so choose. Their position allows them to exert pressure to bring charges, or pressure not to. Careers can be made or undone in the process. If Bill Clinton's memoir is an accurate reflection of his inner life, he came to believe that I was trying to undo his presidency. That's bunk, but the possibility that I or any director would conceivably even attempt to do something like that inevitably makes the job a political appointment, whatever Congress intended, with all the craziness that entails.

On one of my first days as director, I happened to ask my staff how the FBI hiring policy worked in terms of gay people. We have no special policy, I was told. Everyone is treated the same. Well, I went on, what if you're doing a background check and find out that someone is gay? Oh, came the answer, we stop processing the application. Whoa, I said, that's got to change. It was, first of all, a matter of compliance. We were subject to equal employment opportunity provisions just like any other agency. But beyond that, it was a matter of fairness and of image and, yes, of politics. Even as a neophyte I could see that we'd get pummeled in the press if word got out that we were tossing those applications in the dead-letter file. It was during that first week, too, that I got all my assistant directors in the office and noticed—as if anyone could have failed to—that they were white males every one. That had to change, too, to assure a better balance of advice but also because I wanted the FBI's leadership to reflect the nation we served. I was later proud to appoint the first Hispanic and female assistant directors.

That much I could understand, but I never really got used to the sheer politics that invested what seemed to me basic, everyday, practical decisions. I had been director for perhaps a year when I happened to mention in an internal report that because of some budget cuts, we were having to limit the number of rounds that agents were firing, not just at the training academy but also at the quarterly qualifying sessions on the range that every agent—the director included—has to go through if he wants to continue to carry a firearm. Simply put, we didn't have enough bullets to go around or, under current budget restraints, the money to buy more. Naturally, Washington being Washington, the internal report got leaked to the press. Next thing I knew Leon Panetta, who had just moved over from heading the Office of Management and Budget to become White House chief of staff, was on the phone. I liked Leon a lot, we got along very well. But Leon hadn't called to chat.

"Why would you put in a report that the FBI doesn't have enough bullets?" he demanded to know. "It makes the administration look bad!"

I don't know what Leon expected my reaction to be. Would I boil over? Start screaming? Be contrite? He had been around Washington a long time, and I respected him greatly. I imagine he had seen just about everything. For myself, though, all I could do was laugh at the absurdity.

Once I'd settled down, I explained that I had requested more money for bullets for the same reasons the Pentagon asks for more ammunition in its budget requests—because we didn't have enough rounds, and because the agents were complaining about it, and because if you're asking people to discharge firearms in the line of duty, you need to provide them with the best training possible for their own sake and for the safety of the populace generally. But that was being reasonable, at least by my lights, and when politics intervened, reason was often the first thing thrown overboard at both ends of Pennsylvania Avenue. In this case, though, my unreasonable-reasonable budget request was actually approved, and the Bureau thereafter always had more ammo than it knew what to do with.

Another example of the budget process at work: by the middle of Bill Clinton's second term, I was lobbying hard for a long-range aircraft to supplement the ancient Citation jet the Bureau had at its disposal. We were doing everything we could to round up terrorists around the world and witnesses to terrorist acts, and to convince the governments of the host nations to let us carry them back to the United States. Often we failed to find our quarry or to win approval. That's the nature of the business. But when we succeeded, we were commonly given a narrow window to remove the suspects, sometimes as little as twelve hours. In those circumstances, we would have to scramble for a military aircraft to do the transport. If one wasn't available, we would start calling friendly CEOs of American corporations to see if we could hitch a ride to Karachi or Doha or wherever we had to go on their corporate jet. (I can't name the CEOs we approached for obvious reasons, but Ramzi Yousef, for one, was flown out of Pakistan on a private corporate jet under very tight time constraints.)

To me, the situation was ridiculous, so I began lobbying for a Gulf-stream G-5. The price tag wasn't cheap—about $40 million—but the need was obvious. Since the White House clearly wanted nothing to do with my G-5, I carried the case to Congress, to Ted Stevens of Alaska, who was then head of the Senate Appropriations Committee, and to Richard Shelby of Alabama, chairman of the Senate Intelligence Committee. Both of them agreed to see what could be done about the matter, and that's when I got my first-ever call from the new director of the Office of Management and Budget in May 1998.

"You can't do this," he told me in no uncertain terms.

"What do you mean, I 'can't do this'?"

"You're not authorized to make that request."

I told him that we needed the aircraft and tried to make a quick case as to why, but he was unmoved.

"We've done an analysis," he finally said, "and our view is you don't need it."

"Well," I said, working hard to contain the white rage that was starting to build in me, "what's your background in counterterrorism?"

No surprise: he didn't like that, but I didn't much care for what he had to say either.

A few weeks later, George Tenet and I went up to the House Intelligence Committee together to discuss our budget needs. Somewhere in the course of the hearing, the chairman said, "Oh, by the way, Director Freeh, do you guys need a long-range aircraft?"

It was a slow pitch, right over the middle, and I stood up to hit it out of the park, but I got a little too carried away. George, after all, needed a G-5 as badly as I did, and he had been chastised also by OMB just as I was for excessiveness, so I decided to go to bat for both of us.

"Yes, Mr. Chairman," I answered, on my feet and eager to score, "we desperately need the aircraft, and for some reason, we can't get the people at OMB to approve it." Then I turned toward George, and added, "He needs one, too, and he needs one more than I do."

George looked up at me and laughed, but I probably should have kept my mouth shut because he got the G-5 before the FBI did. I later would rib George—a close friend and excellent CIA director—that he should name his plane for the FBI.

E very year we would go through these ridiculous budget exercises. The Bureau would formulate what budget we thought we needed, then send the budget on to the Department of Justice with the expectation that our figures would be reduced to what we actually needed. Justice would then send it on to the Office of Management and Budget with the notion that it would be reduced further, and OMB would send it on to Congress in the same spirit so that if, finally, we had guessed right at the front end and submitted numbers sufficiently greater than what we actually wanted we might ultimately end up with what we needed. That's how the process worked.

It was obvious to me and to many others that wiretapping statutes had fallen dangerously behind telecommunications technology. Wiretapping is a critical tool of law enforcement, used at all levels to penetrate the veil of secrecy that surrounds terrorists, organized crime, white-collar crooks, kidnapping plots, drug traffickers, and on and on. What's more, the requirement that wiretaps be court-authorized serves as a critical check on excess eavesdropping. But by the early 1990s, cellular technology and other forms of digital communication had moved beyond the capacities of the old analog-based wiretapping laws and procedures. Without new ways to tap into new technologies, we were in danger of going deaf, on both the criminal and the national-security sides.

Jim Kallstrom, a great New York agent and longtime friend and colleague, told me about this problem within days after I became director. So I went to Webb Hubbell—then the associate attorney general, before legal troubles derailed his career in government—and explained the problem. Webb was very receptive. He understood our dilemma and arranged a meeting with John Podesta, an assistant to the president and later chief of staff himself, so I could garner support within the White House. John Podesta offered little help or interest.

"The White House is not going to expend any political capital on this issue," he told me. "It's too sensitive. We'll get all the privacy groups on our case."

We wouldn't if we framed it right, I said. It's not about privacy. It's about expanding our technical ability, not our authority. But John's mind, and presumably the White House's behind him, was made up on the matter. So we did it on our own. We went office to the office on Capitol Hill and explained why the Communications Assistance for Law Enforcement Act (CALEA), as it became known, was critically needed and why it wouldn't infringe on any law-abiding American citizen's privacy. We also fought tooth and nail with the telecommunications industry along the way because complying with the provisions of the act was going to require some accommodation on its part. And one by one, we began to win because we were right on the issue and because, whatever the politics, what we were proposing was just plain common sense. Tom Constantine, then the DEA administrator and one of the most respected law enforcement leaders in the nation, stood by the FBI shoulder to shoulder and made a huge difference. We also got the invaluable help of the executive director of the International Association of Chiefs of Police, Dan Rosenblatt, who enlisted hundreds of local and state police leaders from across the country.

Democratic senator Pat Leahy of Vermont, a key member of the Senate Judiciary Committee, came onboard, as did Don Edwards, the powerful House Democrat from California. Edwards was a former FBI agent but not a natural supporter of court-authorized wiretapping. Pat Leahy, on the other hand, was an experienced prosecutor and understood like few in Washington the dangers faced and sacrifices made by law enforcement officers. Once when our family was visiting him and Marcelle in Vermont, a border patrol officer was wounded on duty, and Pat rushed to the hospital, where I watched him hold the wounded officer's hand. Pat was one of the finest leaders I met in Washington.

Conrad Burns, a Republican senator not predisposed toward us, held out until the Montana State Law Enforcement Association, and particularly the sheriffs, began deluging his office with faxes, and more faxes, and still more. Senator Burns could count, and he was hoping to be able to campaign in the next election without picking up a moving-violation ticket from every sheriff he had disappointed. (I happened to be in Senator Burns's office when the faxes started pouring in. We could see his resistance weakening with each new towering stack his secretary carried into the office.) The act we proposed was finally passed in October 1994, without the White House raising a finger, and America is a safer place for it.

Here's one last example of what I'm talking about because it shows how thoroughly our political landscape gets defined by narrow self-interest. By 1994, we had determined that we needed to place an FBI legat with the U.S. embassy in Moscow. Russian organized crime was on the rise globally, and the U.S. was not exempt from its reach. Today, Brighton Beach next to Coney Island looks like a Hollywood set for a gangster movie, except all the thugs are talking Russian, but even back then, a decade ago, the trend lines were unmistakable, and so were the problems. Just as with the Sicilian gangsters who started pouring into New York in the 1960s and '70s, we didn't know the language this time either, and we were having trouble building trust within the community. A Moscow Legat could open up lines of communication with police and other law-enforcement agencies there. We could begin to share information that would give both nations a leg up in the fight against this common enemy, and we'd have someone to call when American citizens disappeared on the streets of Moscow, as was beginning to happen with alarming regularity.

I knew it would sound strange in certain corners of Washington—even at the Bureau—to talk about an FBI agent in Moscow, but to me, the need was pressing and the reasoning obvious. So I ran the idea by Tony Lake, then the national security adviser, and waited to see what the response would be, and the response was not long in arising.

"Can you come over and talk about this?" Tony asked. "Woolsey is all upset."

Thus came to pass one of the crazier meetings I was to attend during my eight years as director. Jim Woolsey, then head of the

CIA, Tony Lake, and I gathered for lunch in Tony's office, and Woolsey protested.

His message was something like "Russia is ours," after I had explained what lay behind my proposal.

"I don't want agents only in Russia," I shot back. "I want one in Budapest and in Bucharest," and on and on.

"But we have officers in all those places," Jim said, aghast.

"They're spies! We need police officers."

While Jim was reeling from that, I went on to explain that FBI Legats scattered throughout the former communist world were only phase one of the plan. I also wanted to set up a police training academy. I'd already spoken with officials in Hungary about the academy, and they were willing to cosponsor it and help find a location in Budapest. As I talked on, I could see that the CIA director was beginning to warm to the idea.

"You might have a point," he finally agreed.

"Sure, I do," I said, inspired to even more oratory. "Training their police will strengthen our relationships throughout the region, and it will be good for the people in those countries as well. The more the police know about scientific investigations and forensics, the more likely they are to look for fingerprints instead of beating someone up to get a confession. We'll teach the police there the same way we do at Quantico. Good training enforces the rule of law."

By now, Woolsey was practically out of his seat with excitement. He would provide all the necessary equipment, then rig the equipment to find out what they're talking about. The CIA could recruit police right through the academy! I said the FBI would never do that.

Tony Lake had long before taken to studying the ceiling. He didn't want to be any part of this train wreck, but when Jim and I were through miscommunicating, Tony gave me the White House's go-ahead for the Moscow Legat and promised to coordinate, which he ably did. Within four years we had opened legat offices every-where from Moscow to Tallinn, Estonia, to Riyadh and Islamabad and Almaty in Kazakhstan. It wasn't always easy to convince officials in places like New Delhi that the FBI and the CIA weren't inter-changeable, that we wouldn't be operational, and that—Jim Woolsey's notions notwithstanding—we were actually trying to help their law enforcement agencies, not penetrate them. (I was never able to convince the Chinese of that although a legat was eventually ad-mitted after I left in June 2001.) But far more often than not, we suc-ceeded and in the process began to build a global network of trust.

The brains and excruciatingly complex work necessary to ex-pand from seventeen to forty-four legats in eight years were sup-plied by Bob and Jim Bucknam. Their incredible skill, diplomacy, and tenacity were responsible for this historic transformation of the FBI. Dick Holbrooke, one of the country's most brilliant diplomats and global thinkers, also gave us continuous guidance and helped forge our foreign strategy.

We also began training what would become a river of thousands upon thousands of foreign law-enforcement officials in a downtown Budapest building that had once been a military-police barracks, then home to a cavalry regiment, and finally, in the communist era, a headquarters for the secret police. That's the kind of irony I'll take any day, but none of it ever could have happened if the usual poli-tics of self-interest had prevailed.

Later, with the counsel of my friend and mentor Elie Wiesel, the FBI set up a multinational task force in Bucharest known as the Southeast European Cooperative Initiative (SECI). This thriving, highly successful regional task force—the first organized police effort in the region—is dedicated to stopping the sexual trafficking of women.

———

For a decade now I've been taking an informal poll among people outside the Bureau who ask me about its work: how many FBI agents do you think there are? Often, I'll provide a few numbers just to create some context. Chicago has a police force of 12,000 officers. New York City uses 44,000 officers to police all five of its boroughs. And the FBI? Often, I'll get estimates in the 60,000 to 100,000 range, sometimes higher. In fact, the FBI makes do with less than 12,000 agents, fewer than Chicago to police a whole nation and increasingly the world.

The public tends to think of the Bureau as a vast national police force armed with unlimited powers and a sweeping mandate to peek under virtually everyone's tent flap whenever it wants to. The reality is far different. The American people never wanted a national police force—the occupying British army soured them on that idea before America was ever born—and they don't have one or want one now. Nor does the FBI have an unlimited mandate or even a very rational one. That's why the loony notion of a domestic, MI-5 style secret police force to fight terrorists will never be accepted by Americans.

The Bureau has grown reactively far more than it has grown logically. We've had to constantly stretch old legislation to cover new conditions. Too frequently, also, we have been a dumping ground for popular causes that everyone in Congress can rally behind but that few in power want to fund. (The "Deadbeat Dads" legislation of the mid-1990s comes quickly to mind, a laudable cause given the number of fathers who fail to meet their court-ordered support payments and the hardship that can follow, but a responsibility for which Congress added not one thin additional dime to the FBI's budget.) More often than not, powers have been granted to the Bureau grudgingly, not willingly; after the fact, not before it; as a corrective, not a preventive. As director, I sometimes thought I was running a huge crisis-intervention unit, except that each new crisis seemed to add permanent responsibilities to the

Bureau's purview without necessarily expanding the resources to take them on.

In a sense, all this is nothing new. Up until the early 1930s, the FBI basically consisted of a bunch of accountants crunching numbers for J. Edgar Hoover in the hope of catching the Al Capones of the world cheating on their taxes. Agents weren't even authorized to carry firearms. If they wanted to make an arrest in, say, Chicago, they had to call local police officers to go with them. Then along came the bank-robbery boom of the Great Depression, especially across the Midwest. Machine Gun Kelly, Pretty Boy Floyd, Ma Barker, Bonnie and Clyde, John Dillinger, the whole mess of them—they were the terrorists of their day. The automobile—the getaway car—was the new technology that made it work, and just as with terrorists today, a ruthless disregard for life was the glue that held it all together.

One day in 1933 outside the Kansas City train station two unarmed FBI agents and a couple of local policeman were escorting a captured bank robber when a posse of his confederates ambushed the party, freed the felon, and left one of the agents and several of the policemen dead. In response, Congress gave agents authority to make arrests, work bank robberies, including pursuing the thieves across state lines, and the right to carry firearms. And thus the Bureau has grown ever since.

The bank-robbery terrorists of the Great Depression became the Soviet spies of the Cold War who became the domestic terrorists of the mid-1990s and the global terrorists of century's end. The car, the cutting-edge crime technology of the Bureau's birth years, yielded to the plane, the cell phone, the computer. And at every step along the way, the FBI has had to adjust and often wait for Congress to catch up with it and provide the relevant legislation. Systematic this is not.

It was the famous 1957 meeting of Mafia chieftains in Appalachia, New York, that awoke America to the pervasive role of organized crime in the economy and in society generally and years later led Congress to enact the Racketeer Influenced and Corrupt Organizations (or RICO) Act. And it was RICO that gave the Justice Department and the FBI greatly expanded powers to pursue the capos and dons and corrupt union heads and their business allies down all the rat holes where they were used to hiding out.

Similarly, it took all the horrors of the civil-rights movement—the murders in Philadelphia, Mississippi, ugly school-door confrontations, and too much more—to finally compel the creation of a Civil Rights Division within the Justice Department and an investigative and enforcement wing within the FBI. Meanwhile, the concept of civil rights keeps subdividing and expanding, and with every new interpretation, the Bureau gains more responsibilities. Today, the Bureau's broad civil-rights agenda includes the National Church Arson Task Force, the Freedom of Access to Clinic Entrances Act, Hate Crimes Working Groups, compliance with the Hate Crimes Statistics Act, as well as more traditional duties, including civil-rights violations by law enforcement officers.

The Bureau led the investigation into the brutalization by New York City police officers of Haitian immigrant Abner Louima. We did the work that resulted in the indictment for civil-rights violations of eight guards at the Corcoran State Prison in California. The Bureau was out front in the investigations of the death of James Byrd, Jr., the African-American dragged behind a pickup truck and finally decapitated in Texas in the summer of 1998, and Matthew Shepard, the gay college student murdered in Laramie, Wyoming, that same fall. We also led the investigation that resulted in a nearly twenty-year prison sentence for Lemrick Nelson after he had been acquitted by a local jury for the murder of Australian doctoral candidate Yankel Rosenbaum during the 1991 riots in the Crown Heights section of Brooklyn. Charles Price, also found guilty in the attack, was not even charged in state court.

During my tenure, we also set out to correct historic civil-rights wrongs: cases where murders were never prosecuted, or ones where likely suspects were never brought to trial or were let off by hung juries or outright acquitted. It took fourteen years to win the first conviction for the 1963 murders of four girls in the infamous bombing at Birmingham's Sixteenth Street Baptist Church: an Alabama Klan leader known as Dynamite Bob Chambliss, who died in prison without ever admitting his guilt. I'd visited the church. I had been inspired by Frank Johnson and sworn in to office by him. I wanted us to go after the rest of the murderers, to finally close the books on that awful day, and we did. In 2001, Thomas Blanton Jr. was convicted in the murders and sentenced to life in prison, where he soon died. The next year the last of the bombers, Bobby Frank Cherry, drew a mandatory life sentence. He had lived free for forty years, his crime a barely concealed secret. To me, that was an insult to the very concept of justice for all citizens.

The FBI does the jobs no one else can do and the ones no one else wants to do. Corrupt police can have a devastating impact on a community because they erode faith in the rule of law. Yet some state attorney generals have historically been loath to take on such cases, in large part because they set them at odds with law-enforcement agencies they have deal with on a regular basis. We went after police corruption time and again during my years as director, in my old stomping grounds in West New York and in dozens of other police departments all across the nation. As with crime generally, the crimes committed by police officers are often linked with the trade in illicit drugs. Roughly half of all the convictions won in FBI-led police corruption cases during my time as director involved drug-related offenses.

We took on corrupt politicians, too, like former Louisiana governor Edwin Edwards. Edwards was the very definition of a charming rogue. The agents working the case all liked him, as did the voters of

Louisiana. He'd been elected to four terms as governor, three of them consecutive. Edwards's political career took a slight setback in the mid-1980s when he was indicted for fraud and racketeering. After a hung jury in the first trial, Edwards was acquitted of the charges in 1986. He regained the governor's office in the early '90s and resumed his old habit of using it for personal gain. Along with his son and several other associates, he extorted millions of dollars from people seeking licenses to set up riverboat casinos in the state's waters. Among those to appear against him was Edward DeBartolo Jr., the former owner of the San Francisco 49ers, who testified that Edwards hit him up for $400,000 for a license, plus a 1 percent interest in the casino once it was up and running. In the end, a jury of Edwards's peers agreed with the government's case and the ex-governor was sentenced to ten years in prison. Only the FBI could successfully pursue such a case.

Before the September 11, 2001, attacks on the World Trade Center and Pentagon, the largest single area of responsibility for the Bureau was white-collar crime, an all-purpose phrase that covers a multitude of sins. One of the most frustrating of all crimes in that broad category was the one involving trade secrets, frustrating because so much money was at stake and because existing laws were so inadequate to the task. Oftentimes, the cases involved a former employee trying to make off with some corporation's intellectual property. We nabbed a onetime contractor for Gillette who had stolen trade secrets related to the development of a new razor, a potential loss to Gillette of hundreds of millions of dollars. But in a surprising number of cases, foreign governments, many of them our putative allies and friends, specifically instructed their intelligence services to go after and secure trade secrets that would give their own companies a decided advantage over American competitors.

(Good espionage can drive the research and development budget down to near zero.) Targets included pharmaceutical formulas, enzymes, computing software and applications—billions of dollars of intellectual property in the aggregate, not to mention the loss of jobs from the lost revenues and the forfeiture of American leadership in critical areas of technology.

In all, we identified about forty-three nations that were so instructing their security services and, in most cases, using their own U.S. embassies as bases of operation. The People's Republic of China surprised no one, but some of our closest allies bordered on the shocking.

Just as shocking were the antiquated laws we had at our disposal. For hundreds of years, trade-secret laws belonged to the states. If someone stole the plans for your better spinning wheel or improved mousetrap, you could sue them in state court, or the state could prosecute, but federal entities were almost powerless to intervene. That might have made sense in a preglobal business environment, but in an economy where foreign governments were among the biggest perpetrators, it hamstrung us to no end.

We tried to get around the matter by invoking a variety of federal statutes—mail fraud, wire fraud, and the like—but the fit was sloppy at best. In one case, in Massachusetts, we charged a group of intellectual-property thieves with the transportation of stolen goods in interstate commerce, a crime to be sure and one for which we had jurisdiction, but a stretch all the same. The judge read the statute; looked at our case; reminded us that the law applied to goods, not ideas; and threw us out of court. Rightly so, I think.

Finally, we drafted a new trade-secrets statute at the FBI; ran it by the Justice Department, which was fine with the idea, and the White House, which didn't give us much support. We called the bill the Economic Espionage Act and took it to Congress. That's exactly what it was—spying meant to gain an economic advantage, not a military one—but the State Department was appalled at the name. You can't call it "espionage," they screamed; ambassadors all around town will be rushing for their smelling salts. Let's make it the Economic Security Act instead. But we held our ground, and the statute passed—a landmark federal trade-secrets law that has gone a long way toward protecting American commerce from foreign spies.

Health-care fraud, antitrust cases, bank fraud, and embezzlement—they all routinely consume tens of thousands of agent hours, with trillions of dollars hanging in the balance.

By the mid-1990s, the FBI was estimating that health-care fraud and other abuses were costing consumers on the order of $100 billion annually, a staggering figure, yet just as had been the case with trade secrets, there was no pertinent federal legislation governing a broad set of relevant crimes. Congress, as it frequently does, had fallen way behind the curve. Again, we were using outmoded laws—the interstate transportation of stolen property statute and others—to bring cases against a whole new class of crime and criminals. We needed new legislation, new funding and manpower, new forfeiture and civil-fine provisions. Again, it was the FBI that drafted the necessary new criminal provisions for the Health Insurance Portability and Accountability Act of 1996, and we didn't waste any time in taking advantage. Health-care convictions jumped more than threefold between 1992 and 1997. Eleven physicians in San Diego pled guilty to conspiring to commit medical fraud against insurance companies. Another eleven doctors in New York were charged with taking kickbacks in exchange for Medicare referrals for equipment and other services. In Miami, we indicted seven doctors, a dozen nurses, and twenty other people on similar schemes. SmithKline Beecham Clinical Laboratories Inc. paid the government $325 million to settle charges that it had filed false federal claims. Damon Clinical Laboratories paid $119 million; the Laboratory Corporation of America, $187 million in criminal fines and a civil settlement. And on and on it went.

Under the aegis of Operation Broker Bust, we brought charges against twenty-seven real-estate professionals, including mortgage brokers and accountants, who were securing mortgage loans with false information provided to lending institutions. Under Operation Rogue Brokers, we won indictments against twenty-five investment brokers who were defrauding their clients. Operation Checkmaster, targeted against check and credit-card fraud and counterfeiting, has won hundreds of indictments, arrests, and convictions.

In one of the greatests examples of individual initiative and persistence I was to witness during my eight years as director, two FBI agents working out of our small regional office in Decatur, Illinois, caught the scent of a price-fixing scheme at Archer Daniels Midland Company and wouldn't let it go.

The office seemed almost too small to undertake such a gigantic criminal case. There were other duties and responsibilities that had to be seen to. Moreover, ADM had a powerful national presence. Not only was it then the forty-eighth largest publicly held company in America, it also sponsored *This Week with David Brinkley* and was a major political donor. Some of ADM's principal beneficiaries were among the most powerful political brokers in Washington.

In spite of everything, these two remarkable agents, Brian Shepard and Bob Herndon, spent more than two years gathering evidence that ADM had conspired with Japanese and Korean companies to fix the price and volume of a feed additive for livestock. With help from their fellow Decatur agents and from the Bureau's Atlanta and San Francisco divisions, they were also able to make the case that ADM had engaged in price fixing in high-fructose corn syrup and in citric acid. By the time the matter ended up in my office, the case was backed up by more than a hundred audio and video recordings of the conspirators planning to evade existing laws. In the end, Archer Daniels Midland paid more than $100 million in criminal fines for violations of the Sherman Antitrust Act and an additional $300 million in civil fines—again, benchmark figures. In 1998, an Illinois court found three former executives of the company guilty on one count each of violating the antitrust provisions. Had these dedicated agents not been so determined to see justice done, I doubt that we ever would have gotten there. FBI agents—even just two of them—can make a difference.

Ever since agents were empowered back in the 1930s to carry guns and cross state lines, bank theft—whether by fraud or embezzlement, or by blasting the vault door off its hinges—has been one of the Bureau's key responsibilities. Bad guys go where the money is, and banks exist to warehouse the stuff. In a global economy, though, banks have even greater criminal utility. We ran down a series of New York City banks that were being used to illegally funnel billions upon billions of dollars out of the former Soviet Union. Thanks to computers, you don't even have to show up at a bank anymore to rob it. In one celebrated case, Vladimir Levin, a Russian computer expert based in St. Petersburg, and a gang of associates used stolen passwords and identification numbers and an off-the-shelf PC to transfer $10.4 million from Citibank into their own accounts strewn all over the world. Eventually, after Levin was arrested in London and extradited to the U.S., all but $400,000 of the money was recovered by the FBI.

Another Russian, Alexey Ivanov, used a stolen credit card to open an account with a San Diego-based Internet service provider, then hacked his way into a Los Angeles e-bank and two credit-card processing companies. When he was indicted on fifteen criminal counts relating to the scheme, Ivanov already had trials pending in two states on similar charges. Hacker crooks are like vampires; you have to drive a stake through their heart to slow them down. And even then you better keep some cloves of garlic hanging around your neck.

When I set up the FBI academy in Budapest, I insisted that computer training be a significant part of the program. IBM responded by generously donating an entire classroom dedicated to teaching police from around the world about computer crime—a tremendous boon for law-enforcement agencies everywhere because computer crime is a borderless phenomenon. Japanese crime syndicates have used Russian hackers to blast their way into police databases so they can monitor efforts to rein them in. In Italy, the Mafia and associates hacked their way into one bank's computer network and diverted more than $100 million in European Union aid to mob accounts. Michael Bloomberg was two years shy of becoming mayor of New York City when two guys from Kazakhstan tried to extort money from him by threatening to expose security holes on his Internet-based financial news service. The FBI stopped them and made the case.

To combat such crimes and the potential threat they posed to vital national interests, we set up the Computer Investigations and Infrastructure Threat Assessment Center in 1996 and two years later folded that into the National Infrastructure Protection Center, also located within the FBI. We worked to beef up the relevant statutes, and we worked mightily to augment and enhance our own expertise. Even then, though, it sometimes didn't do any good. Nearing the end of the Clinton administration, we had a series of cases in which young teenage hackers were crashing the computing systems of U.S. Internet-based companies. Among those responsible, we learned, was a fourteen-year-old Canadian boy, but that's where the trail ended. In Canada, what he had done wasn't a crime. We couldn't even interview the young man about it because of his age.

"Well," I said when I found that out, "can we hire him, then?"

But of course we couldn't do that either. In the end, we were oftentimes being taught this end of the business by teens and even preteens from around the world.

Computers, the Web, the Internet, e-mail, instant messaging—they're all great. They level the playing field: a simple PC and an Internet connection can give the poorest people on earth access to the same information available to a Ph.D. candidate at Harvard or the Sorbonne, Oxford, or MIT. Thanks to the World Wide Web, entrepreneurs have been able to launch a myriad of businesses with virtually no overhead and market their goods globally, not just locally. My guess, though, is that of all the criminal subsets of society that have benefited from the connectivity, none has benefited more than sexual predators. The Internet takes the lock off the door. Chat rooms let predators cozy up to the desks and bedrooms where kids are typing away on their keyboards.

Crimes against kids strike a special chord with me as they do with most people. You don't have to spend much time talking with someone like John Walsh to appreciate the devastation that comes when a child is murdered or to admire his and Reve Walsh's determination to turn their son Adam's death into a better world for all children. Adam was six years old when he was abducted and brutally killed in Hollywood, Florida, in 1981. Out of that terrible experience and the news reports it generated came the Missing Children Act of 1982, the Missing Children's Assistance Act of 1984, and the Adam Walsh Child Resource Center, which has since been merged with the National Center for Missing and Exploited Children (NCMEC), where Ernie Allen and John Rabun do a stellar job for all of us. As director I assigned agents to the center on a full-time basis. You do not have to spend a long time reading the history of Megan Kanka, the seven-year-old New Jersey girl raped and murdered by a two-time sex offender, to appreciate the need for the so-called Megan's Laws at both the state and federal level that help to track and identify those who serially prey on children.

To me, the Internet posed an especially insidious threat to kids because it can be so easy for predators to use cyberspace to hide their identity while they slowly rope in their prey. Worse, as I looked around the Bureau, it became apparent to me that we weren't doing nearly enough, or doing it the right way. Rather than go after Internet predators, we waited for state and local law-enforcement agencies to ask for our help, then sent agents out. To remedy matters and to insert ourselves more directly into the fight, we launched a program we called Innocent Images out of our Baltimore office. It wasn't a huge undertaking, at least initially, just a couple of agents who would go into chat rooms posing as young teens to see what might happen. We weren't after pornographers or casual perusers of the chat rooms, even ones who like to talk dirty to kids. Our main goal was to rope in what are called travelers, predators who after a few cyber chats want to meet a child in a mall or a motel. In too many instances, travelers had lured kids into sexual liaisons and far worse.

I'm not sure anymore what I expected Innocent Images to turn up by way of numbers, but whatever it was, it was insufficient to the reality. It was like happening upon some incredible trout stream never before visited. The fish just couldn't stop taking the bait. The more people we put on the program, the more cases we made. A little publicity followed. Surely, I figured, word would get around, and the bait taking would slow down. But no.

I said as much one day to one of our young agents working the Internet for Innocent Images.

"This can't last, can it?"

"Watch this," she answered as she plunged into yet another chat room.

"Hi," she typed in, "I'm Amy, I'm thirteen, and I'm lonely. Is anyone there?"

Within seconds, she had ten hits. Then she changed course dramatically.

"I'm not Amy," she pecked in. "I'm a twenty-eight-year-old FBI agent."

But that didn't stop things for a moment.

"Yeah, right," came the responses. "Where can I meet you?"

We were laughing watching the screen, but it wasn't humorous in the least.

Soon we were franchising the program around the country, to our own field offices, naturally, but also to state and local law-enforcement organizations that had heard about Innocent Images and wanted a version of their own. To pull the loose threads together, we also set up a Crimes Against Children coordinator in each of our major field offices. To this day, the program has never received a great deal of notice, but to me it's law enforcement and the FBI at its best.

It simply is not possible to do a job like being the FBI director in normal business hours. Too much is going on. There are too many demands on your time, too many angles that have to be covered, but I was determined to lead as normal a life as I could—for myself and my family—under the circumstances.

When I wasn't on the road, I'd generally wake up about 5:00 in the morning, throw on my sweat clothes, and take off jogging from the front door of our house out in Great Falls for about three miles. Afterward, I would shower and dress, then come down to the kitchen and make lunches for all the kids who were then headed to school. I was happy to do it—that hour of the morning was dead time for me, and I was giving Marilyn some much-needed assistance.

But I also used my duty to slip little notes into the lunches: "Be sure to study for your Spanish exam this afternoon," "Don't forget to turn in your trip money," that kind of thing.

The notes drove the kids crazy, but they must have made an impression because they still talk about them. Maybe they even learned something from the reminders and encouragements. Our oldest, Justin, is in his final year at the United States Naval Academy as I write; the next in line, Brendan, is studying filmmaking in California.

As a rule, I'd wake Marilyn around 6:30, just as the sun was rising. By then, John Griglione would be waiting outside in our Chevy Suburban.

By 7:00 most mornings, I'd be at my desk in the Hoover Building, going through e-mails, teletypes from the overseas offices, the newspapers, other reports that had come in overnight. At 8:00, the FBI's senior executive staff—eight to ten people in all, some permanent, some rotating in and out as the situation demanded—would gather in my office for a daily update. More briefings and meetings filled much of the rest of the day.

I could have cocooned myself in my office, been constantly busy, and rarely left, but I made a point of doing just the opposite. Around lunch, I'd head up to the cafeteria, not really to eat and not in the midst of some phalanx of high-ranking officials but just to walk around by myself and chat casually with the people I ran into. I tried to leave the building on my own most days, too, even when I didn't have an official meeting scheduled somewhere else. I'd stop at a nearby Au Bon Pain for coffee or wander across the street to the Justice Department, walking alone, again chatting with the agents and FBI personnel I ran across. I wanted everyone to know that I wasn't off in some unapproachable privacy zone.

At first, I could tell it was a big deal. What's up with the director? But soon enough, we got used to each other's company, and I was the better informed because of it. I'd do the same thing when I went down to the FBI Academy at Quantico or visited our field offices—sit down with agents, who do the real work for the FBI, without their special agent in charge (SAC), so I could better understand what the job was like at street level. This was the best way to get real-time and unfiltered information about our organization. It was also thrilling to have the routine privilege of talking to and thanking the always impressive men and women of the FBI. Over my almost eight years as director, I visited each of our fifty-six field offices several times.

During the course of an average week, I might meet with two or three foreign officials who were visiting Washington: the head of the French intelligence service, say, or a South American delegation. Sometimes I'd meet with ambassadors. Attorney General Janet Reno and I got together at least once a week, almost always in her office, and almost always I came by myself, not with a whole detail of FBI brass. As the counterterrorism threat grew, I'd meet at least once a week with CIA director George Tenet at my office, or in Langley, or in the office set aside for the CIA chief in the Old Executive Office Building next to the White House. As I said, George and I became close friends and I have great respect and affection for him. There were other meetings on a more or less regular basis: with the drug czar, with the national security adviser, with assistant secretaries of this and that. Our law-enforcement brief stretched in innumerable directions and overlapped with nearly every department and agency in Washington, or so it sometimes seemed. For reasons I'll get into later, I almost never met with Bill Clinton or even talked with him, but communication with the White House was constant.

I made it a point to leave the office whenever I could by no later than 7 P.M. Marilyn and I had things we needed to spend time on, and I wanted to be home with my family in any event, but there was a second reason. Washington operates by an odd macho code of hours. If I stayed past 7:00, so would most of my top people, and if

I announced that I was coming in on a Saturday morning to catch up on some work, practically the entire staff would come in then, too. The only way to get people to go home was to leave myself, so I did. Maybe once a month, I would quietly drive down to the office on a Saturday and work until midday.

The children were through with dinner most nights when I got home, but I'd help with their homework, do baths, get them to bed, and sometimes go out to a school or church meeting. Then the rest of the workday would begin. I had a tiny office at home that the FBI technical people had fitted with a safe and secure communications. I'd settle in there for more paperwork or to meet with one of my staff or an agent who would stop by on some particular matter. Obviously, the postage-stamp home office was in some ways just an extension of my large one on Pennsylvania Avenue, but the kids knew their dad was at home, downstairs, while they slept. That made a big difference to me.

By midnight or 1:00, I'd finally get to bed. Do the math, and you'll see that I rarely slept more than five hours. I had been doing that for a long time, and I'll probably pay a price for it someday, but for me, five hours has always seemed just about enough bedtime. Almost invariably, the morning run served to revive me. I never took a sick day the entire time.

As crazy as it seems, I could have worked a lot more—traveled extensively, hung around the White House all weekend long. More than a few people in the administration did, and they often complained the whole way that they had no time left over for their families, that their marriages were suffering, that they didn't "have a life." My guess is that at least in some cases they wanted that lifestyle, but official Washington is a work-obsessed city. People get caught up in that. They're only happy if the world is in perpetual crisis, and if it's not, they act as if it were. To my mind, it's a pathology.

My own feeling is that if I had put in any more hours on the job,

I would just have been spinning my wheels, and I didn't want to let it come to that. To help make sure it didn't, I filled a long wall in my office with my kids' drawings—eight years' worth of them by the end, a reminder to me every time I looked up at them that there was another reality out there, that life didn't begin and end in this large box I occupied halfway between Capitol Hill and the White House.

In much the same spirit, Marilyn and I never discussed my job when I got home in the evening. It was our unwritten rule, religiously followed. The small window of time I had between my downtown workday and my at-home one was an FBI-free zone. Marilyn had two more children during my time as director: Liam Patrick and Colin Michael. (Appropriately, Colin was born at the same hospital in Reston, Virginia, where we took his brothers dozens of times to be patched up after one household disaster or another.) As a mother of six boys, Marilyn performed flawlessly. She had wanted to be a juvenile probation officer and had majored in criminal justice at Mercyhurst College in Erie, PA. This fortunately dovetailed with raising six boys. But she still had more than enough on her plate, and we had plenty of family matters to discuss without dragging in my small daily victories and setbacks. The kids caught the spirit, too. I can think of maybe one or two times they asked about my work, no more.

Off-loading anxiety or passing on gossip is not part of my nature in any event, but if I had an issue I was grappling with, something I couldn't quite wrap my mind around, I had plenty of resources: the senior officials who worked for me, some of whom I had known for decades; fellow judges, my old network from the U.S. Attorney's Office for the Southern District of New York, including Bob Fiske; for big matters, Bill Webster, who had served as head of both the FBI and CIA and was always a willing and wise listener; sometimes for the biggest items, the first President Bush.

It was also impossible in my role as FBI director to ignore the threats to my family and to me personally. I said no to the escort cars, the security trailer in the backyard, and the armor-plated behemoth to chauffeur me around because Marilyn and I didn't want the Freeh family living in a bubble at the end of the street. We were in the leafy suburbs of Washington, D.C., not along the Green Line in Beirut or the Green Zone in Baghdad. I also didn't want to be surrounded by a posse-size security detail the way other directors had been—in part for the same reason but also because if someone did come after me, I didn't want a lot of other people hurt or worse. I was the target, not anyone else.

But I tried to be no more stupid than I had to be. By the time I took over as director, I'd had a lifetime's worth of exposure to the dark side of the human psyche. My friend Giovanni Falcone and his wife had been blown up in Sicily. I had visited with Helen Vance not long after she was badly wounded and her husband, Judge Robert Vance, gruesomely murdered by one of Roy Moody's mail bombs, and I still call Helen every year on the anniversary of that attack. Whether it was true or not, I had to assume that bad people had me on their radar screen. I had put bin Laden on the FBI's "top-ten" list and oversaw his investigation, indictment, and fugitive hunt. I always assumed my family and I were big targets.

The mail took care of itself. Every package and envelope addressed to our house was intercepted by the FBI and cleared before being delivered to our home. In one form or another, that's standard operating procedure these days for high-ranking government officials.

The children were another matter. During my eight years as director, Marilyn and I never stopped worrying about their safety. Short of putting them into something like a witness protection program, there was no way to protect the kids completely, and if I had been inclined to such radical measures, I wouldn't have taken the job in the first place. In the world we live in, zero risk doesn't exist.

I felt much the same about having agents following the boys around school all day. It's just not a natural way for a kid to grow up. Instead, we opted for small, practical fixes. Because predictable routes are the most vulnerable moment for an attack or abduction, our people followed the children to and from school. We also made sure the administrators and teachers knew about our concerns for the boys' welfare, and we're still grateful for the excellent job those school officials did in setting up and maintaining procedures to screen anyone coming into the buildings. The Fairfax County, Virginia, police also patrolled the house several times a day and were our first responders in case of emergency.

On family trips we did everything we could to leave quietly, arrive without fanfare, and keep a low profile while we were enjoying ourselves, but that didn't always work. We were down in Hilton Head, South Carolina, on vacation when one of the little ones gouged himself somehow. I was sitting with him in the hospital, waiting for someone to sew him up, when a couple of local deputies brought in four manacled prisoners for treatment.

"Wait a minute," one of the prisoners said after he'd eyed me for a while. "I know you from somewhere."

"Naw," I told him, "we're from out of town."

"No, no," he persisted, "I've seen you!"

"Of course, you have," one of the deputies finally piped up. "He's the FBI director."

"Thanks," I told him. Another cover blown.

For my protection, John Griglione and I had that machine gun in the console of our Suburban for the commute into and out of town, and I carried a 9-mm handgun with me everywhere I went when I left home or the office: as I walked out on Pennsylvania Avenue to get a cup of coffee, to meetings with the attorney general or in the White House or at the CIA, on planes and trains, at church, at school plays, driving the family car on vacations, in the evening when I worked at my home office. Just about the only times I ever took off the gun were when I slept—and then it was on the nightstand, just a hand's reach away—and in the early morning, when I went jogging. (That's not entirely rational, I realize, given that I was running alone down darkened streets, but some things you just have to take on faith.)

In truth, I assumed that if very capable people did decide to come after me, they would probably succeed whether I was packing my trusty 9-mm or surrounded by agents willing to lay down their lives for me or not, but I kept it close at hand all the same, both for protection and as a constant reminder never to let down my guard. Over the years, I suspect that mind-set has become a more general habit of personality.

Think of yourself as running a company that produces everything from applesauce to zippers; a company with 535 members on its board of directors, three-quarters of whom must run for reelection every two years; then imagine yourself reporting as CEO up through a chain of command with a dozen different agendas, under constant media scrutiny, knowing that every memorandum, every piece of paper, every smallest secret is in constant danger of being leaked. And then give your employees weapons and send them out to perform the country's most dangerous work. Give yourself a firearm, too, and work like a dog from sunup to well after sundown, and you'll have some idea of what the FBI director's job is like. Most important, keep in mind that everything the FBI does every day impacts directly on the nation's safety and precious liberties. In sum, every bit of our work is controversial.

Every day brought some amazing, sometimes frightening new twist to the old imperatives of law enforcement. And that was just when things were fairly calm, when the Bureau was in the midst of doing what it does for a living, not what earns it front-page head-lines and scathing editorial comment. When the TV cameras started rolling, when there were call slips from every major newspaper and television news outlet stacked on my desk, when bombs were exploding in public venues and spies were crawling out from under the woodwork—that's when the job *really* got demanding.

How did I get through it? That's an easy one. The calm and steadfast nature of Marilyn and the 28,000 FBI heroes—agents and other personnel—who did their difficult jobs superbly with fidelity, bravery, and integrity. They made the temporary occupant of the director's office look better than he ever was.

One agent of very special note was John Collingwood. When I first met him at FBI headquarters in 1981, he appeared to be a shy, retiring lawyer of few words. I later saw him as the FBI's champion on the Hill and with the media, a man who was able to snatch victory from the jaws of defeat every time. John thrived on crisis, and with eternal optimism and flawless judgment on the most sensitive issues, he was the FBI's beacon in every storm. Immensely respected and trusted in Congress, the FBI, and throughout the media, John always came up with the right solution to the worst problem. I recall many stints at the witness tables on the Hill—I testified more than any other official in D.C.—where after feeling particularly beaten up at a hearing, John would put his arm around me and say, "This is great. You got killed, but we'll get a lot of money to fix this." He was right.

". . . and the Guy's Bob Hanssen"

I'm surprised that April 19,1996, is not a day that the nation pauses to remember and mourn. Pearl Harbor Day and D-Day—December 7 and June 6—are engraved on the national conscience. September 11, I'm sure, won't pass in my lifetime without some public event marking the destruction of the World Trade Center towers or the attack on the Pentagon. But April 19—the date of the worst terrorist attack ever inflicted on the United States by its own citizenry—goes virtually unrecognized except in Oklahoma City.

For an amateur, Timothy McVeigh was an accomplished bomber. With maybe 80 percent of the explosives that terrorists used on Khobar Towers, McVeigh managed to rip apart the nine-story Alfred P. Murrah Federal Building in Oklahoma City and kill 168 of his countrymen, nearly nine times the number who died in the Saudi attack.

For me, the Oklahoma City bombing was an eerie preview of what I would see fourteen months later in Dhahran: the same army of law-enforcement officers and rescue workers crawling all over the crime scene (some of them in fact the very same people), the same red paint outlining the human remains that had yet to be collected for fear of destroying vital evidence, the same random debris scattered far and wide. But there was one difference I'll never forget. The Murrah Federal Building had housed a child-care center. So much of the litter that lay around seemed to have come from there: pieces of construction paper, broken toys, little backpacks. Seeing it was devastating. Watching little bodies being pulled from that wreckage was worse.

I arrived roughly twenty-four hours after the bombing. I wanted to give our people time to set up without having to worry about looking after the director. The Monday-morning quarterbacks and second-guessers must have arrived on the next plane because they started complaining not long afterward and haven't quieted down completely yet.

In fact, the Oklahoma City bombing is probably as good a place as any to begin dealing with how I ran the FBI.

My view of the director's role was to be in the field with the "street agents" whenever I could, especially when the stakes were high, but I didn't rush off to Saudi Arabia or to Yemen, to East Africa or to Oklahoma City because I love airplanes or for the frequent-flyer miles—government servants don't get them. And I certainly didn't rush off because I wanted to be away from my family: that was the worst part of it. I made sure I was on location in those places because that's what I understood, and still understand, the job to be.

As director, I could be significantly involved in a maximum of maybe twenty-five cases at any given time. That doesn't mean I ignored the hundreds of others that were trying to bubble their way up to my office, but the simple reality of the position and of the limits of human attention is that no more than two dozen or so major cases could fit on the radar screen simultaneously: a major white-collar crime case; a big civil-rights case; an investigation of a high-ranking government figure, a terrorist attack involving loss of life, cases of a similar magnitude. Those are the ones I would be briefed on regularly, the ones about which I would request additional information, the ones sometimes I would get involved in more directly—requesting a better prosecutor, pushing through a search warrant or providing greater resources, doing liaison with a foreign power if that was called for, and occasionally also making sure I was on the ground at and around the crime scene because only there can you really see and sense what needs doing.

Oklahoma City is a case in point. Finding the immediate perpetrator was hardly a challenge at all because as good a bomb maker as Timothy McVeigh was, he was a lousy criminal when it came to avoiding arrest. Less than an hour and a half after he had laid waste to the Murrah Building, McVeigh was stopped for speeding in Perry, Oklahoma. If that wasn't stupid enough, he had a gun jammed in his waistband. Guns aren't rare in that part of the country, but the policeman who pulled McVeigh over had the good sense and training to smell something fishy about this one, and to detain McVeigh until he could check things out. Meanwhile, a very different type of policeman—Jim Norman, a bomb expert we had flown in from New York City—had uncovered an axle from the truck used in the bombing some two blocks from the explosion (and think of that: two blocks!) and was using the vehicle identification number stamped on it to trace the truck back to the Ryder agency that had rented it and from there to Timothy McVeigh. McVeigh was just about set for a bail hearing when the Bureau's National Crime Information Center connected the dots and the police had their man. If McVeigh had walked from the bombing to the nearest precinct station and turned himself in, he couldn't have made it much easier.

But as far as we were concerned in those first days and weeks, McVeigh was only the first part of the puzzle. Our assumption was,

and had to be, that the bombing was possibly the handiwork of organized terrorists, possibly from the Middle East. The attack resem-
bled too many others whose origins were well established: the
bombing of the U.S. Marine barracks in Lebanon in the early 1980s
and the bombing of the World Trade Center in New York only a
few years earlier, to cite the most obvious examples. What's more, a
federal building was a natural and symbolic target for a foreign force
intent on harming the United States. In truth, too, I think it was
simply hard for any of us to really fathom that an American
citizen—a military veteran at that—could hold such hatred for his
country that he would slaughter wholesale so many innocent people, children among them.

That's the mind-set with which I arrived at Oklahoma City, the
lens through which I was viewing the case, and by those terms, the
legal effort on the ground simply wasn't sufficient. The lawyers on
hand at the local U.S. Attorney's Office were undoubtedly competent people, but the office lacked a cadre of prosecutors experienced
in crisis situations. The pace was too leisurely. Search warrants were
dripping out; other court applications were being created and pro-
cessed far too slowly. To pick up the pace, I detailed my chief counsel,
Howard Shapiro, to sit out in Oklahoma City and hold people's feet
to the fire. Howard had been with me in Atlanta when we took over
the investigation of the mail bombings that would eventually lead us
to Walter Leroy Moody. He knew how to get things done on the fly.

I never thought for a moment that my decision to put Howard in
charge would be popular, and it wasn't. I was micromanaging, which
nobody likes the boss to do. Inevitably, I was insulting the attorneys
in place out there. I would have been sore myself had I been in their
shoes. But I wasn't running a popularity contest. I was overseeing
the investigation of a probable conspiracy that resulted in horrific
deaths, and the better a conspiracy is organized, the faster it breaks

apart and disappears once the crime has been committed. Speed is everything—speed and pressure.

That's also why I insisted we investigate Terry Nichols. McVeigh had been living on the Michigan farm owned by Nichols and his brother, James. The two of them—McVeigh and Terry Nichols—were close friends. James Nichols had bought fertilizer and fuel oil, critical components of the bomb that had destroyed the Murrah Building. None of it was perfect. Friendship isn't a crime, and just about every farmer buys fuel oil and fertilizer at one time or another. I certainly took my hits for pressing law-enforcement officials to arrest and charge Nichols: hits from our own field-office people who didn't want to charge him and who didn't like being overruled any more than the U.S. attorneys liked having a baby-sitter assigned to them; hits from a federal judge, too, who thought the Bureau had gone over the line. But if the conspiracy was bigger than what we had found to date, I wanted maximum pressure put on the subject (or subjects) and their lawyers.

It was Timothy McVeigh himself, by the way, who persuaded me that the conspiracy didn't go beyond what we had uncovered. The more he talked, the more we learned about him, the more it seemed evident that his was largely a self-conspiracy, abetted by Terry Nichols and to a lesser extent by McVeigh's old army buddy Michael Fortier, who had foreknowledge of the bombing plot but failed to act on it. But that was six months out, just about the time we were ready to take McVeigh to trial. Until then, it was my duty and obligation to assume the opposite and to act based on that assumption. Any competent FBI director, I hope, would have done the same.

On June 2, 1997, Timothy McVeigh was found guilty of murdering in cold blood 168 of his fellow citizens, then perhaps the most heinous crime on American soil in the twentieth century. Eleven days later, he was sentenced to death by lethal injection for his crimes. By year's end, Terry Nichols had been convicted in a separate trial on manslaughter and conspiracy charges for which he would be sentenced to life in prison with no possibility of parole.

Unfortunately, though, that wasn't the end of Timothy McVeigh. In early May 2001, a week before McVeigh was to be executed, we told his lawyers that the FBI had inadvertently withheld more than three thousand pages of documents. On May 11, Attorney General John Ashcroft delayed McVeigh's execution for a month, and on May 15, we expanded our search for more documents. No one was happy about the mix-up, and if Ashcroft was upset with the FBI, I never saw or heard it. He was concerned about the delay, sure. I was, too. I was also disappointed by what had caused it, and in testimony before the House Appropriations Committee on May 16, I took full responsibility for the failure. I was in the driver's seat. We should have done better. But a little perspective, please.

Investigations of the sort we undertook in the wake of the Oklahoma City bombing are a massive effort, unimaginable to someone who has never been in the middle of one. This case alone generated some 3.5 tons of evidence, nearly a billion separate pieces of information. FBI agents conducted more than 28,000 interviews and examined 13.2 million hotel reservations, 3.1 million Ryder truck rental records, and 628,000 airline reservation records. Storing so much information, sorting it, reporting it—they were all Herculean tasks. We did not perform well on a very tiny portion of it this time. Our technology was not up to the challenge. Some of our field offices sent in summaries of the information without the underlying documentation. Some wrongly concluded that the information they held was so extraneous to the task at hand that they never submitted it at all. Other mistakes of judgment were made. Human error happens, and I deeply regretted it and still do, not because justice was compromised—it clearly wasn't—but because the errors marred an otherwise exemplary investigation and because the delays at the end delayed the punishment of a horrendous act.

Timothy McVeigh's lawyers naturally seized on the withheld records as a last chance to save their client, but both they and attorneys for Terry Nichols ultimately agreed that not a single one of those missing 3,135 pages of documents was relevant in the least. More important, judges so found.

As for me, I regarded our celebrated mix-up more as a sign of strength than of weakness. The missing material was discovered by manually, painstakingly inventorying our records—post conviction and post appeal—and comparing the results to discovery lists of exhibits that had been given over to the defense lawyers. No court compelled us to undertake that exercise, and no one intentionally kept back anything once it was under way and the discrepancies found. Had the finders kept quiet about the discovery, no one outside a tiny circle would have ever known. But that was what was so rewarding about how the matter was handled once the omissions were discovered. No one sat on the information. No one tried to push it off into a dark corner or sweep it under the rug. The FBI did exactly what the public should expect. It gave full disclosure.

Over the course of the eight years I was director, I had spent hundreds of hours at Quantico and in the field offices, telling our people that honesty was more important than the successful result of a case. For eight years I had been preaching accountability, assuring agents that it was okay to make mistakes so long as we acknowledged and learned from them. And this time we did it and took our lumps. The FBI was no longer an imperial culture. I'll take some credit for that.

In the end, too, justice was done. On June 11, 2001, Timothy McVeigh was executed in Terre Haute, Indiana. Nichols later admitted his guilt and no other conspirators surfaced. The FBI was totally vindicated.

———

Washington is filled with lightning-rod jobs, from the presidency on down, but when it comes to taking heat, day in and day out from a multiplicity of directions, I'll stack the job of FBI director up against any other position in town.

The pecking order that goes with the post almost guarantees you'll remain in close combat. I reported to two judiciary committees, two appropriations committees, two intelligence committees, as well as to the attorney general and the president. I happen to think that's a good thing—a lot of people *should* be keeping an eye on the nation's law-enforcement apparatus and on its top cop—but no other agency head in Washington has reporting obligations on that scale.

No other agency that I can think of operates with our degree of transparency either. Like the FBI, the CIA also has a raft of reporting responsibilities. Like us, it gathers intelligence, a messy business in the best of times. (The best sources are generally not the best citizens, no matter what country you're talking about.) But the CIA gets to hide behind a veil of secrecy when needed. I testified so often before congressional committees that I wore a rut in the pavement between the Hoover Building and Capitol Hill, and with very few exceptions those were public appearances. But no one on the Hill or elsewhere expected George Tenet to sit down in an open committee session with the tape recorders humming and the cameras whirring, and defend every last detail of some action his agency had taken. Given that CIA activity can sometimes involve "lethal findings"—basically, licenses to kill signed by the president and approved by Congress—almost no one on the Hill even *wanted* transparency from the mother ship out in Langley, Virginia. Some things are best left unsaid in public.

Not so the FBI. We're a law-enforcement agency. At the end of the day, we don't get to appear before secret tribunals and explain away our actions. We have to go before a court and a jury, and judges and juries expect and should expect us to abide by both the spirit and letter of the law.

FBI directors in my view should be judicious but not so cautious they won't take necessary risks. We took plenty of risks during my tenure, both domestically and abroad. We went after Archer Daniels Midland. We snatched Ramzi Yousef, who was under indictment for murder in the first World Trade Center attack, from a hotel in Pakistan and just missed nabbing Khalid Shaikh Mohammed in Qatar. We thought outside the box when it was appropriate, and we fought for the tools that would let us operate outside the box and redefine it to the advantage of all Americans—digital wiretap authority, for example.

But the FBI isn't the KGB. We can't just go barging in someplace because we have suspicions or even because we're 99 percent certain of what we'll find. We can be creative, sure, but we can't take liberties and perform experiments on the basic laws of the land. Court warrants, chains of custody with regard to evidence, indictments, due process—these obligations trace back not just to our own enabling statutes but to the very legal foundations of the Constitution, of our nation. Beyond such enduring restraints, any number of congressional committees over the years have imposed very exacting conditions on what our agents can and cannot do. During my time as director, Janet Reno and I added our own further strictures consistent with what we thought the intent of Congress and the courts to be. All that circumscribed our actions, but it also guaranteed, to the extent that guidelines can govern human behavior, that the FBI under my guidance would behave judiciously. I make no apology for that. To my mind, people should demand nothing less.

Simply put, the FBI that I inherited in the late summer of 1993 needed to improve credibility and trustworthiness. Some of that was historical. Probably no government agency in history has ever been better served by television than the Bureau was by *The F.B.I.,* which debuted in 1965 and ran for nine seasons, 234 episodes in all. With Efrem Zimbalist Jr. starring as the incorruptible inspector Lew Erskine, the show treated the Bureau so reverentially that J. Edgar Hoover allowed scenes to be shot on location in its old headquarters at DOJ. But even as the cameras were rolling, the wheels were coming loose.

Hoover's obsessive pursuit of the American Communist party led him to embrace a broad array of covert measures known as the Counter Intelligence Program—the infamous COINTELPRO. Unable to distinguish legitimate social protest from communist agitation, Hoover ended up going after iconic American figures, including Martin Luther King Jr. In 1975, the COINTELPRO excesses were dragged to the surface by the Senate Select Committee to Study Government Operations with Respect to Intelligence Activities, known as the Church Committee after its chairman, the late senator Frank Church of Idaho. Mark Felt and others were convicted and later pardoned for running illegal FBI operations. By then, everyone knew that the Bureau—now under Hoover's successor, L. Patrick Gray—had also grossly failed to exercise its political independence in the wake of the Watergate break-in.

But it wasn't just past history that was haunting the Bureau when I took it over in September 1993. Waco and the horrible images of that consuming fire were still fresh in the public's memory. So was the FBI's standoff at Ruby Ridge, Idaho, with Randy Weaver and his family. Thanks to the newly embraced Internet, the disaffected could commune on-line, trade wild accusations about the Bureau and its actions, link them to some alleged global network, and spawn a whole new generation of off-the-wall conspiracy theorists. (Timothy McVeigh was one of them.)

Inevitably, all this had an effect on the public at large and on the

media. The FBI labored under a presumption of guilt, not innocence. For some Americans, we were the heavies, the government
thugs. As director, I never knew where I was going to be pressed
from next—the media, Congress, the public generally.

S ometimes it was the backside of a case that jumped up and bit
us from behind. The Branch Davidian standoff didn't happen
on my watch. If it had, I probably would have given the attorney
general different advice on how to proceed and would have followed the playbook I used with the Freemen in Montana. As I told
Bill Clinton when we first talked about the director's job, the government, not David Koresh, had time on its side. But the fact that I
was a federal judge working out of a Manhattan courthouse on the
day all hell broke loose in Waco, Texas, didn't prevent the case from
keeping my attention while in office.

The Freeman siege was resolved peacefully without a shot being
fired. I applied a formula of patience and the first-time use by the
FBI of third-party negotiators: non-government people with whom
the fringe Freeman identified. I will always be grateful both to Senator John McCain and then Congressman Bill Richardson who generously offered to act as our negotiators. Both of these fine public
servants never sought any credit or publicity for their offer—a testa-
ment to their character and integrity. They should be recognized
here. Not surprisingly, the Freeman matter ended without bloodshed
and so, of course, generated very little press as a result. No inquiries,
hearings, bombast, or even a thank-you to our agents for a job well
done. My only regret and deep sadness there was the accidental death
by car accident of Kevin Kramer, one of our best young agents.

Of the many issues that lingered long after the smoke had
cleared in Waco, the one that absolutely, positively wouldn't die was
whether military CS—or gas—canisters had been fired by govern-

ment forces surrounding the Branch Davidian compound on the final morning of the standoff and, more specifically, whether the canisters had ignited the conflagration that killed Koresh and seventy-four of his followers. I admit that the matter was not high on my must-attend-to list. The canister story had been kept alive by the conspiracy-theory networks and given added legs by lawyers pushing a wrongful-death suit. To me, that sounded like the usual pack of suspects. The evidence we had available to us suggested that the canisters had never been used. As for the fire itself, I never thought there was the least chance that it had been ignited by anyone other than Koresh himself.

When documents did finally surface, six years after the fact, that indicated we had in fact used the gas canisters, I went to Janet Reno and told her that we needed an outside investigator to take a fresh look at the whole scenario of the final hours at Waco and see how the canisters might have fit into the story line. Janet agreed, and she was able to convince John Danforth, the distinguished former Republican senator from Missouri, to head up the investigation.

I wasn't any happier about this last-minute discovery than I had been when the missing McVeigh documents were found. I was even less happy when Danforth took FBI agents detailed to him and sent them secretly into our own headquarters to secure a group of files for his investigation. To me, going through the back door not only added to the general hysteria surrounding the Waco aftermath, it also was utterly unnecessary. We didn't have the files under lock and key. All they had to do was walk in and ask for them, but courtesy, if nothing else, might suggest they announce themselves first. I called Danforth and told him as much.

"Look," I said as best I can remember, "if you think you need to act in this manner, unilaterally, without any notice to us, then we're not going to stand in your way. But to get all the records you want, it might be more productive to call me and let us help you with that."

That, at least, put a stop to the cat-and-mouse games. Far more important, Danforth determined in the end that, while the canisters had indeed been used, they had been fired several hours prior to the onset of the blaze at targets far removed from the fire's origins. Bottom line: the deaths at the Branch Davidian compound had been caused by the messianic lunatic who had brought his followers there in the first place. That's the point, not the wild speculation; but long months passed in the director's office where the emphasis seemed to be exactly the other way around.

Other times, compelling evidence intersected with political correctness in ways that served, to my mind, to hamstring the entire judicial process. I'm thinking specifically of Wen Ho Lee.

The Bureau had no choice but to investigate him. We had information suggesting that, in 1982, Dr. Lee had contacted a suspected spy. Given that Lee was a mechanical engineer helping to develop nuclear bombs at the Los Alamos National Laboratory in New Mexico, that information alone was alarming, but it was only the beginning of the trail. Later, we learned that Lee, who was Chinese born, had failed to report a possible relationship with a key figure in China's nuclear program. In 1998, he told us that he also had been approached by nuclear scientists from China. Furthermore, he had gone to extraordinary lengths to download, copy, and remove materials from a secure national laboratory: forty hours of work stretching over seventy days. Even after Lee's security clearances were stripped at Los Alamos, he made attempts to reenter the weapons design area, including one try at 3:30 A.M. on Christmas Eve of 1998, not exactly a normal work hour.

Investigating people with profiles such as Dr. Lee's—people with access to vital, extremely sensitive information—is a basic law-enforcement responsibility of the FBI. We would have been guilty of gross negligence had we ignored his actions. But we didn't try and convict him in the court of public opinion before any criminal charges could be brought. To the extent that happened to Wen Ho Lee, it was the work of *The New York Times,* which took a leak from a congressional committee and blew it up into a four-thousand-word front-page story that ran March 6, 1999. That's what launched things, not the FBI. The *Times* all but acknowledged as much in a grudging 1,680-word "Note from the Editors" that ran on page two of its September 26, 2000, edition.

Frankly, I was surprised at the *Times:* The reporting was unconscionable. But I was also fed up yet again with the way leaks drive the process in Washington, and this time I decided to act. I proposed to Janet Reno that we convene a grand jury and drag before it everyone who had been in a position to leak the Wen Ho Lee story to *The New York Times.* I would go first. The rest of the investigators and other officials could come behind me. I'd seen grand juries shake loose this kind of information before. Even if that didn't happen, I thought we would be sending an important message: you leak at your peril.

Note that I wasn't out to get the reporters involved. Journalists are supposed to go for the story, but we didn't have to make it so damn easy for them to get it. Not surprisingly, of course, Janet and the administration behind her had no real stomach for any of what I proposed.

The simple fact, though, is that once the Wen Ho Lee genie was out of the bottle, nothing could get it back in. The fifty-nine-count indictment that was eventually returned against Lee—with my great support, I hasten to add—was viewed by some as further evidence that the FBI was piling it on. The fact that, after the indictment and at our urging, he was held nine months in solitary confinement added inhumanity to the charges against us, and never mind that the odds of Dr. Lee trying to flee to China at that point had he been free were, to my mind, astronomical.

Inevitably—and with the urging of Lee's lawyers, who knew an opportunity when they saw it—several Asian-American groups got involved. The FBI was persecuting Lee based on his ethnicity. One of the judges we had appeared before got swept up in the hysteria and declared, entirely inappropriately, that the FBI was embarrassing the nation by pursuing Wen Ho Lee. As sometimes happens in high-profile circumstances like this, the suspect became the victim.

Finally, as political pressure built to free Lee, Janet Reno called a meeting over at the Department of Justice to say that she was prepared to abandon the indictment and let Dr. Lee plead guilty to a relatively minor charge of mishandling classified documents. The case, she felt, was just too weak to pursue. I disagreed, and I let my feelings be known. We ought to take this guy to trial, I argued. The case was much stronger than anyone at the meeting other than my fellow FBI agents realized. No, we didn't have a confession. No, we didn't have fingerprints. And, yes, we had made some mistakes of our own along the way, but our people had done an incredibly painstaking job of building a powerful computer forensics case against Lee.

They had shown that he had access to vital information kept on the computers at Los Alamos. They'd detailed his late-night downloads at the lab even after his clearance had been suspended. Lee contended through his lawyers that, yes, he had moved the information onto tapes, but had subsequently destroyed the tapes, so our agents spent days pawing through the sites where his home garbage would have been dumped and found no evidence whatsoever of what he alleged had happened.

"There's no jury in the world that would believe his explanation of why he had downloaded that information and then destroyed it," I told Janet and her assistants. "And even if they did, he was still technically admitting to all the elements he had been charged with."

It was all to no avail. Janet had clearly made up her mind prior to the meeting. In addition to the felony guilty plea, Lee agreed to submit to interviews as to where the classified information he had improperly accessed had disappeared to, and that's where the case ended. The gods of political correctness were satisfied. The firestorm died down, but in the end I didn't feel that justice was served.

Occasionally, also, justice—at least as we conceived it—was forced to take a backseat to larger geopolitical interests. I was in my office at the Hoover Building one day in mid-August 1998 when Sandy Berger and George Tenet came to see me. It was the only time that the two of them had shown up together at my door. They didn't have to tell me something big was up.

The CIA director and national security adviser had come to apprise me of an operation then in its final planning stages. Targets were to be struck simultaneously in Afghanistan and Sudan in retaliation for the bombing a week earlier, on August 7, of the U.S. embassies in Nairobi, Kenya, and Dar es Salaam, Tanzania. Afghanistan, I understood. The embassy bombings were the work of al Qaeda forces loyal to Osama bin Laden, who had taken refuge with the Taliban regime in Afghanistan, and the bombings had been lethal in the extreme, leaving 260 dead and thousands injured. I was becoming increasingly frustrated by the Clinton administration's unwillingness to confront Iran on the Khobar Towers bombing. Here, finally, we seemed ready to take a stand consistent with what had become obvious to me. We were already involved in a global terrorist war.

Better still, the CIA had come into possession of intelligence that seemed to indicate bin Laden would be meeting with his senior staff on August 20 to assess the damage from the embassy attacks and begin planning new assaults. We were set to use U.S. Navy destroyers stationed in the northern Arabian Sea to rain seventy-five Tomahawk missiles down on the al Qaeda camp where the meeting was supposed to take place and hope for the best. I couldn't have agreed more.

A simultaneous attack planned on a Sudanese pharmaceutical factory suspected of turning out lethal gas troubled me far more. For starters, I wasn't much convinced by the evidence that Sandy and George laid out. The U.S. had basically been blind in Sudan for several years, ever since our embassy and the CIA station in Khartoum had been closed down for fear of terrorist attacks. George's people had managed to entice an agent to collect some soil samples some distance away from the main entrance to the factory, and the soil had shown traces of a chemical substance used by the Iraqis in the production of nerve gas. But apart from that and some vague intimations of a financial connection between bin Laden and the factory, there wasn't much else to go on.

I thought it was a slim dossier to launch an attack over, but I had more immediate concerns. The Bureau had a huge contingent of agents, laboratory experts, forensic experts, and other specialists on the ground in Africa at the two embassy sites, 471 people in all at the height of the investigation. Only about one in ten Kenyans is Muslim, but about a third of all Tanzanians are, and in Zanzibar— part of the United Republic of Tanzania—virtually everyone is a Muslim. I was worried about retaliation against our people if we went ahead with an attack on an African Muslim state, and I insisted that if we did go after the pharmaceutical plant, I be given notice far enough in advance of the exact timing of the missile launches so that we could put protective measures in place.

There was a third element, too. Sudan had detained two people we suspected of being part of the embassy bombings. Even as the

U.S. was planning to level the factory, John O'Neill was negotiating on the Bureau's behalf in New York City with the Sudanese ambassador to the United Nations, and the ambassador had opened talks with his own people back in Khartoum about turning the two individuals in question over to the Kenyans, so that they could ultimately be turned over to us for trial back in the United States. Was it really necessary to do this strike, I asked, given that it would in all likelihood spell the end of that effort?

The answer, of course, was yes. Tomahawks got launched in both directions—at the al Qaeda camp and, from the Red Sea, at Sudan. Whether the intelligence was wrong or the missiles less accurate than expected, Osama bin Laden lived to attack another day. In Sudan, the factory was obliterated, but little evidence has ever been found to suggest it was manufacturing the lethal gas in question or any other weapons-grade chemical compounds. As feared, the attack drove a stake into John O'Neill's effort to broker a deal with the ambassador.

On the positive side, the FBI was given the heads-up we asked for. I was on the ground in Dar es Salaam on August 20, 1998, taking a meal break with some of the agents who had been working there, when my old friend and able deputy, Bill Esposito, called from Washington. He'd just heard from the White House and the CIA that missiles would be striking their targets in Aghanistan and Sudan within the hour. I had my senior people pull the rest of our contingent together.

"Look," I said, "I've got some news for you." Then I told them about the missile strikes. Except for me, the room was absolutely silent. By then, the attacks were imminent. We took extra precautions of our own in the hours and days ahead to keep our people safe, but the crime scenes in Dar es Salaam and Nairobi were already being protected by heavily armed, company-strength U.S. Marine FAST teams. To my great relief, there were no attempts at retaliation against either site.

The Centennial Park bombing that marred the 1996 Summer Olympics was another case where I directly intervened to prevent what would have been a legal catastrophe.

Richard Jewell had originally been one of the heroes of the Centennial Park bombing. A security guard hired to protect a light and sound tower at the popular late-night meeting site, Jewell had been the first person to alert police to a suspicious knapsack shortly before the bomb inside it exploded. After the blast, Jewell had helped police clear the park. So far, so good, but Jewell also had gone out of his way to tell television reporters about his efforts. More than one "hero" has been known to create the circumstances of his own heroism, and Jewell was beginning to fit that profile. Statements by some of his co-workers raised further suspicions. I wasn't in Atlanta, but when a draft application for a search warrant to be served on Richard Jewell crossed my desk back in Washington, I responded that the evidence seemed sufficient for probable cause.

It wasn't that I was convinced Jewell was the man. If anything, I was unconvinced, then and later. To me, he never quite seemed to fit the facts. But a search warrant isn't an accusation. It's a judicial order to acquire evidence and other information that will help decide whether to move forward toward an indictment or to move on to other suspects and other lines of inquiry. That's where we were with Richard Jewell when the *Atlanta Journal-Constitution* got wind of the search warrant, added two and two and came up with five, and named Jewell as our prime suspect. Thus, just as with Wen Ho Lee, a choreographed media circus ensued that would take two long months to die out.

Unfortunately, at just about the same time, we compounded the difficulty by getting too cute by half. Agents had originally asked Jewell if they could interview him at a local restaurant. Since Jewell agreed to come along voluntarily and since a restaurant hardly constitutes "custody"—he could walk out whenever he wanted to— there would have been no need to apprise him of his Miranda rights to have a lawyer present.

Then the plan changed. Rather than use a restaurant, agents asked Jewell to come down to the Atlanta FBI office and take part in a bogus training film about how to interview a "first responder." Jewell once again said yes, came of his own free will, and of his own free will began to answer the questions that interviewers had been planning to ask over sandwiches and coffee.

Technically, I suppose, that still let us off the hook in terms of his Miranda rights, but when I found out what was going on, halfway through the ruse, I didn't like the misleading way it had been orchestrated. The arrangements for the interview, the setting it was taking place in, the fact we were tricking the guy—the whole production began to suggest a nonvoluntary situation. This was an FBI office. Guys sit around with guns strapped to them. On top of that, if Jewell was the guy, we were risking tainting the case right at the outset. What's more, we had an incipient media blowout on our hands, and I wanted to make sure things were done more than right. Not only had people been killed and injured—one dead from the bomb, another by heart attack seemingly as a result of the explosion, and 120 wounded—they had been killed and maimed in the public eye, on a hallowed stage. The world press corps was camped out within walking distance of Centennial Park, desperate to fill column inches and broadcast minutes. (The heart attack victim was a Turkish cameraman racing to film the event.)

For me, the situation had reached critical mass. Read him his rights, I said, not to any great hosannas of praise either in my office or down in Atlanta. Why, people asked? But I was through explaining. Because that's my directive, I answered. It was only when they asked him to acknowledge in writing that he had been read them, as required by the statute, that he glommed onto what was happening and shut up tight.

I've read in the years since that if we had continued the ruse, Richard Jewell would have told FBI investigators enough that they could have cleared him then and there. Maybe so. I don't have a crystal ball. But given the choice between deceit and transparency, I'll take transparency every time.

I was galled by what had happened, and I agreed when three FBI supervisors were reprimanded by Justice Department investigators for their role in the questioning of Richard Jewell. As I wrote in an internal FBI memo on the reprimands, "No prosecutor could go into court, and no director of the FBI could go before Congress, and claim that necessary constitutional warnings are adequately conveyed by telling a suspect that he is an actor in a training video and that he is being presented Miranda warnings 'just like it's (a) real official interview.'" Inevitably, the memo was leaked to the press almost before the ink was dry.

But as happened with the flap over the McVeigh records and Wen Ho Lee, I was mostly galled by the fact that the controversy drew attention away from what the FBI does best: exhausting tens of thousands of work hours on solving crimes that no other agency has the training or resources or resolve or corporate culture to take on. Led by John Behnke, Tracey North, and Todd Letcher—all veterans of the Moody case—agents ultimately conducted more than twenty thousand interviews in the Centennial Park bombing. They studied and cross-referenced and matched up innumerable photos and video camera stills and individual frames from TV and newspaper coverage. (*Everyone* was recording the Olympics in one way or another.) And in the end, after two years of the most minute examination and cross-comparison, all those dedicated and unbending agents had made their case against their man, Eric Robert Rudolph.

By then, Rudolph was already on the FBI Most Wanted List for a 1998 bombing at a Birmingham, Alabama, abortion clinic that had killed an off-duty policeman helping to guard the facility and seriously wounded a nurse at the clinic. Soon, additional charges relating to other Atlanta area bombings, at a lesbian nightclub and a women's clinic, would be added to the list.

Another half decade would be needed to hunt Eric Rudolph down and finally close the books on the Centennial Park bombing, almost two years after I had left the director's post, and for that, too, the FBI has taken flak. But Rudolph was willing and able to live virtually like a wild animal in the rugged mountains of western North Carolina. The area had been a stronghold of a hate group that called itself the Army of God, to which Rudolph belonged. He grew up there. As Osama bin Laden has proven, even the most committed manhunts in the world can fail to flush a prey when it's hunkered down in a harsh terrain, protected by its own kind. And Rudolph clearly had the genes of the maniacally committed. Back in 1998, his brother sawed off his own hand, on videotape, to protest the FBI's pursuit of his sibling.

Had a local police officer in Murphy, North Carolina, not spotted Eric Rudolph one evening eating out of a Dumpster behind a supermarket, he might still be at large. But the point to be made is that, as with Khobar Towers and so many other cases, the FBI never gave up. We never stopped looking for Eric Robert Rudolph, and because we didn't, we created the conditions that led to the lucky break that finally brought a crazed murderer to ground. That tale might begin with Richard Jewell and a foolish trick in the Bureau's Atlanta office, but that's the background static, not the story itself. Rudolph has now admitted to his crimes, but the FBI's overwhelming evidence would have gotten him in the end even if he hadn't.

The Unabomber was a case study for me in how the media can not only drive events but sometimes precipitate them, which is why I will forever associate the names Ted Kaczynski and Dan Rather.

I was working my first big case as an agent when Kaczynski mailed his initial bomb back in 1978, a package device supposedly being returned to Northwestern University professor Buckley Crist. Suspicious—he'd never mailed the package in the first place—Crist turned the package over to campus police, who opened it, causing minor injuries to one officer. Other bombs followed. Some went to airline officials; others were meant to explode in flight. Fortunately, Kaczynski wasn't much of a bomb maker, at least in the early days. Then in 1985, he did his first serious harm. A graduate student at the University of California at Berkeley lost four fingers and the use of one eye. Later that year, a California computer store owner was killed by a bomb loaded with nails and other shrapnel. Two years later, in 1987, Kaczynski struck again. A similar bomb was sent to a computer store in Salt Lake City. Then he went to ground for seven years. His first victim when he surfaced again was Yale computer scientist David Gelernter. Gelernter survived but lost part of his right hand. Kaczynski followed that up by maiming geneticist Charles Epstein. In 1994, he killed an advertising executive; in 1995, the president of a forestry association.

Clearly, the attacks were increasing in frequency and in accuracy. Whoever the Unabomber was, he had learned how to make an effective bomb, and his list of enemies was growing. But that was about all we had to go on. Most bombers are driven by some obvious if demented cause. Kaczynski, it turned out, had one, too. He had declared war on modern society and particularly those who were by his malicious lights abusing technology. But until Kaczynski sent his first anonymous letter to the press in 1993, we had not the remotest clue who was behind the attacks, and the letter provided little help. The writer credited the attacks to an anarchist group he called FC. Indeed, "FC" had been inscribed on the bombs regularly since 1985, but we had no idea what that stood for. (The answer, once we got it, was simple in the extreme: "Freedom Club.")

We'd dubbed the case Unabomb—an amalgamation of "university" and "airlines," his favorite targets—and we had a special task force dedicated to finding the Unabomber, but that, too, was going nowhere. Using every kind of matrix and analytic tool they could think of, the agents had assembled a massive computerized list of anyone and everyone who might have some kind of lethal grudge against the specific people attacked, against computers, against universities, against the airline industry, and on and on. Just assembling the list was the work of thousands of agent hours; checking it increased the workload exponentially. Every time I look back on the case, I'm amazed by the perseverance our people showed, the sheer dedication in the face of so little positive feedback. The FBI task force was led by agents like Terry Turchie who didn't know the meaning of giving up, yet Ted Kaczynski's name wasn't even on the list. He was below everyone's radar.

When Kaczynski had a new bomb to send, he would bicycle down from his cabin to town, then hop a bus to someplace like San Francisco, where he would mail his lethal devices before scurrying back to his hidey-hole in Montana. Like Walter Leroy Moody, he left no forensic trail, and like Eric Rudolph he seemed able to live on air and bark and beetles. And then Theodore Kaczynski made his pivotal mistake, without which we never would have caught him. He mailed to *The Washington Post* and *The New York Times* a 35,000-word "manifesto" and claimed he would cease his bombings if the document was published verbatim by one of the newspapers or by a major national magazine such as *Time* or *Newsweek*.

The manifesto was rambling, the reasoning tortured, but the minute I started reading it, I felt certain someone, somewhere would recognize its author. The syntax, the diction, the logic—they were all so singular, as full of idiosyncratic quirks as any fingerprint. The problem was how to get it published.

Newspapers don't like to be bossed around, and they don't like setting onerous precedents. I can remember sitting in the office of Arthur Sulzberger Jr., the publisher of *The New York Times*, with Donald Graham, who had succeeded his mother, Katharine, as publisher of *The Washington Post*, hashing matters over with the fourth estate. Publish this and we'll be hostage to every nut with a cause, the two of them argued. Fail to publish it, I countered, and people might die, perhaps your own employees, or their families and loved ones. The Unabomber has shown an affinity for airplanes in the past. He might really bring one down this time. More practical issues intervened, as well. Publishing a 35,000-word document would require a special section. Paper, ink, typesetting time—none of it's free, and no advertisers were going to be rushing to fill this insert with quarter pagers. Publishers have to answer to their stockholders, too, and Sulzberger and Graham were both conscious of that, as they had to be. Graham said that in the end it came down to a matter of "public safety."

It was obvious to me, too, that neither publisher wanted to be in the position of aiding and abetting the FBI, but I couldn't help but note the irony involved. A quarter of a century earlier, the government had unsuccessfully moved heaven and earth to keep these same two newspapers from publishing the "Pentagon Papers." Now I was trying to move heaven and earth to get them to publish a document they would have just as soon left alone.

"This might be the only time in history the FBI has begged you to leak something for us," I told them.

I don't know if it was true, but I suspect so, and ultimately my argument carried the day. Against the economic self-interest of both papers, against the widespread opposition of some of their top editors, and, to be honest, to my great surprise, Sulzberger and Graham struck a deal. The *Post* would publish the manifesto, and the *Times* would share the cost, maybe $40,000 in all.

On September 19, 1995, right at the tail end of a three-month deadline imposed by the Unabomber, the manifesto finally saw the light of day, in an eight-page supplement to the *Post* amended three days later by an additional two paragraphs, seventy-two words in all, that had been inadvertently dropped by a typist. Media critics, by and large, were appalled. The *Post* and *Times* had caved. Their pages were going to be Crackpot City from now on. Armchair criminologists climbed on board, too. The Unabomber, whoever he was, was chortling over his success.

Maybe my stomach should have been churning, too. I'd gone way out on a limb to talk America's two most influential daily newspapers into this. If the manifesto didn't flush out someone who could identify its author, the FBI was going to have plenty of crow to eat and could have made powerful enemies in the process. But from the moment I opened my *Washington Post* that morning, I knew we'd done the right thing. Some professor or student was sure to recognize the quirky style of a former mentor or mentee, and it wouldn't take long. It didn't, but what almost floored me was that it was Ted Kaczynski's brother who dropped the dime.

I've got two brothers I dearly love. I can only imagine how wrenching it must have been for David Kaczynski to see his brother's tortured style and psyche spread all over those pages, and then to decide to turn him in. But I like to think that, under similar circumstances, I would have had the courage to do much as David did. First, he contacted a lawyer, and the lawyer contacted us. His anonymous client, he said, was prepared to identify the Unabomber, but he wanted concessions, the chief of which was that the government would not ask for the death penalty. We didn't agree entirely, but we did say we would take the request into strong consideration, and ultimately we did. With that, we had the Unabomber's name, corroborating evidence such as it was, and an address: a backwoods cabin outside Lincoln, Montana. But the weirdness was not done, not by a long shot.

I was sitting in the FBI's operations center on April 2, 1996, the day before agents armed with search and arrest warrants were to descend on Ted Kaczynski in Montana, when one of my chief lieutenants shouted over to say that Dan Rather was on the line.

"Here we go," I said.

So I got on the phone, and Dan, whom I had met a couple of times, came right to the point.

"Listen," he said, "we know all about Kaczynski, where he is, all that, and were going to have some people go out there and film the search."

"You can't film the search!"

"Well," he said, "that's what we'd like to do."

"You're going to get someone killed," I told him. "First of all, and I know you're not going to answer this, I'd like to know how you found out about this."

We'd been mobilizing people to move out to western Montana for days, but not on the scale that would attract media attention. Now I was enraged, not at Dan—I'd been in Washington long enough to know that the place leaks like a water mattress at a porcupine convention—but at his source. The operation had been relatively tightly held; whoever had talked was clearly intimately involved in the operation. Dan Rather, though, wasn't about to hand over CBS's stoolie.

"Well," he said, "you know, we have good sources."

Right.

"Don't worry," he went on. "We're just sending one truck. It'll be low profile."

"Dan, this is western Montana. You can't do that! There's no way for a news truck to be unobtrusive."

And so we went on, the CBS news anchor and global media figure assuring us that his reporters and soundmen and camera crews would be quiet as church mice, and me assuring him that this wasn't going to happen. Finally, we struck a deal. CBS would give us a couple hours to do the search before it set up, and we would give the network some exclusive interviews in return. Dan Rather couldn't have been more honorable on his end once the deal was struck. For our part, we burst into Kaczynski's cabin unannounced by satellite dish trucks and found a wealth of evidence awaiting us, everything from fabricated explosive devices to the original of the manifesto and the typewriter used to produce it. And with that, one of the most frustrating cases the FBI had ever worked on—an eighteen-year wild-goose chase that had spanned the tenures of five directors and acting directors—was ended. Today, Ted Kaczynski, who murdered three people with his bombs and injured twenty-three others, is behind bars for the rest of his life.

Once in a rare while, too, a case went so deep to the bone that I couldn't help but feel raw anger.

I'd been FBI director for only a few months when some of my top people dropped by to brief me on one of the most highly classified operations the Bureau had ever undertaken—so restricted that, even though I ran the place, no one could tell me the code word. Fine, I said, talk on, and the story was almost too incredible.

For years, it turned out, the Bureau had had two agents living in a small Georgetown row house and posing as just another set of urban upwardly mobile DINKs (double income no kids, for those who forget the shorthand of the '90s). These two, though, were more in the mining business than in anything normally associated with Washington. Out of their basement ran a tunnel that had been dug at huge effort and public expense with an eye to penetrating the then new Soviet embassy built on one of the city's highest points, a place known locally as Mount Alto. (I should point out that this was in stark contrast to Moscow, where the new U.S. embassy had been built in a hollow surrounded by KGB listening stations. Beware, in other words, of democracies bearing gifts.) Naturally, my staff, or that part of it that was allowed in on the secret, was enormously proud of this fact.

"We're right under the code room!" they told me, practically bursting out of their suits.

"Oh yeah?" I said, wondering where this was headed.

"And all we have to do is go up a little farther and we'll be in the code room!"

"So why don't you do it?"

"Well," came the answer, "we think their instrumentation will detect us if we do that."

"How much money did we spend on this?"

"Millions of dollars."

"How long?"

"Years."

"And you're to the point where you're almost there but can't get there?"

"That's right—we can't get there. We think it would be best if we filled in the tunnel."

"How much?"

"Millions."

"How long?"

"Years. Do you want to see the tunnel before we begin?"

I told them no. I was already having a vision of a string of D.C. streets collapsing on top of our tunnel, creating an urban chasm that would point right from the Russian Embassy to our little row house—and from there, a second furrowed line of responsibility that would point directly to my seventh-floor office. Indeed, one evening I had dinner at the embassy and realized that I was treading softly on the floor.

I had no way of knowing it at the time, but that was my first introduction to FBI agent Robert Hanssen and his treasonous sideline. Hanssen had already told the Russians about our tunnel, long before we determined we would never be able to use it. As for Bob Hanssen himself, we had already met once, briefly: he and I and our families attended the same Roman Catholic church, St. Catherine's in Great Falls, Virginia. On one of the first Sundays after I had become director, he made a point of stopping me after mass and introducing himself. Over the next eight years, I would have virtually no direct contact with him, but his shadow hung heavily over my tenure.

Oddly, given that the Soviet Union basically went out of business in 1989, the 1990s were the Decade of the Turncoat Soviet Spy. Aldrich Ames, a thirty-one-year veteran of the CIA, and his wife, Rosario, were arrested by the FBI in 1994 and charged with conspiracy to commit espionage. Ames had offered his services to the Soviets in 1985 while serving as chief of the Soviet branch of the CIA's Directorate of Operations. In the eight-plus years that followed, he had done untold damage to the Agency and his nation, and in the end he was sentenced to life in prison without parole for his crimes. (Rosario Ames drew sixty-three months in prison for abetting his espionage.)

A year later, in 1996, we arrested Harold Nicholson, a veteran CIA operations officer and former chief of station in Bucharest, as he was attempting to leave the U.S. to meet with agents of the Russian intelligence service. Eventually sentenced to twenty-three years in prison, Nicholson was the highest-ranking CIA official ever convicted of espionage. In both the Ames and Nicholson cases, the arrests were the fruit of significantly improved ties between the CIA and FBI, across the ranks and especially at the top. From day one, I had a great working relationship with John Deutsch, who was heading the CIA when these espionage cases popped, and with George Tenet, who succeeded him.

The FBI came in for its own black eye in 1996 when Special Agent Earl Pitts, a counterintelligence officer and a thirteen-year veteran of the Bureau, was charged with espionage, attempted espionage, and communication of classified information, all of it over a five-year period beginning in 1987. On more than one occasion during the covert phase of our investigation, I walked past Pitts while traversing the corridors at Quantico and did a good rendition of hello as we passed each other. Pitts drew a twenty-seven-year sentence for his activities.

Other arrests came down, as well. Late in 1998, we nabbed ten people who had been conducting espionage for the government of Cuba. About the same time, David Sheldon Boone, an army sergeant assigned to the National Security Agency, pled guilty in Alexandria's U.S. district court to conspiracy to commit espionage for the KGB. We caught a husband-and-wife team that had been spying for the East Germans; both were convicted in 1998 of four counts of espionage. By then, the cold war had been in cessation for almost a decade, but you wouldn't have known it from our National Security Division.

The irony of breaking a spy case is simple. Finding a spy is terrible news. Not finding a spy is worse but not news.

Try as we did, though, it was clear by 1997 that one mole was eluding us. We knew he was highly placed within the American intelligence community, probably in Washington, D.C. We knew he had been compromising important operations to the KGB over a long period of time, perhaps since the mid-1970s. We even had a code name for him: Graysuit. But we had no clue who Graysuit was.

We had set up a huge team of CIA and FBI officers and agents, and located them off-site from both facilities, mainly at the old Washington Navy Yard. To make sure we weren't inviting the fox inside the henhouse, we polygraphed and otherwise individually screened everyone who went into that team, and we kept the operation quiet enough, despite its size, that only an incredibly well-placed mole—someone extremely close to George Tenet or me—could have known of its existence.

The arrests and subsequent interrogations of Ames, Nicholson, and Pitts had filled in many of the blank spots in our espionage files: cases where someone recruited by either the Agency or the Bureau had been compromised, killed, or arrested by the Russians, or ones where we had opened an investigation only to have the subject tipped off and skip town. But plenty of unexplained cases still remained, and those are the ones the team concentrated on. Still, by the end of the decade Graysuit was as big a mystery as he had been two years earlier.

It was just about that time, late in 1999, that George Tenet and I held one of our regular meetings on the matter with our respective espionage and national security chiefs. We have news, they said. Our staffs have determined that the mole in all likelihood is somewhere inside the CIA. All the pieces, all the signs pointed that way.

"Too bad," I told George, half in jest. "Three strikes and you're out." But, of course, it was my strike, not his. I just didn't know it yet.

Frustrated and determined finally to stop the bleeding, George and I came up with a plan, something that hadn't been tried before. We would pool our financial resources, come up with a reward large enough to garner attention among the new capitalists of the old People's Paradise, and basically buy the mole's identity. The sum we finally settled on was a seven-figure payment. That, we figured, should be enough to turn up some KGB equivalent of Aldrich Ames, especially if we supplemented the cash reward with additional incentives such as residency, protection, whatever was necessary.

Once we had the money set aside, we had task-force analysts pore over their files and identify five senior KGB officers, all retired, who were likely to have had access to Graysuit's identity in the normal course of their operations. Then we sent task force members over-seas to approach each of the targets individually. The pitch was as simple as the plan: we are from the FBI and the CIA. We think you have information that would be very valuable to us, and we are willing to pay for it.

One ex-KGB officer we contacted responded just as directly: go screw yourselves. Officer two wasn't a lot more gracious. He might have information, he said, but he never returned any calls after that—and not surprisingly, either. The Soviet Union might have been gone by then, but selling out an asset as valuable as Graysuit was an almost certain death sentence if you were caught.

Officer three took the bait: I can help, he said. His price was pretty much what we expected: the cash reward, U.S. citizenship for himself, and relocation to the U.S. for his mother. Fine, we said. Give us Graysuit, and it's all yours. He couldn't, the officer said. He knew him only by his Soviet code name, Ramon, but he had plenty of records and other information that related to Graysuit, all of it lifted from Lubyanka, the infamous KGB headquarters. That's what he was proposing to sell us for several million dollars plus other con-siderations: not our mole but the path to his door.

"No way," George Tenet and I both said when word got back to us. After all, we were kids from Queens and Jersey City—not easily fooled. First, we weren't about to hand over any reward based on this guy's representation that he had the goods that might get us what we were after. Second, *no one* walks out of Lubyanka with anything without at best getting his hands chopped off. Third, it just smelled too much like a scam. In truth, though, we had nothing better to go on, so we told the agents who were in contact with officer three to string him along until we saw what he could produce. A good thing we did, too, because when agents met with him in October 2000, on neutral ground in a European country, he turned over a remarkable amount of material: dates and times of meetings, amounts of payments, other detailed records and files, all of it smuggled out of what had supposedly been one of the most secure locations on earth.

I'll never forget being in my seventh-floor office at FBI headquarters a week or so later when Neil Gallagher, my longtime colleague and able national security chief, popped in.

"What are you finding?" I asked him. The material had just arrived at our laboratory on the third floor, where it was being evaluated forensically.

"You've got to come down and see," he said. And so I did.

The documents, Neil told me, appeared to be authentic. As advertised, they did everything but name Graysuit, but that wasn't what he had dragged me down to the third floor to show me.

"There's a tape recording," Neil said.

The Russians, it turned out, wanted to find out who this guy was just as much as we did. They had been doing business with him for two decades and paid a bundle of money along the way. Even though the information he provided was very good, it offended their professional pride not to know who they were dealing with. Not only did Graysuit never meet with his handlers or contact them; they were never able to even get a photo of him, despite plenty of efforts on their part, but finally they got him to talk on the telephone, and that's what our source had handed over to us: a casette of that conversation.

"And?" I asked Neil.

"And the guy's Bob Hanssen."

As I mentioned, I'd had almost no professional contact with Hanssen during my then seven-plus years as director. He'd spent the last five years detailed to the Office of Foreign Missions and the Department of State. But I had that earlier contact with him through my church, and by the fall of 2000 I had a second personal connection to him as well. We each had a son attending the same Catholic school, The Heights School, in Potomac, Maryland.

We couldn't just go out and arrest Bob Hanssen. We wanted to catch him in the act of espionage. To that end, we started surveillance on his computer, his car, his phone, anywhere and everything that he might use to contact the Russians and transport himself to them. (We didn't yet know that he never even told his handlers when he made drops or what he was dropping. He would simply stash the documents in one of several predesignated spots, and the Russians would leave the money in the same place for later retrieval.)

Meanwhile, the headmaster of The Heights School had asked me to give a talk at the annual father-son night in December 2000. Not surprisingly, Hanssen was part of the official committee waiting to welcome me when I arrived that evening. Just to overwhelm the event with irony, the headmaster had also asked me to talk about a particular topic: ethics and integrity in government. There I was on the small stage, waiting to speak and knowing that the man sitting in front of me had sold his nation down the river; and there Bob Hanssen was, sitting by his son in the front row, not having the least idea that we had finally cracked his cover. I don't think I ever showed it that evening—I certainly hope I didn't—but the longer I sat, the angrier I got, not just at the fact that the man had betrayed his country for money (as much as $600,000 in the aggregate) and smeared the agency I led but also that he had betrayed his family. His crimes were going to come crashing down not just on his own very deserving head but also on the head of the unsuspecting boy sitting next to him as well as his wife and the rest of his family. To me, that was almost as unforgivable as the espionage itself.

As we had with the Clinton administration, we briefed the incoming Bush team on the pending arrest. Andy Card, George W. Bush's chief of staff in waiting, was particularly concerned that we not haul Hanssen in on Inauguration Day. But he needn't have worried. We waited for Graysuit to make a drop so we could catch him in the act. When he finally did—on Sunday night, February 18, 2001, in the woods near a bridge at a local park in Vienna, Virginia—we arrested him on the site. Then we waited another day and a half before announcing the arrest, in the hope that we could nab one of his Russian masters picking up the goods. They didn't, but at least we had cut the cancer out from inside us. Right after we arrested Hanssen, President Bush called me in our operations center and asked that I convey his thanks to the FBI personnel involved. It was the first time since I became director that a president—and Bush had been in office less than thirty days—had ever thanked the FBI for protecting the country.

In announcing the arrest February 20, I also announced that Judge William Webster—not only one of my predecessors but also a former CIA director—had agreed to lead an inquiry into the Bureau's internal security functions. There's probably no way to foolproof any organization against a determined traitor, but we have to make it as hard as possible for any such person to get in a position to sell out his country. In that announcement, I also let my own feelings show. Bob Hanssen and I had been in different training classes, but we'd joined the Bureau within a year of each other. What he had done was personal with me.

Since becoming director over seven years ago, I have administered the FBI oath to each graduating class of special agents at the FBI Academy. Each time, I share the pride and sanctity of those words when new agents swear to "support and defend the Constitution of the United States against all enemies, foreign and domestic" and to "bear true faith and allegiance to the same."

Regrettably, I stand here today both saddened and outraged. An FBI agent who raised his right hand and spoke those words over twenty-five years ago has been charged today with violating that oath in the most egregious and reprehensible manner imaginable. The FBI entrusted him with some of the most sensitive secrets of the United States government and instead of being humbled by this honor, Hanssen has allegedly abused and betrayed that trust. The crimes alleged are an affront not only to his fellow FBI em-

ployees but to the American people, not to mention the pain and
suffering he has brought upon his family. Our hearts go out to
them. I take solace and satisfaction, however, that the FBI suc-
ceeded in this investigation. As an agency, we lived up to our re-
sponsibility, regardless of how painful it might be.

One more thing Bob Hanssen did to my tenure as FBI director: he was mostly responsible for extending it another six or so months longer than I had intended.

I had expected to announce my retirement after the November 2000 election. That would have been seven years plus a few months in office, and that seemed enough to me. The new president would appoint the next director for a ten-year term, and I would stay on briefly for the transition. Besides, the oldest boys were just about to reach college age. Once again, I was pressed by family circumstances to earn something beyond a government wage.

Then, of course, the November election didn't end, and didn't end, and didn't end. We had identified Hanssen by mid-November. By December, when the Supreme Court found itself inserted into the middle of the election process, Hanssen was very much on my mind. No matter where we brought him down or how, his arrest was going to be a large black mark on a Bureau I had devoted a sizable chunk of my adult life to. I couldn't let my successor bear that burden. I'd have to do it myself. By then, too, a light was at long last beginning to shine at the end of the long Khobar Towers tunnel. I had briefed President Bush on the case and Iran's involvement. His response was immediate and fearless: "Go make the case." Appropriately, he followed up on his father's earlier and critical efforts to get FBI access to Saudi witnesses. The Khobar families and I will always be thankful to him for his leadership. If there was a chance of seeing that resolved on my watch, of seeing the families come to closure, I had to stick around, especially if my presence might help to make the difference. We were also still in the middle of a long, hard-fought campaign to gain the funding so that we could begin to upgrade our technology, and we were making significant improvements in our counterterrorism capabilities.

All those factors weighed in my decision making, but there was a final reason, too, for staying on past the end of the Clinton administration. The president's and my relationship was toxic by that time. Not only was he actively hostile toward me, he was hostile to the FBI generally. My departure might be one last opportunity for retaliation. Quite frankly, I was worried about whom he might appoint as my successor, even on a temporary basis.

CHAPTER 9

Bill and Me

I never expected to be Bill Clinton's best friend in Washington. We had gotten along well when I came down to the White House to talk about taking the job as director. My Rose Garden introduction to the media was a joy. The president had been as deft with my children as he was with me. But Bill Clinton is a master politician—as I wrote earlier, maybe the best of his generation. Winning people over is what masterful politicians do.

It was obvious to me, even in that first meeting, that we had differences of temperament. He seemed to wear his heart on his sleeve. I'm more cautious by nature. Maybe because of my training as a federal prosecutor, I've learned to keep a check on my emotions. There were times I literally wanted to strangle the people I was trying to put behind bars. Roy Moody, to cite one obvious example, is an odious human being, a remorseless killer. But losing my temper at him in the courtroom wouldn't have done the cause any good, nor would justice have been truly served if I had been anything less than fair in prosecuting Moody. That's a hard line to walk, but over the years, I had come to edit my responses carefully before I spoke.

Bill Clinton is almost the opposite. Like his big sprawling autobiography, he himself is big and sprawling and, basically, unedited. That was his strength as a politician, but it was also his great weakness as president.

But if I didn't expect to be pals with the president, I did think we would have plenty to hash over. He had been a law professor briefly before he started pursuing elected office. The first post he won was as Arkansas attorney general. He was so articulate, so obviously smart, and in our initial interview, he appeared to have a deep interest in law enforcement and an almost encyclopedic knowledge of some of the crises the FBI had faced in recent years: Ruby Ridge and, especially, Waco. Drug-enforcement issues, the Wall Street prosecutions—he was on top of everything. An activist president was certain, I thought, to take an active interest in the Bureau and its leadership. Again, I was wrong.

Someone asked me not long ago how often I met with the president early in my service as FBI director, before things turned sour between us. To the best of my recollection, the answer is one time, maybe two, maybe three times in the entire seven-plus years I worked under Bill Clinton. Add in phone calls, and the total might climb to half a dozen, on the outside. Jim Woolsey, who took over the CIA at the start of the first Clinton administration, had the same experience: virtually no meetings, virtually no calls, essentially a wall of silence.

At least in those early days, I don't think it was personal. Politics is what drove so many of the Clinton people and, I have to assume, the president himself. He just wasn't very interested in intelligence gathering or in law enforcement, and that meant he wasn't very interested in Jim Woolsey or me.

It did become personal, though, even though we were so seldom in each other's company. Oddly enough, Tom Hanks is one of those who helped drive an early wedge between the president and me.

BILL AND ME

———

Floyd Clarke, who was briefly acting director of the FBI before I took over the job permanently, left me two great parting gifts: the wisdom of his long years with the Bureau and his secretary, Wanda Siford, who knew where all the secret switches were that get things done in large bureaucracies. No director has ever been better served than I was by Wanda and Noreen Gawley, and believe me, I needed them both.

It was Wanda who called me one day fairly early in my tenure, so excited she could barely contain herself.

"You and Marilyn have been invited to the White House by the Clintons," she said, "a dinner and a private screening with . . . Tom Hanks!"

"You'll have to decline for us," I told her.

"What?"

"Decline."

I could already hear the response at 1600 Pennsylvania Avenue. That was the least of my problems, though. The greater issue was Marilyn.

"Are you going to tell her?" Wanda asked.

"Nah," I said, "I don't think so."

"You better. She might hear about it later."

That sounded like advice I couldn't ignore, so that evening I gathered my courage up, waited for an opening, and dropped the news.

"Listen, Marilyn," I said, "we got invited to the White House to have dinner with Tom Hanks and the president and some other people, but we can't go."

"What do you mean, we can't go?" she asked.

After all, this was supposed to be one of the side benefits of having a spouse who had an exalted position like mine. Sure, the job just ate up time, but every now and again some really neat, memorable moment came your way in reward: a state dinner, one of those galas at the Kennedy Center, or an intimate little meal and movie screening with the First Couple and a famous star like Tom Hanks.

"I can't explain it," I told her. "We just can't."

Perplexed, I think, might be the right word to describe Marilyn's reaction, but in fact, I really couldn't tell her why.

The FBI is an investigative agency; it says so right in the name. And the two absolute requirements of a good investigator are to remain independent and to maintain confidentiality. That was the hurdle. Marilyn didn't know it, but she and I couldn't socialize with Bill Clinton because he was already the subject of a criminal investigation.

I had barely gotten used to my new office furniture back in late 1993 when the head of the FBI criminal division dropped by to ask if he could brief me on an Arkansas savings and loan case. Sure, I said, go ahead. Thus I first learned in detail of the soon-to-be-famous Madison Guaranty Savings and Loan and of its owner, Jim McDougal, and thus, too, I first glimpsed the tip of the iceberg that would come to be known as Whitewater.

The whole case is way too complicated to go into here. McDougal had bought a small savings and loan early in the 1980s, renamed it Madison Guaranty, and watched it sink along with the rest of the industry during the S and L debacle that hit a few years later. That was a common tale in the mid-1980s, but Jim McDougal had friends in high places in Arkansas.

As the world was soon to learn, McDougal and his wife, Susan, were old pals and business partners with Bill and Hillary Rodham

Clinton. In 1978, the four had spent more than $200,000 in borrowed money to purchase land along the White River in the Ozarks region of northwest Arkansas. The idea was to subdivide the property and sell it to retirees looking for a quiet place in the country, but soaring interest rates and a sour economy caught up with the plan almost before it was hatched, and both the Clintons and Mc-Dougals lost money on the deal.

Faced with another investment gone sour, Jim McDougal now sought permission from the Arkansas Securities Commissioner to offer preferred stock in Madison Guaranty and to launch a subsidiary that would provide brokerage services. The commissioner, a lawyer named Beverly Bassett Schaffer, was a niece of Dale Bumpers, a former two-term governor of the state who was by then serving the third of four terms in the U.S. Senate. Schaffer also had been appointed to her post by, naturally, Governor Bill Clinton. To second his effort, McDougal had a lawyer at the Rose law firm, the state's leading attorneys, write a letter explaining and supporting the stock proposal. That lawyer, of course, was Hillary Clinton, the governor's wife. Like a river at a delta, Whitewater would fork out from there in dozens of directions, but that was for later.

I wasn't at all sure what kind of case could or should be made against the Clintons out of all this Madison Guaranty mess, but by the time the briefing ended, two large issues seemed to be looming in front of us. Issue one was jurisdictional. The Madison investigation was under the aegis of the Justice Department, but for some truly weird reasons, Justice was working the case with the inspector general of the Department of Labor. No, I said, that doesn't make any sense. At one level, I would have preferred that the whole business just disappear, but if the case had any merit, if it was going to be pursued any further, then it belonged under the FBI's Criminal Division. I wasn't just fighting for turf, I was trying to ensure that the people who were most experienced with the issues at play were the ones who handled the investigation. That's what the Criminal Division does. Placing the matter there was not only the most logical solution, it was clearly the fairest for all parties involved.

Issue two was broader. Listening to the briefing, I could see us walking down a path that ended up with a sitting president of the United States as the subject of a criminal investigation, perhaps even the subject of a criminal prosecution. That could automatically trigger the independent counsel statute, and even though I was only a few months into my job, I knew that would change almost everything about my relationship with the White House and Bill Clinton, on both a professional and personal level. On that front, at least, I was prophetic in the extreme.

I made my own mistakes in trying to find a working balance with Bill Clinton. I lacked subtlety at times. I had an insufficient appreciation for the nuanced life of southern politicians. I never learned to do good ol' boy. My part of New Jersey is a long way from Hope, Arkansas.

Hard on the heels of my briefing on Madison Guaranty Savings and Loan, the White House sent over a personal pass for my use. Under other circumstances, I would have been flattered. Personal passes let you come and go at 1600 Pennsylvania Avenue without having to be logged in. The passes were given out to cabinet officers as a matter of routine. Beneath that level—and I was—they're a gift of sorts, a way of saying that you're a key part of the team.

By then, though, a personal pass was just what I *didn't* want. If the FBI was going to be involved in an investigation of the president, as seemed possible, I wanted every visit I made to the White House to be part of some public record. I was just starting law school when the Watergate scandal broke. I remembered all those shadowy late-night meetings with Richard Nixon, all those "What did you talk about?" and "Who was there?" grillings before the congressional committees. I didn't want to go through that myself somewhere down the road, and I didn't want that kind of taint to attach itself to whatever waited ahead when this scandal broke, if it was a scandal, if it broke at all.

So I sent the pass back with a polite but fairly terse note, expressing my thanks and simply stating that I didn't mind signing in when I came calling, and that, I was to find out much later, offended Bill Clinton mightily even though, so far as I knew, I had been a virtual nonentity to him up to that point. Not only was returning the pass a personal affront to the president, it was seemingly a declaration of open hostility on my part. I later heard that some of the Clinton people understood that wasn't the case and tried to tell the president as much, but to no avail. The president's mind was made up.

In retrospect, I should have better explained my reasons, sugar-coated the action and taken more care to try to preserve my relationship with the president even as I was intentionally distancing myself from him. But was I wrong to have returned the pass? No, not at all.

I was the nation's top cop. The president and his wife might or might not have been involved, however marginally, in an act of bank fraud; or they might simply be good friends and former business partners of someone who was involved in bank fraud; or it was possible no fraud had been committed at all. Until the matter was sorted out, I had to be accountable for every trip I made to the building where the president worked and lived. That meant no personal pass, but it also marked the end of any hope I had of establishing a close working relationship with my boss. Less than half a year after Bill Clinton had wooed me into taking the job of director, the president was seriously beginning to wish that I had said no.

———

The problem, of course, was that with Bill Clinton the scandals and rumored scandals, the incubating ones and the dying ones, never ended. Whatever moral compass the president was consulting, it was leading him in the wrong direction, and he lacked the discipline to pull back once he found himself stepping into trouble. Worse, he had been behaving that way so long that the closets were full of skeletons just waiting to burst out. Whitewater grew like mold through the entire first term. Travelgate went away, finally, but Gennifer Flowers and Paula Jones never really did. The women, the wheeling and dealing down in Arkansas, Webb Hubbell's legal troubles, Vince Foster's suicide—they were always there as background static.

We added our own mess to the pile by incorrectly sending the president's staff more than four hundred FBI file summaries of people who had had White House security clearances during the Bush and Reagan years. It was a goof, plain and simple, as Ken Starr's office eventually confirmed, but it was embarrassing all the same. Still, if the ethical climate at 1600 Pennsylvania Avenue had not been so suspect, "Filegate" never would have provoked much more than a mild gasp.

I didn't help matters either by the way I handled the Larry Potts promotion. I had known Larry since my U.S. attorney days when we worked together down in Atlanta on the Moody case, and I had the highest regard for him. He'd had a distinguished career in the FBI, rising to the rank of assistant director before I came on the scene, and he had every right in the normal course of affairs to expect that I would make him my number two, the deputy director, at some point after I took over the top post. But Larry was also a Bureau lightning rod. He had supervised two of the FBI's most controversial undertakings in the early 1990s, the siege at Ruby Ridge, in Idaho, and the one at the Branch Davidian compound in Waco. Both had attracted plenty of media scrutiny and outside criticism, and a lot of that had attached to Larry.

From what I knew, Larry was getting an unfair rap, but when Floyd Clarke announced at the end of 1993 that he would be vacating the deputy director's post, I thought the time wasn't yet right to elevate Larry. I wanted to let all the controversy die down before I did that. Otherwise, the promotion would turn into yet another media circus. So I picked David Binney for the post. Understandably, Larry was very upset about being passed over, and he told me so. I explained my reasons to him, told him the furor needed more time to die down, and in effect promised him the deputy director's position when David left. That was my mistake. David Binney quit less than a year after accepting the job, to become director of corporate security at IBM, and, as promised, I named Larry Potts to succeed him while the controversy over Waco and Ruby Ridge was still raging. Ten weeks later, in mid-1995, I had to pull Larry out of the job and transfer him to one of our training units.

The promotion-demotion was an embarrassment to the FBI, Larry, me, and to Janet Reno, who had approved my selection. It reflected poorly on the administration generally. This was an important post, responsible for day-to-day operations of the Bureau, not some Ping-Pong ball to be knocked all over the place. Most of all, though, my mistake was unfair to Larry Potts, and for that I feel deep regret.

Bernie Nussbaum, who had been my first connection to the Clinton White House and my best friend in it, resigned after only fourteen months as White House counsel. Whether Bernie left on his own or was nudged toward the door, I still don't know. I've never asked, but he'd had a rough run. Vince Foster's suicide, our bungling with Filegate, the flogging he took in the press when it was revealed that he had met with officials of the Resolution Trust Corporation over the Madison Guaranty criminal referrals—Bernie got it from all sides. What's more, his strategy for protecting the president wasn't working. Bernie was a top Wall Street lawyer. He was used to circling the wagons, locking the doors, and denying everything when things went bad. Offer up nothing. Make them get it out of you. My feeling was that the president needed to be disclosing more, not less; he needed to be more forthright with the American people about the charges and insinuations flying around him. Bill Clinton wasn't a corporate CEO; he was the leader of a nation. There's a big difference.

Bernie also never got over the fact that the president had failed to follow his advice to resist an independent counsel to investigate Whitewater. That more than anything else, in my opinion, is what made Bernie head for the door, but it was a door that would get plenty of use. In eight years in office, Bill Clinton ran through six White House counsels, a telling index of just how troubled his tenure was. But none of them had Bernie's depth and high integrity.

For me, Bernie's departure was a serious loss. As I wrote earlier, there's a special bond between those of us who have come out of the U.S. Attorney's Office for the Southern District of New York. Bernie was proud that he had recommended me for the job, and he would remain so even after Bill Clinton had changed his mind on that one. For my part, I was proud that Bernie had thought I was up to the task, and of course, it's always nice to have someone you trust and like inside the lion's den. But Bernie's departure did leave me feeling slightly abandoned. I still had plenty of channels to the Oval Office. Leon Panetta, John Podesta, Mack McLarty, George Stephanopoulos—I was on good terms with all of them despite our occasional differences over particular issues. Every one of them was a pro, but none of them was Bernie, and that became a problem as the first term wore on. Also in Bernie's departure I was struck at how easily Clinton played hardball politics even with his loyal and closest friends.

An FBI director should be able to go directly to the president, sit down with him and say, You should know about this. I wish that I had been able to do that. We had vital business to discuss. But almost from the very beginning, I felt uncomfortable spending private time with the president. There was always some new investigation brewing, some new calamity bubbling just below the headlines.

The president's frequently expressed point of view was that his troubles stemmed from political enemies who wouldn't leave his past alone and a special prosecutor he never should have agreed to. The White River real-estate deal was a decade and a half old by the time Bill Clinton moved into the Oval Office. He'd first met Gennifer Flowers even before that, in 1977, when she was a local television reporter and he was a wet-behind-the-ears attorney general. The commodities deal in which Hillary allegedly made a sweetheart $100,000 profit—another fork in the river as Whitewater flowed along—dated back to the late 1970s, as well. Paula Jones was old news, and a gold digger, too. As for Robert Fiske, the former U.S. attorney from New York whom I had recommended Janet Reno appoint as special prosecutor, he was "the worst presidential decision I ever made," Clinton writes in his memoir.

I don't happen to agree with him on all those points, and not at all on the matter of a special prosecutor, but the campaign contribution investigation that dogged the beginning of the president's second term was none of those things. It was new; the makings were homegrown in the White House, not back in Arkansas; and Bob Fiske had nothing to do with it.

On November 24, 1997, I sent to Attorney General Janet Reno and to Deputy Attorney General Jamie Gorelick—and to those two only—a twenty-seven-page memo accompanied by a two-page cover letter in which I provided an overview of an ongoing FBI investigation into allegations of illicit fund-raising during the 1996 presidential campaign. In addition to the facts of the case, I outlined the provisions and requirements of the independent counsel statute and recommended that the attorney general invoke it in this instance. By now, it should go without saying that word of the memo leaked to the press almost instantaneously.

It wasn't long before Dan Burton, the Indiana Republican and chairman of the House Government Reform and Oversight Committee, was demanding that Janet provide him with a copy of what I had written. Janet's refusal touched off a war of words between the two of them that almost earned her a contempt of Congress citation. (Most of the words in this "war" were fired by Burton, who is rarely without something to say when he's riled up. Janet tried to keep a dignified silence through the ordeal.) But I didn't write the memo to stir up the war.

Nor did I write the memo to make myself even more of a persona non grata at the White House. The president had assured me before I took the job as director that I would be immune from political pressure. That was my bottom line on the professional side, and he had agreed to it wholeheartedly. But he obviously had second thoughts when my political immunity crept too close to his own skin. Bill Clinton stopped talking with me just about the time word of my memo surfaced, and he didn't speak to me again until shortly after the USS *Cole* was attacked almost four years later, and then only a few words.

I didn't even write the memo with the thought that anyone was "guilty" of anything. As I told Chairman Burton when he pressed me, unsuccessfully, to divulge the contents of the memo before his committee:

"In recommending to the attorney general that an independent counsel be appointed, I did not and do not believe that any particular person has committed a crime or is a target of a grand jury, or even has done anything improper. I recommended appointment of an independent counsel to investigate whether crimes may have been committed, but nothing more should be inferred from that recommendation."

And I certainly didn't write the memo as an act of partisan politics. To be sure, appearing to buck President Clinton won me GOP fans on the Hill, but believe me, it wasn't always thus. As the Democratic commentator Mark Shields noted on PBS's *The NewsHour with Jim Lehrer* just as the memo flap was hitting its high point: "Six months ago Republicans—I mean, the majority of Republicans—were calling for [Freeh's] scalp on Capitol Hill. You name the offense . . . he was a bum. Now he's the pinup boy." Don't worry, I would be a bum again.

I wrote that memo for the simplest of reasons: because I felt that as FBI director, I had to write it. "Soft money" appeared to have seeped into the 1996 presidential and congressional campaigns, in staggering quantities, and from alarming sources, including the People's Republic of China. Not surprisingly, the great bulk of the money seemed to have ended up in the Clinton-Gore reelection coffers. The presidency is the biggest prize, and Bob Dole never appeared to have much of a chance against Bill Clinton. Everyone likes to back a winner, at the highest level possible.

The Bureau had been looking into what we called Campcon (campaign contributions) since early 1997. By November, when I sent the memo, we had divided the investigation into three distinct but interrelated matters. To quote from the memo that almost earned Janet Reno a contempt citation, those three matters were:

- an aggressive campaign fund-raising operation developed and executed by a core group of individuals from the DNC [Democratic National Committee] and the White House, including the president, the vice president, and a number of top White House advisers.

- allegations of illegal conduct by a myriad of opportunists and other individuals who gained White House access in order to further their personal, business, and political interests.

- efforts by the PRC [People's Republic of China] and other countries to gain foreign policy influence by illegally contributing foreign money to U.S. political campaigns and to the DNC through domestic conduits.

As noted in item one, above, the president and the vice president were equally subjects of the investigation. If anything, the onus of the allegations seemed to be falling more heavily on the VP than on his boss. But Bill Clinton and Al Gore were anything but equal in their understanding of my motives and those of the Bureau. The vice president got it; Clinton did not.

Granted, I was on much closer terms with Al Gore than I was with the president. I was a member of the vice president's Air Safety Commission. My wife, Marilyn, served on the committee for the Race for the Cure, the fund-raiser for breast cancer research that Tipper Gore had been instrumental in launching. Al and I both ran in the race several times. I also was good friends with a wonderful Mississippi lawyer named Frank Hunger. Frank's wife—Al Gore's sister—had recently died of cancer, and Marilyn and I had gone to the memorial service. Afterward, we'd been part of a small dinner party at the Gores' vice-presidential mansion on the grounds of the U.S. Naval Observatory.

I couldn't talk directly to the vice president about the allegations any more than I could talk directly to the president. They were, after all, subjects of the investigation. But I did hear from people in the White House that Al had said to the president and his protectors, "I don't know why you're so upset at Freeh. He's just doing his job." Certainly, his conduct toward me reflected that attitude. I have always had tremendous respect for Al Gore, and in this instance, an investigation found no evidence of any improper activity.

Hillary Clinton, I think, got it, too. I had almost no dealings with her, socially or professionally. Like the president, though, she had been the subject of our investigative attentions and might well have resented it. But on the one occasion when I did spend some time with her—at the May 2000 funeral services for Cardinal John O'Connor, the Roman Catholic archbishop of New York—I had no sense of hostility on her part. (John Cardinal O'Connor, Navy admiral chaplain and the best archbishop New York ever had, was a great friend and teacher. Over the years he had personally expended great efforts, prayers, and real help to dozens of FBI agents and their families—especially to me. Later, Cardinals McCarrick and Law continued this special ministry to the FBI family, who revered both of them.) By chance, Hillary Clinton and I sat side by side and shared a hymnal that day. She seemed perfectly at ease.

Not so her husband. With him, it always seemed to be personal.

"I didn't believe Freeh was foolish enough to think the Democratic party would knowingly accept illegal contributions from the Chinese government," Clinton writes in his autobiography; "he was just trying to avoid criticism from the press and the Republicans, even if it damaged our foreign policy operations."

That's his take. Maybe he has even convinced himself it's true. Certainly, I've seen the charge made often enough, by the president's defenders and apologists, that it no longer angers or surprises me. But Clinton couldn't have this more wrong.

Men and women I was being paid to oversee and for whom I had the highest regard had uncovered without any direction on my part a troubling pattern of very aggressive fund-raising that included shadowy figures such as John Huang, and questionable practices such as overnight White House stays for the largest donors. We didn't know if illegal acts were involved, but the Campcon Task

Force had turned over a rock and found a situation highly conducive to illegal acts with lasting consequences—acts that might subvert the integrity of our political system if they went unchecked. I believe I would have lost the respect of the agents who served under me had I not pursued the investigation further. What's more, I believe I would have deserved to lose their respect had I failed to do so. It might have come as a surprise to the man who hired me, but I didn't take the job of FBI director so I could roll over and play dead whenever it became convenient for the White House.

To me, the only logical way to carry out the investigation and insulate it from political influence was through invoking the independent counsel statute. Janet Reno and I happened to disagree on that. She felt the investigation could be left in the hands of a special prosecutor appointed by and responsible to the attorney general. We hashed the matter over in the way we hashed over many matters during our joint tenures: very civilly, very thoroughly, very legally tethered. We both felt strongly about the matter—we both felt strongly about many matters—but it was never personal with either of us.

I happen to think Janet got bad advice on the matter from her Public Integrity Office. Others, including Pat Moynihan, the late Democratic senator from New York, agreed with me. In effect, sticking with a special prosecutor meant that the attorney general and the director of the FBI would be simultaneously investigating the president and vice president and reporting to them, and I didn't see how we could do that. Furthermore, the law provides a reasonable alternative in such dilemmas: independent counsels who are appointed by and report to the courts.

That's the route I thought we had to take with Campcon, and finally, after much debating back and forth, I wrote a twenty-seven-page memo plus cover letter (and I literally did write most of it myself) stating as much and summing up the case as I saw it. That, of course, is the document that found its way to the press and set Janet at odds with Dan Burton, touching off yet another firestorm that never should have been. (Another thing that's impossible to understand until you actually sit in one of Washington's hot seats is how *much* leaks drive the news cycle in the capital and in the nation as a whole.)

Was I right, even though I didn't prevail? Maybe not, if outcome is the only measure. Although a grand jury did meet on Campcon, although indictments were issued and cases brought and made, the president and vice president were never charged; and I have no reason to think they might have been, had an independent counsel handled the investigation instead of a special prosecutor. To that extent, my argument was largely academic. But process counts, too, and maybe counts more in the long run than outcome. An independent counsel would have given the public confidence that the case had been seen through in the right way, not in a political vacuum—there is no such thing with matters like this—but at least within a reporting hierarchy that encouraged free and open investigation. To me, that was the point: not the journey's end but how we got there. This time, I lost.

The last thing in the world I would have wanted going into the office of director of the FBI was to conduct a criminal investigation of the president. I never considered it a possibility when I was weighing whether to take the job, never contemplated it, never threw it into the balance. The lost resources and lost time alone were monumental. There was always this cloud of confusion about how to insulate my office and the Bureau and the Justice Department from the president to whom we reported. Under the shadow of the almost constant investigations, so much that should have been straightforward became problematic in the extreme.

We were in the midst of Campcon when Secretary of State Madeleine Albright asked for a briefing on our case findings prior to a trip she was about to make to China. The request was perfectly appropriate. China was obviously under our scrutiny. What's more, we had uncovered in the course of the investigation information that a secretary of state should know. Everything we were learning suggested that the Chinese intelligence services, presumably with support from the highest reaches of the PRC government, had devised and liberally funded a campaign to influence and compromise elected American officials. That's a big deal, with potentially big consequences, but for Janet Reno and me, Madeleine's request was also a big headache. Although she had never been part of Campcon—indeed, hadn't been a part of the Clinton administration until after the 1996 election was over—Madeleine Albright reported to the president just as we did. How much could we tell her, then, about an ongoing criminal investigation into the activities of her boss? Finally, we gave her the briefing she requested but refrained from disclosing what would be grand jury material.

We went through basically the same song and dance a second time with Jamie Gorelick, then the deputy attorney general. Jamie took the stance that we had to share everything we were learning in the course of Campcon with the White House because national security was at stake. I found her request completely inappropriate, way out of line. I was in Egypt when all this came to a head, so Jamie, Janet Reno, and I hashed it out over the phone. My argument was simple. We couldn't be put in the position of sharing the details of an ongoing criminal case with the subjects of that investigation. Janet struggled with the matter but came down on my side, so we constructed a compromise briefing that gave the White House the necessary national security information but excised the criminal elements.

As part of that decision to keep the president's people in the loop on our investigation, we sent two fairly senior FBI agents over to the National Security Council to bring Rand Beers up to speed on our findings. (A council member under multiple presidents, Beers in all likelihood would have become national security adviser had John Kerry won the 2004 election.) Sometime afterward, Bill Clinton wandered into the White House press room and got asked by a reporter how his administration could have allowed the Chinese government the opportunity to influence an American presidential election. Granted, the president must have been feeling under siege by then. Ken Starr had begun his investigations. We were still doing ours. But his answer that day in the press room was a miracle of dissembling. If the FBI had just told us about what was going on, he said, we would have taken steps to make sure there was no undue influence. Next thing I knew, the reporters were on my doorstep, wondering why the FBI had been so derelict in its duty.

It's not in my character to lose my temper. I don't yell, scream, pound the table, curse. I have never done that, as everyone who has ever worked with me knows. That's just not my personality. But I came awfully close to doing all those things when I heard about the president's response. First, I called in the two agents who had briefed Rand Beers. Listen, I said, this is very important. What did you tell him? They said, we told Beers the Chinese Ministry of State Security—their CIA—had formulated a plan to influence the U.S. elections. Are you sure? I asked. They were. Then, since it was inconceivable to me that Rand Beers wouldn't have conveyed what he had been told up the chain to the president, I helped to draft a press statement that said, in effect, the White House was lying.

"Are you sure you want to go with this?" one of my top aides asked as were looking over the statement. "Maybe we should just forget about it."

"No," I said, "I don't want to let it go." And I didn't. We issued the press release as drafted. Later the White House corrected its earlier statement with as little fanfare as possible.

———

I felt as if I had gotten myself involved in some schoolyard drama: *Yes, you did. No, I didn't.* Then, just when I thought things couldn't get any more outlandish, along came Monica Lewinsky and turned the White House into a theater of the absurd.

Monicagate, or whatever you want to call it, was in Ken Starr's bailiwick, not mine. He had been the court-appointed independent counsel for several years by then, and as mandated by law, he carried out his investigation independent of any government agencies. The FBI detailed agents to Starr's office. We continued to pay their salaries while they worked for the independent counsel, and we determined their next assignments when they were through. But so long as they were assigned to Ken Starr—and so long as they felt that nothing in the investigation was compromising their own ethics or integrity—the agents reported to him, not me. I have always had tremendous respect for Ken Starr and never more so than during those most challenging times when he proved himself a lawyer of great integrity and trustworthiness.

It was FBI agents assigned to Ken who grilled Monica Lewinsky at the Pentagon City Ritz-Carlton Hotel on January 16, 1998, a moment that some still smolder over. For the most part, it was also these specially assigned agents who pursued the case although the Bureau itself was catching enormous flak along the way. I don't write that to pass the buck or to disavow the conduct of the agents involved. In fact, I can't say for certain how they did behave. I never debriefed them later, and the firewalls erected between the Bureau and independent counsel's staff forbid the sort of regular briefings I might otherwise have expected. I'm very proud, though, that so far as I know, no charges were ever filed with the Bureau's Office of Professional Responsibility about the behavior of the agents on loan to Ken Starr, either from Monica's camp or from the president's side. That's a rarity in any circumstance. I mention the whole business here only to clear up the record because I've been asked more than once how the FBI could have allowed itself to be drawn so deeply into the scandal. We weren't, and we didn't. But we also weren't completely out of the loop or immune to the craziness that followed.

One story should suffice to catch the spirit of those times. In addition to agents, we were statutorily obligated to provide the independent counsel's office with support services—laboratories, technicians, and the like, as needed. It was in that capacity that Ken called me one day. The infamous semen stain had been discovered on Lewinsky's little blue cocktail dress. His investigators needed a DNA sample from President Clinton to see if the two matched up, and he wanted us to obtain one.

"Wait a minute," I can remember saying to Ken. "This is ridiculous. We're talking about taking a DNA sample from the president of the United States to compare with semen on a dress? This is like something out of a bad movie!"

But the bad movie was just beginning. We were obliged to honor the independent counsel's request, so we opened negotiations with the president's people and put together a plan. We would send over to the White House our chief DNA scientist from the lab, along with an FBI agent to serve as a witness, and one of Ken Starr's lawyers just to make sure everything stayed on the up-and-up. To assure this was done in as confidential a manner as possible, the White House insisted that there be no obvious deviation from the president's public activities. Our team was to arrive unannounced, well in advance of a scheduled dinner, and hide itself inside a little antechamber near the dining room. At some point during the meal, the president would excuse himself, presumably to answer a call of nature, and slip into the room where the guys in the lab coats were waiting. They would obtain Clinton's DNA material and send him back to his dinner with no one the wiser. Then our team would wait until everyone had left the White House and sneak out into the night with its tiny portion of DNA from the president of the free world.

It sounds almost simple as I tell it, but it wasn't that at all. The Secret Service had to be involved because they would be expected to accompany Clinton when he left the dinner and because you don't jab a needle into the president of the United States without clearing it first. The White House is also under constant surveillance. Smuggling anyone in and out of it takes intricate planning. Just to make sure nothing went wrong, I asked our chief DNA scientist to come see me in my office shortly before the Great Event.

"Listen," I said, marooned somewhere between dismay, anger, and involuntary humor, "if this thing leaks out, we're all going to be fired. I'm going to fire you, and then I'm going to fire myself. Don't talk about this to anybody. Don't mention it anywhere!" No one did, but the logistics just to achieve what never should have had to be done were unbelievable.

Decorum, reasoning, the dignity of the office—the longer the Clinton second term dragged on, the more farcical it became and the more ass backward everything seemed to get.

As a former prosecutor and federal judge, I take claims of executive privilege very seriously. Just like any citizen, a president has to be free to communicate with his attorney in the knowledge that whatever is said between them will remain confidential. He ought to be able to get the best advice he can on a variety of matters without expecting what's asked and what's said to spill out into the public domain. But Bill Clinton and his lawyers seemed to be inventing some new executive privilege every fifteen minutes or so, both to keep the wraps on potential witnesses and to forestall turning over documents.

It's hard to say when the claims hit rock bottom—there were so many of them—but to me, I think that moment came when the president tried to invoke an "executive protection privilege" to prevent Secret Service agents from testifying before a grand jury during the Campcon investigation. According to the claim, an agent could not testify about what he or she heard the president say or saw him do even if it was criminal because requiring an agent to do so would compromise the security and protection of the president since, in the future, a president might not want to have the Secret Service around when he's committing a crime.

The argument was pure craziness. A dozen comedy writers couldn't invent anything more ludicrous, but of course, the Secret Service had to lend its support and the president's lawyers had to do their bit for it and the court had to waste its own time considering the matter before it did the obvious, which was to throw the "executive protection privilege" out the door. But even that wasn't the worst of it. Claiming so many different and novel executive privileges weakened the existing and necessary ones by stretching the entire concept of executive privilege to the breaking point. And the battles went on, right to the bitter end.

Throughout all this, I continued to have the greatest regard for Clinton's lawyer, the legendary Bob Bennett. One of the best lawyers of our times, Bob's honesty, skill, and humanity was always at its best. We later became good friends.

Given the state of my relationship with Bill Clinton, it was no surprise that the Bureau was kept in the dark about the pardons and commutations the president intended to issue on his last day in office. But that didn't stop us from worrying about what he might do.

Of particular concern was a Native American named Leonard Peltier. By January 2001, Peltier had spent a quarter century in jail, serving two life sentences for the 1975 murders of FBI agents Jack Coler and Ronald Williams. The murders had taken place during the siege at Wounded Knee in South Dakota, on the same Pine Ridge Reservation where the U.S. Cavalry had confronted the Lakotas' ancestors more than eighty years earlier. I remembered the murders well—Coler and Williams were gunned down while I was doing my Quantico training to be an agent—and I remembered the manhunt that netted Peltier and his trial and imprisonment, and his 1979 escape and recapture.

In the years since, Peltier, like the siege at Wounded Knee itself, had become a left-wing cause célèbre: Robert Redford, Whoopi Goldberg, and Nelson Mandela had all called for Peltier's release. Even Mother Teresa had put in a good word for him. I didn't discount their concerns, and I knew that Wounded Knee was a convoluted story. But about Leonard Peltier I had, and still have, no confusion. He murdered those agents, and he deserves to spend the rest of his life in jail. But I also knew that Bill Clinton loved the grand gesture and was particularly susceptible to the tug of the Hollywood crowd.

Back in 1994, when we got word that the Peltier lobby was leaning hard on the president for his release, I prepared several memos for the attorney general to send over to the White House. I wanted to be sure that Janet saw them, that she was familiar with our reasoning, that she knew why we opposed any kind of leniency in Peltier's case. I took the argument public, just to be certain there was no confusion anywhere, and we also spoke to the pardon attorneys, who assured us they would send notice if anything was about to be done. As for myself, I was ready to submit my resignation as director the moment Peltier was freed, whenever it happened. I never told the president that, or sent word through someone who could have told him, but I knew that I could not in good conscience continue to serve under those circumstances.

When the drumbeat on Peltier's behalf ebbed, I breathed a sigh of relief, but as the president neared his last hours in office, many of us in the Bureau worried that he might, in fact, finally free Peltier, this time to get back at what he considered his own abuse at the hands of the FBI. He didn't, but he didn't stint on other insults.

I look back now on the 177 pardons and commutations Clinton issued as his final act of office, and I'm still stunned by the fact that neither the FBI nor the attorney general of the Department of Justice was ever consulted about a single one of them. Clinton pardoned his own brother, Roger, on a 1985 cocaine conviction. He pardoned former Arizona governor Fife Symington, whose high school roommate had later been Bill Clinton's roommate when he was attending college at Georgetown University. Closer to home, he also pardoned his former coinvestor in the White River land deal, Susan McDougal, though not her husband, Jim.

Article II, Section 2 of the Constitution gives the president "the power to grant reprieves and pardons for offenses against the United States," but giving reprieves and pardons out almost as party favors and to some of those closest to him wasn't what the Founding Fathers had in mind. Just as he had tainted the concept of executive privilege through his frequent and inventive use of it, so Clinton now tainted the old and honorable tradition of presidential mercy by his inability to rein in his own instincts, by his penchant for excess.

One name on the pardon list floored me far more than any other: Marc Rich. Along with his partner, Pincus Green, Rich had fled to Zug, Switzerland, nearly two decades earlier, hard on the heels of being indicted on more than fifty counts of fraud, racketeering, and tax evasion. Rich had rigged up an oil-price-fixing scheme during the energy crunch in the early '70s. Later in the decade, he had illegally sold oil to the Iranians when they were holding U.S. citizens hostage in Tehran. He'd cooked his own books and evaded paying taxes on something like $100 million in illegal profits. If he'd been given the maximum sentence on all the counts against him, he would have been serving three hundred years in prison—multiple lifetimes. Instead he was living in the scenic Alps. Nor was he at death's door, which would have at least introduced an element of compassion into Clinton's pardon. Rich was sixty-five years old, in the pink of health, and now he was free to come and go in the United States as much as he wanted and thumb his nose at all those who had spent years trying to get him behind bars.

I was in the U.S. Attorney's Office for the Southern District of New York, serving under Rudy Giuliani, when we went after Marc Rich. Rudy, who would later become the Republican mayor of New York, wasn't consulted on the pardon. Nor was my colleague Sandy Weinberg, who had been the lead counsel on the case. Nor was Janet Reno, who was by definition the government's highest-ranking lawyer and should have had a say in the matter. I had long been beyond the pale as far as Bill Clinton was concerned, but I should have been consulted, too. Rich was a fugitive, after all. He might have been enjoying the life of Riley, but warrants existed for his arrest. It might have been nice to let the FBI know beforehand that we could tear them all up and roll out the red carpet instead. At the least, the president could have given us an advance peek at his plans, but we didn't find out Marc Rich was a free man until the morning of George W. Bush's inauguration.

All that was damning enough—it was worse than that—but Rich's former wife, Denise, was the final straw. A political fund-raiser and a longtime advocate for her ex-husband's pardon, Denise Rich had donated more than a million dollars to the Democratic Party during the eight years Bill Clinton had been president. Even if the pardon had had any merit, the stench of the circumstances should have been enough to dissuade the president. It didn't, of course. That wasn't Bill Clinton.

I'll leave the final word on my ex-boss and the forty-second pres-ident of the United States to one of Clinton's former students from his days as a professor at the University of Arkansas School of Law, Susan Weber Wright.

Although she had been appointed a U.S. district judge by the first President Bush, as I was, Wright had enjoyed a temporary hero status among Clinton supporters when she dismissed a suit against the president by Paula Jones. In that case, Wright had ruled that even if Jones's claims were true, they didn't amount to a violation of her civil rights as the suit claimed. But that didn't end the matter. On January 17, 1998, the president had been deposed as part of the discovery in Jones's suit, and in that session he had denied having sexual relationships with Monica Lewinsky. Eight months later, the president acknowledged in a national address that, while his testi-mony in the Jones trial was "legally accurate," he had indeed en-joyed a relationship with the former White House intern that was "not appropriate" and "wrong."

For Judge Wright, that was enough. She cited Clinton for civil contempt for lying about his relationship with Lewinsky—the first time a sitting president has ever been so cited—and she asked the Arkansas Supreme Court's Committee on Professional Conduct to determine whether the president should forfeit his license to prac-tice law in the state. The committee did eventually decide to sus-pend Bill Clinton's license for a period of five years, embarrassment enough, but it was the words of Judge Wright's April 13, 1999, de-cision that I found so searing.

"The court takes no pleasure whatsoever in holding this nation's president in contempt of court and is acutely aware, as was the Supreme Court, that the president 'occupies a unique office with powers and responsibilities so vast and important that the public interest demands that he devote his undivided time and attention to his public duties,'" she wrote, ". . . [but] there simply is no escaping the fact that the president deliberately violated this court's discovery orders and thereby undermined the integrity of the judicial system."

In case anyone missed the point, Judge Wright drove it home again:

"Simply put, the president's deposition testimony regarding whether he had ever been alone with Ms. Lewinsky was intentionally false, and his statements regarding whether he had ever engaged in sexual relations with Ms. Lewinsky likewise were intentionally false, notwithstanding tortured definitions and interpretations of the term 'sexual relations.'

". . . [T]he President's contumacious conduct in this case, coming as it did from a member of the bar and the chief law enforcement officer of this nation, was without justification and undermined the integrity of the judicial system."

Maybe I'm simply a law freak, a stick in the mud. Maybe I lack an adequate appreciation for the distinctions between the public and private man. Bill Clinton still argues that Ken Starr and all the other prosecutors who went after him were trying to "criminalize" his personal life. It might surprise the ex-president, but I actually have some sympathy for that argument, at least in broad terms. Ken Starr decidedly *was not* among them, but I do think there were people out to get Bill Clinton, people who would stop at virtually nothing to bring him down. You could argue that Clinton didn't have to offer up so many targets, but fair's fair, and the president did get hammered from all sides.

Judge Wright's contempt citation had nothing to do with the relationship per se; it had to do with the president's shameful efforts to cover up the relationship. As an attorney, as a onetime law professor and state attorney general, Bill Clinton knew the rules. He knew what the law and the legal code of ethics required of him, and in an attempt to save his skin, he intentionally violated those rules and sullied the highest office in the land. To me, it was the most devastating moment of my entire tenure as director. I thought and I still think that the presidency hit an all-time low with that citation, perhaps only equaled by Richard Nixon, about as low as a benchmark can go.

If a federal judge were ever to say those same words or their equivalent to me, and if I knew them to be true as Bill Clinton must know them to be, I think I would be so devastated that I might never show my face in public again. The ex-president, however, seems to suffer no such pangs of conscience. Perhaps that says more than I could possibly add here.

Politics is the air Washington breathes, the water it drinks. It also can be the germ that infects you, and in the almost eight years I served as FBI director under Bill Clinton that danger was always present. We were investigating a sitting president during one of the most partisan periods in modern American history. Comity had broken down on Capitol Hill, particularly in the House of Representatives. Charges and countercharges flew every which way, but in all that time, there was never once a Democrat or a Republican who charged publicly that I had politicized the office I held or the Bureau I led or who called for my removal.

The closest anyone came was when Representative Bob Livingston of Louisiana, the Republican chairman of the House Appropriations Committee, got it in his head that my chief counsel, Howard Shapiro, had tipped the White House off to some investigation we were undertaking that might involve administration members. The charge was ridiculous. Howard is both an incredibly able attorney and absolutely honest. But Livingston wouldn't let the matter drop. He wanted Howard to resign or, failing that, wanted me to fire him.

I went up to the Hill for one of the annual Appropriations Committee hearings. Normally a subcommittee chairman handles those matters, but Livingston himself showed up, clearly upset and loaded for bear, and started firing off all sorts of questions about Howard that had nothing to do with the matter at hand. Finally, I called him on it.

"Mr. Chairman," I said, "if you're not happy with what I'm doing, ask for my resignation. You do that, and I'll take it very seriously."

He didn't. In fact, he backed off completely, never raised the issue again, and before too much longer was gone from Congress himself. But no one else called for my resignation either, then or at any other point, despite the deeply contentious political climate. That's not something to be proud of. Keeping the director's office politics-free should be baseline behavior, not the exception. But when I look back on my eight years in the post, I'm pleased that I was able to walk that fine line so successfully.

CHAPTER 10

9/11

I'll never forget one of the last times I ever saw my mother alive. I'd started a new job that very day, as senior vice chairman of MBNA America, the giant credit-card issuer headquartered in Wilmington, Delaware. I had been gone from the director's job for a little over two months by then, but Marilyn and the boys were staying on in Great Falls, Virginia, until the end of the year to ease the dislocation of a move. I was on my own, a temporary bachelor. MBNA and I had agreed that I would work part-time until after my mother died. She had only days left, and I wanted to be by her side as much as possible.

Mom was in the Palisades Medical Center, across the Hudson River from the Upper West Side of Manhattan and just below the bluff of Braddock Park, where I had played so many days as a kid. As I left the hospital that evening, a little after midnight, I looked down the river as I often did to admire the skyline of New York City. As always, the twin towers of the World Trade Center were glittering in the distance, the tallest and last things to be seen looking south across the island. September 11, 2001, was just beginning.

Marilyn was the first person to let me know what was happening. I was finding my way around a new office in Wilmington when she called to say that a commercial airliner had flown into the upper floors of one of the WTC towers. The place was on fire. An evacuation was under way. If I had been more focused on my old life than on my new one at that moment, I might have seen the warning signs more clearly, but like most people, I thought it was just a horrible, horrible accident.

When Dale Watson, the FBI's assistant director for counterterrorism, called forty-five minutes later, the entire terrain had changed. The second tower had been hit. Dale told me that we were in the midst of a major attack. By then, his reaction was much the same as mine. We grieved for the people who had been injured and killed, but we also realized that the moment we had both feared and fought against had finally arrived. Dale and I had seen up close the war the enemy was waging on us in the Middle East and Africa. Now they had brought the fight to our own shores.

If there was any good at all to be found in the mayhem spreading across our television screens, it was that our government could no longer look away from places like Khobar Towers, no longer look away from the ruins of our embassies in Nairobi and Dar es Salaam or the almost sunk USS *Cole*. Because of what had happened and because of where it happened, America would finally have to go to war in return. The events of the next hour or so—the hit on the Pentagon, the plane downed near Shanksville, Pennsylania—only confirmed for both of us what our hearts and minds first told us. (I feel certain, by the way, that the Shanksville airliner was headed for the U.S. Capitol. It's a more powerful symbol abroad than the White House, and al Qaeda was going for the most potent American symbols it could find.)

I drove back to my mother's hospital again that afternoon, a trip normally of about two hours that, on that infamous day, took more than triple that time. From my mother's hospital window, we could see a pall of dust hanging over the site where the World Trade Center had been. Very soon, the victims across the river would start to take on a more personal face. My former international terrorism chief John O'Neill lay dead somewhere inside the rubble. He had been with Dale Watson and me in Saudi Arabia five years earlier, on the heels of the bombing at Khobar Towers. Less than a year earlier, in October 2000, John and I had stood side by side on the deck of the USS *Cole* after it had been attacked and nearly sunk by al Qaeda operatives. FBI special agent Leonard Hatton was also dead in the rubble. Like John O'Neill, Hatton gave his life helping to evacuate those who were still trapped in the towers. Every director bleeds for the violent death of every brave man and woman who served under his watch, and I still bleed for both men. Somewhere in that debris, too, were people I had grown up near and gone to school with.

A few days after 9/11, as the nation was mourning its losses and trying to understand what had happened, my father, my brothers, and I buried my mother. At every level—personal, public, and professional—it was as sad a time as I have ever known.

By now, hundreds of thousands of pages of newsprint, untold broadcast hours, and dozens of books have been devoted to parsing what went wrong on 9/11. Both the Clinton and the Bush administrations have been blamed at least partially, and so has just about every relevant agency under both presidents. The Federal Aviation Administration paid insufficient attention to airplane security. The Immigration and Naturalization Service and the State Department and Customs should have done a better job of guarding our borders. The CIA didn't have ears where it should have been listening or eyes where it should have been looking. At the FBI we lacked technological sophistication, and we let what could have been vital intelligence get trapped in the bureaucracy.

I've added my own accounts to the towering pile of words in testimony before the Joint Intelligence Committees on October 8, 2002, and before the National Commission on Terrorist Attacks on April 13, 2004, and in articles for the *Wall Street Journal*. Along the way I've picked up praise for how I ran the FBI in the eight years preceding the attacks and I've been hit with a few brickbats, too.

In these pages let me summarize what I've learned and what I've come to believe about that worst moment in our current American history: what went wrong at the core, what went right in the margins, and why I think we as a nation were fundamentally unprepared for what happened that day.

First, on the FBI and technology: we were in the Dark Ages. The most basic wonders of the computer revolution had not yet arrived at the Bureau. My guess is that the average twelve-year-old sitting at a desktop PC anywhere in America on the evening of September 10, 2001, had more computing power at his fingertips than almost any FBI agent had available at his or her workstation. That's a pathetic record. We needed improved technological capacity desperately, but it's not like we didn't know it.

For years we had been asking Congress, almost begging it, for the money to upgrade our information technology systems, and for years Congress had been turning us down. The numbers get hard to follow here, but let me try to summarize them because I think the lesson is important. As early as 1992, before I came on board, the Bureau had begun planning for what became known as the Information Sharing Initiative, or ISI. The goals were less than ambitious by modern computing standards, but they're a measure of how far behind the times the Bureau had fallen. We wanted to replace outdated desktops, upgrade network capacity so agents could electronically exchange large files and images, improve our analytical capacities, and allow information sharing with other law-enforcement and intelligence agencies. (That last item takes serious planning, by the way. The last thing anyone would ever want is for hackers to get into our files.) To fund all this, we estimated a cost of about $432 million. Then, once we had the plan together and the development work taken care of, we set out to find the money.

In 1998, we asked Congress for a total of $70 million for new technology: $20 million in basic funding for information technology and $50 million in new budget authority for ISI. Congress gave us $2 million of the requested $50 million, but it forbade us from spending any funds on ISI until we submitted a comprehensive implementation plan to Congress. Two years later we came back again, this time asking for $58.8 million: $20 million for base funding and $38.8 million in new budget authority for ISI. We got no new budget authority this time, and we were again prohibited from redirecting available funds to ISI. Meanwhile, the implementation plan we had submitted (and resubmitted) to Congress was caught up in a meat grinder over whether the work would be done in-house or by outside contractors, how the staging would be handled, and what the ultimate cost should be. When Congress finally did see a plan it could approve, the bottom line was less than half what we had initially proposed, not even adjusted for inflation.

If finding the money was hard, recruiting the people who could help us do the planning was no less difficult. Even relatively mid-level programmers were making fortunes in Silicon Valley in the late 1990s, at least by government pay standards. By an act of sheer good fortune, I was recommended to Bob Dies, who had run network operations for IBM. By even greater fortune, Bob had always wanted to work for the FBI and was looking for a challenge, and Lord only knows, we had that waiting for him. I remember so well Bob's comment after he had completed his first in-depth review of our technology:

"You guys aren't on life support," he said. "You're dead!"

Bob was right, and he would be a large part of the remedy. But we never could have gotten Bob on board had he not had a burning desire to serve his country. For salary, the best we could do was maybe 20 percent of what he had been previously earning. We couldn't pay his moving costs either—standard practice in the private sector but a no-go when someone is being brought in from the outside to fill a government post.

It was Bob Dies who devised the e-FBI plan that Congress finally accepted, Bob who designed the whole Trilogy system that would take us off life support and bring us into the twenty-first century of computing and information technology. But even then, even when we had an expert in shop and a plan Congress had signed off on and an obvious, desperate need, Trilogy was never wholly funded—and this *is* the point—until after September 11, 2001.

Money, though, is not everything. Common sense helps a little, too. Bob Dies was not only great at cutting to the chase, at zeroing in on what needed doing; he also was extremely practical. The system he devised was capable of meeting all our needs, of upgrading us to the levels necessary, but it was also fitted to the reality in which we, and he, had to work. In automotive terms, Bob designed us a highly reliable Chevrolet fitted perfectly to a Chevy frame. Problem was, the FBI later insisted on a Cadillac: all the bells and whistles, all the amenities, just put it on the existing chassis as best you can. Bob kept telling them they couldn't do it, that the extras would overwhelm the base. For his troubles, they drove him out the door, but that didn't stop his prediction from proving absolutely right. Last time I looked, the Bureau was paying $2 million to an outside research firm in a final effort to see if anything could be salvaged from its $170-million computer overhaul.

Even without adequate information technology or the funding to procure it, we weren't ignoring the threat of foreign terrorists in the United States and beyond our borders. Far from it. Ever since the 1993 attack on the World Trade Center, the Bureau had been all but obsessed with terrorism and its proponents.

Thanks to excellent investigative work by FBI agents and skilled prosecution by the U.S. Attorney's Office in New York, Sheikh Abdel Rahman, the head of a terrorist organization known as the Islamic Group, has been in prison since 1995, serving a life sentence plus sixty-five years for his lead part in the first attack on the World Trade Center. More important, as all of our CT agents knew, Rahman was the spiritual leader for the al Qaeda leadership. That same investigation uncovered and thwarted further plans by Sheikh Rahman to blow up tunnels, bridges, and landmark buildings in Manhattan, including the United Nations headquarters—the so-called Day of Terror plot.

Two of Rahman's associates in the 1993 attack, Ramzi Yousef and Khalid Shaikh Mohammed, escaped to Pakistan before we could apprehend them, but we never stopped pursuing either man. In 1995, FBI agents snatched Yousef out of a guesthouse in Pakistan known to be sponsored by Osama bin Laden and returned him to New York, where he was tried and convicted not only of the earlier World Trade Center bombing but also of a plot to destroy eleven U.S. airliners in flight over the Pacific. A year later, in 1996, our agents and the CIA narrowly missed grabbing Khalid Shaikh Mohammed as he was about to travel from the Qatari capital of Doha to the United Arab Emirates. We believe he was tipped off, but however he got away, it was a slipup with tragic consequences. Almost seven more years would pass before KSM, as he's known in the business, was run to ground, during which time he is believed to have masterminded the 9/11 attacks. But it wasn't for want of trying that we failed to get him.

In June 1997, FBI agent Brad Garrett seized Mir Aimal Kasi in a hotel in Pakistan and brought him back to the United States for trial. Four and a half years earlier, on January 25, 1993, Kasi had stood outside the entrance to the CIA headquarters in Langley, Virginia, and murdered in cold blood two employees while wounding three others. At Kasi's request, Garrett stood by his side as he was executed at the Greensville Correctional Center in Jarratt, Virginia in November 2002.

The rapid expansion of our overseas FBI legat offices, from seventeen to forty-four during my eight years as director, gave us unprecedented access to resources that had previously been denied to us. When forensic evidence suggested that the USS *Cole* had been attacked with an explosive manufactured in Russia, I called the director of the FSB, the internal security force carved out of the old KGB, and with his cooperation and that of his explosives experts, we were quickly able to pin down the source, an immense help in that case and a large step forward generally in the global effort to combat terrorism.

We shared freely from our end as well. FBI agents in New York procured and relayed to Egyptian authorities intelligence that resulted in the October 19, 2000, arrest of Alaa Abdul Raziq Atia, who was wanted for the 1997 massacre of fifty-eight foreign tourists and four Egyptian nationals at the popular Luxor pyramid site. Atia is also believed to have been plotting to assassinate Bill Clinton during the president's visit later that month to the summit on Middle East violence at Sharm el-Sheikh, the posh tourist center on the Sinai Peninsula, beside the Red Sea.

To open up lines of communications that would keep us in contact with intelligence and security agencies around the globe, I visited sixty-eight countries during my eight years as director and met with 2,100 foreign leaders: presidents, prime ministers, kings, emirs, my coequals, George Tenet's coequals, anyone who would see me who might be able to shed light on where the terrorists were hiding and what they were planning. I sometimes caught flak for those trips, just as I caught flak for rushing to Dhahran and East Africa and Aden. One critic suggested that having once been an agent myself, I was obsessed with the "culture of the field." But having once been an agent, I also knew that there's no substitute for looking someone in the eye—a thug, a world leader, it doesn't matter—if you want to take his or her measure and establish the sort of connections that can grow and spread. Washington headquarters are full of desk jockeys. I never hoped to be one of them.

Again, budget restraints hurt us. For fiscal year 2000, for example, we requested funding for 864 new counterterrorism positions within the Bureau at a cost of nearly $381 million. Congress approved five positions, funded to the tune of $7.4 million. Over the three fiscal years 2000–2002, we asked for a total of nearly 1,900 special agents, analysts, and linguists to enhance our counterterrorism program. In all, we got seventy-six people to fill those critical gaps, during a time when terrorist activity against the United States, both here and abroad, was clearly in the ascendancy. We desperately needed Arabic and Farsi speakers for our New York City office, where the bulk of the counterterrorism work was handled, but except for one brief exemption granted and later withdrawn by Congress, we couldn't pay higher than the mandated government salary for that position, an almost laughable figure given the competition in New York for such skills.

Officially, we were the lead government agency in fighting terrorism; in reality, we were allotted 3.5 percent of the total counterterrorism budget. Officially, too, there wasn't a man or woman in

Congress who wasn't four-square against the bad guys, but this was pre-9/11. Partisanship, not partnership, was the order of the day on Capitol Hill. To his great credit, Bill Clinton introduced the 1996 Anti-Terrorism Bill HR 2703. To its discredit, the House stripped the bill of just about every meaningful provision, then passed it overwhelmingly. Even today, post-9/11 and despite endless testimony from me, Congress refuses to grant law-enforcement agencies the authority and the resources to break down encrypted messages.

We were in a constant process of reallocating the Bureau's resources and reconfiguring its infrastructure to help us combat terrorism. We established a Counter-Terrorism Center at FBI headquarters and made certain it could work in tandem with the similar center at CIA headquarters. In 1999, we were finally able to move into our new Strategic Information and Operations Center so that, when the next crisis arrived, agents wouldn't be tripping all over each other and having to make sensitive calls on open lines.

In the 1980s, the FBI formed its first Joint Terrorism Task Force, bringing together expertise from multiple agencies to identify the roots of radical-fundamentalist terrorism in the United States. As the foreign terrorist threat mounted in the '90s, we tripled the number of such task forces so that we could better share intelligence and related information and operations with other federal, state, and local law-enforcement agencies. Simultaneously, we were setting up a National Defense Preparedness Office and organizing and carrying out countrywide, regional, and local training exercises to help prepare for terrorist attacks.

We poured vast amounts of resources, human and otherwise, into preventing violence at the sort of target-rich, high-profile venues terrorists crave: U.N. gatherings, World Cup matches, the national political conventions, Super Bowls, the 2002 Winter Olympics in Salt Lake City, and so many more. In 2001, in my final months as

FBI director, I recommended setting up an FBI training facility in Central Asia, similar to the one we had established in Budapest in 1995 and a second academy we were then launching in Dubai. The reasoning was the same as it had been six years earlier. We need the liaison and the critical points of contact that the training academies foster. Without them, we risk being blind and deaf.

As for Osama bin Ladin and al Qaeda, from at least the mid-1990s on, they were constantly on our radar screen, and at the highest level of concern. Working side by side with the CIA, we secured a June 1998 indictment charging bin Laden with plotting to murder American soldiers in Yemen in 1992. A year earlier, a clandestine CIA–FBI team operating quietly out of an unmarked building in Alexandria, Virginia, under the code name Alex Station had begun tracking the al Qaeda leader around the globe. In 1998, the group came up with a plan to snatch bin Laden out of a compound in Kandahar, Afghanistan, using U.S. Special Forces, FBI agents, and Afghani local forces. The scheme worked its way up the chain of command until it was finally killed by the military, which owned the assets that were to have been used. (George Tenet and I happened to agree that the chances of success were extaordinarily low, especially without Pakistan's cooperation.)

On August 7, 1998, al Qaeda forces attacked the U.S. embassies in Nairobi and Dar es Salaam. By November, we had secured a second indictment against bin Laden, charging him, his military commander, Muhammad Atef, and others with murder in those bombings. Five months later, in April 1999, we placed bin Laden on the FBI's Top Ten Most Wanted List, where he remains as of this writing. Simultaneously, we created a bin Laden Unit at FBI headquarters. Arrest warrants were flying around the globe for him. Like us,

Interpol was on the highest alert. Our own investigations jump-started similar ones all across Europe and in countries around the world, and every one of them filled in pieces of the puzzle.

Nor did we delude ourselves as to what Osama bin Laden and his organization might be capable of within our own borders. During the course of several major trials of al Qaeda members at the U.S. District Courthouse in lower Manhattan—my old court—we closed streets, brought in cement trucks as barricades, set up checkpoints, and employed hundreds of heavily armed New York City police officers and FBI agents to protect the courthouse and surrounding areas. The trials went off as planned, and the defendants, charged in the bombings of the East African embassies, were found guilty as we knew they would be.

In the early spring of 2000, I flew to Pakistan, and on April 6, the U.S. chargé d'affaires (we had no ambassador then) and I met with Pervez Musharraf. The meeting had originally been set for Islamabad, but we were diverted to the military headquarters at Lahore for security. It was, in a way, an odd setting. Although he also served as commander in chief of the army, having recently consolidated power, Musharraf was dressed in a business suit, yet the compound was martial in the extreme, decorated with military awards and trophies, and photographs of fighting units and their leaders.

I'd arrived with two goals. The first was to secure Musharraf's approval for a Pakistani intelligence officer to come to New York and testify against one of the suspects in the attacks on the East African embassies. The man in question had fled to Karachi after the bombings. There he had been detained by a border-patrol officer and subsequently turned over to the intelligence officer. Under interrogation, the suspect had made an incriminating statement, and that's what we wanted the officer to testify about. The Pakistani intelligence chief, who was also at the meeting, wanted to know if his officer's identity would be protected. No, I told him, we couldn't do that. Nonetheless, Musharraf agreed, and the suspect was later convicted for his part in the attacks.

The larger goal, by far, was to ask for Musharraf's personal assistance in helping us capture Osama bin Laden and bring him to justice for his role in the mass deaths at Nairoti and Dar es Salaam. Afghanistan was a no-man's-land. The Taliban had closed ranks around the al Qaeda leader. Musharraf and his intelligence chief had the sway to break that cycle and open the door for us if Musharraf so chose.

"I have some arrest warrants for bin Laden," I told the Pakistani leader. "You're probably the only person on earth who could serve these warrants right now."

Musharraf laughed and asked me to tell him more. I used the time to lay out what I felt was compelling evidence that proved al Qaeda's and bin Laden's involvement in the East Africa attacks. Musharraf was extremely engaged, very charming, and very knowledgeable about our interests. He resisted my suggestion that we permanently base FBI agents in his country—even the moderate political parties would be upset by that, he told me—but Musharraf readily agreed to let us send a second team, including additional FBI agents and an assistant U.S. attorney from New York, back to Pakistan to brief his staff in greater detail so they would know that our case was very factually based. Those briefings did take place, but in the end Musharraf refused to help. Taliban leader Mullah Omar, he said, had given his personal assurances that Osama bin Laden was innocent of the East African bombings and had abandoned terrorism. It was nonsense, but without Pakistan's assistance, Osama bin Laden was snug as a bug in a rug. The point, though, is that we never, ever stopped going after him.

And yet, of course, none of our efforts averted what was to

come. None of what we did stopped nineteen terrorists from hijacking four commercial airliners on September 11, 2001, and flying two of the planes into the World Trade Center towers, a third into the Pentagon, and a fourth—but for the bravery of the passengers aboard—into the heart of the nation's capital. We had rolled up an astounding array of terrorists, thwarted dozens of plots, increased our knowledge of terrorist networks exponentially. Thousands of men and women, our agents and others, had spent tens of thousands of hours in the hunt. Some had risked their lives time and again. But nothing we tried, nothing we did, prevented Osama bin Ladin from funding 9/11 or Khalid Shaikh Mohammed from planning it or Mohammed Atta and his coconspirators from carrying it out.

The question is, why?

If you had been able to look hard into President Bush's eyes on September 11th, in those first few minutes after he learned of the second hit on the World Trade Center towers, I believe you would have clearly seen a president coming to understand under the worst of circumstances that an entirely new paradigm is at play: that we are at war and that we had been at war without acknowledging as much to ourselves for half a decade; that the towers then being destroyed were not the opening salvo of a new global conflict but the culmination of a series of steadily escalating acts of a preexisting one.

I'm proud of the way I ran the FBI from September 1993 to June of 2001 and immensely proud of the people who served with me in the Bureau. But I still fault myself for many shortcomings during my tenure as director. Anyone who runs an organization as complex as the FBI and so much in the public eye and doesn't find fault with his performance is living in a fool's paradise as far as I'm concerned. You can always do the job better in hindsight, and if nothing else, 9/11 gave us all cause for that.

I regret that I was never able to convince Congress to fully fund our technological initiatives. I'm embarrassed that on the afternoon and evening of September 11, 2001, FBI agents had to send photos of the suspected terrorists via express mail service because they still lacked the computing power to scan and send images. I was no longer there, but I should have done better on my watch. In hindsight, the Bureau might have been more responsive to the July 2001 memo sent by one of our agents in Arizona, raising a red flag about the number of Middle Eastern men enrolled in U.S. flight schools and suggesting the Bureau query civil aviation schools around the country about their Arab or other Muslim students.

But there were roadblocks to the latter suggestion. Given existing federal privacy rules, we probably would have had to secure subpoenas to get the schools to open up their rolls. Even then, the task wouldn't have been easy. Most of the pilots in the world are trained in the United States because English is the most common language of air-traffic controllers and the Internet. Among those being trained were plenty of Arabs and people of Arab origin who were doing nothing more than paying good money in the hope of a better job.

But in theory—and I stress *theory*—if we had been able to do that, and if we had connected that information with the arrest the next month in Minnesota of Zacarias Moussaoui, the French-Moroccan who aroused a flight instructor's suspicions when he asked to learn how to fly a commercial airliner, and then tied that to the two al Qaeda cell members living in San Diego and to the earlier warnings that terrorists were plotting to use commercial flights as kamikaze planes, and used all that to get our North American Aerospace Defense Command, or NORAD, forces pointing inward inside of looking outward for foreign-launched air attacks, then perhaps 9/11 never would have happened, or would have happened at a lesser scale.

Believe me, I've asked myself plenty of times what I could have done to better prepare the Bureau to connect those dots. We had proved time and again—with the failed "Day of Terror," with the never-realized plan to blow up nearly a dozen commercial jets in flight over the Pacific—that good investigation leads to prevention. Maybe this time, it would have done so again. But the hard reality is that we simply did not have the operational and tactical intelligence in hand to make a 100 percent convincing case, and we lacked the political will and determination to close down our air-traffic system for even a single day with anything less.

The realization that we were at war altered the equation entirely. Until that moment, we dealt with terrorist attacks against U.S. targets as if the assaults were a law-enforcement issue like organized crime or white-collar crime. We were sifting through bomb sites, looking for the forensics that would help us secure indictments, then arming ourselves with arrest warrants. I don't know an agent who thought that was sufficient to the cause, or anyone who believed that a criminal investigation was a reasonable alternative to military or diplomatic action, but those are the tools we had available to us, the ones our legal system and our political system outfitted us with to wage the war on terrorism.

The enemy meanwhile was arming itself with trucks loaded with five thousand pounds of explosive, with suicide boats and 747s packed with our own people. Our warrants could help us snatch a Ramzi Yousef and bring him back to the United States to face justice. Their trucks and boats and planes could rip the face off a military barracks, split open embassies, topple the tallest towers in Manhattan, and set fire to the very headquarters of American military might. That's what we learned on 9/11: al Qaeda is not the Cosa Nostra, and Osama bin Laden is not a John Gotti or a Ted Kaczynski.

I had been in dozens of meetings before 9/11, sessions called

specifically to discuss terrorism. We all saw the problem. I can remember Senator Bob Kerrey using the phrase "acts of war" long
before the country was prepared to admit that's what they were.
We knew what steps to take, too. I'd served on the White House
Commission on Aviation Safety and Security—the so-called Gore
Commission, chaired by the vice president—convened to improve
air safety in the wake of the crash of TWA 800. Our report, issued
in February 1997, warned that the airline industry and operations
were vulnerable at multiple points to hijackings and terrorist attacks, but basically nothing was done about it. Politicians were
worried that the public wouldn't tolerate long lines at security
checkpoints. The airlines didn't want to spend the money to beef
up their own defenses. Appalled by the prospect of greatly increased user fees to help offset the proposed multibillion-dollar
changes, the Aircraft Owners and Pilots Association questioned the
commission's independence and objectivity. What should have
been a big step forward in the fight against terrorism devolved into
the usual inside-the-Beltway brawl.

I'd seen the evidence of the ongoing war with my own eyes, too,
at Dhahran, in East Africa, on the USS *Cole* at the Port of Aden, and
elsewhere. But until 9/11, we lacked the political leadership and
more important the political will to do what had to be done, and that
ran right across both administrations I served under.

During my scant five months in the first George W. Bush term, I
found the White House better organized than it had been under Bill
Clinton. Not surprisingly, I thought the new president had a more
personal touch than his predecessor. I was pleased that the Bush
team had been far more supportive than the Clinton one in going
after the Khobar Towers bombers and winning indictments against
them. But the nation's fundamental approach to Osama bin Laden
and his ilk was no different after the inauguration of January 21,

2001, than it had been before. We were fighting criminals, not an enemy force.

The Joint Intelligence Committees said as much in a report issued in December 2002: ". . . neither President Clinton nor President Bush nor their National Security Councils put the government or the Intelligence Community on a war footing before September 11th."

As a measure of our unwillingness to look reality square in the eye, the 2000 presidential campaign spoke volumes. Osama bin Laden and al Qaeda had repeatedly declared war on the United States—in a 1996 fatwa and again in 1998 in a more strongly worded directive to kill Americans anywhere. And they had backed up their words with bloody deeds. They were a clear and present danger, yet not only did we refuse to declare war back on them, we virtually refused to discuss the matter in public.

I will always remember standing on the deck of the USS *Cole* in mid-October 2000. A suicide boat had attacked the navy guided-missile destroyer, blown a forty-five-foot hole in her port side, and killed seventeen U.S. sailors. The explosion had rolled the side of the ship up as if it were the lid of some giant sardine can. In front of and below me, our agents and navy personnel were working with unbelievable care and respect as they removed human remains from the tangled mess of steel. It was monstrous, a clear act of war by a sworn opponent of the United States, right in the middle of a heated presidential campaign. Yet within forty-eight hours, the *Cole* had virtually disappeared from the news cycle. As for the campaign itself, the attack was a nonissue. I can't recall either candidate ever raising it, or the larger terrorist threat it spoke of, in any serious, ongoing way.

I had been the one who had gone to Pakistan in 2000 to ask for Pervez Musharraf's help in capturing Osama bin Laden because, before September 11, 2001, bin Laden was a law-enforcement issue. We had outstanding warrants against him. That was our reason for pursuing him. If our government had a different mind-set, the secretaries of state and defense would have been in Lahore with me, or instead of me. Or perhaps Sandy Berger. But that wasn't the case.

Yes, we had gone after bin Laden with a salvo of Tomahawk missiles back in 1998. That was the one exception, in retaliation for the embassy bombings in East Africa. Otherwise, he was always a legal problem, a fugitive from justice. Even the ambitious 1998 Alex Station plan to snatch bin Laden from his lair using Special Forces, FBI agents, and Afghani troops turned on the indictments we held. The Justice Department and the FBI were the ones with the standing to go after him because before 9/11, bin Laden was, by our government's definition, an international criminal, not an imminent national-security threat. Afterward, we saw him for what he was, the head of a shadowy army intent on carrying the terror war to our shores and murdering as many Americans as he could, anywhere the opportunity presented itself. The change in mind-set changed everything with it.

A small but telling example of what I'm talking about: it must have been early in 2000 when Brian Stafford, then the director of the Secret Service, called to ask for my help. Shortly after the Oklahoma City bombing in 1995, the section of Pennsylvania Avenue that runs in front of the Treasury Department, the White House, and the Old Executive Office Building had been closed to vehicular traffic, but the decision had never been popular with D.C. politicians or with commuters. The traffic that used to regularly rumble past the White House had been shuffled off to the streets to the north, creating new rush-hour choke points.

Local officials also didn't like the message sent by the concrete barricades at either end of that historic stretch of Pennsylvania Avenue. They feared tourists would be scared to visit a city that acted as if it were under siege. The barricades didn't sit well with some on the Hill either. America couldn't look scared. Aestheticians and prominent architects were tut-tutting over the barricades as well. The long-range plan was to create an attractive pedestrian mall in front of the White House, but for the moment, those chunks of concrete were plain ugly.

Finally, the White House itself had begun to buckle. D.C. mayor Anthony Williams and Eleanor Holmes Norton, the District's non-voting Democratic representative, had joined the fray. Pressure was building to let the cars roll by once more. That's why Brian Stafford had called. He wanted my help in convincing the White House that the barricades were necessary. I had our people do a computer simulation of what would happen if a van packed with bomb materials (Timothy McVeigh was our model) exploded as close to the White House as it could get with the barricades removed. According to our simulation, the entire West Wing would have been blown away, pulverized, incinerated, and everyone within it killed. Brian Stafford took those results to Sandy Berger—whose office happens to be in the West Wing—and the agitation to remove the barricades disappeared. But that's a good index of where most people's heads were prior to 9/11. As far as the White House was concerned, blocking off Pennsylvania Avenue was about politics, not national security.

We took the threat of terrorism very seriously as the end of the millennium neared. The celebrations planned across the nation and around the world to mark the flip-over from 1999 to 2000 were target-rich environments, rife with symbolic value. Terrorists love to play on apocalyptic fears. Al Qaeda in particular had shown in East Africa and in Yemen that it was capable of staging complex attacks beyond its own base, and of course a fatwa had been issued, religious authority to kill.

As events turned out, we were right to be concerned. Al Qaeda had planned a three-prong attack meant to span the globe. Ahmed Ressam was assigned, among other less lethal tasks, the job of bombing Los Angeles International Airport. Had he not been stopped by U.S. Customs inspectors as he tried to enter Washington State via ferry from Canada in a car packed with explosives, Ressam might even have succeeded. Instead, he was found guilty by a federal jury on nine counts of plotting terrorist attacks against millennium celebrations along the West Coast of the United States.

Jordanian intelligence services quashed an al Qaeda cell that had been charged with reducing to rubble the Amman Radisson, whose four hundred rooms had been booked almost entirely by Americans and Israelis gathered to celebrate the millennium. Other sites in Jordan had been targeted as well. One terrorist had boasted that there wouldn't be enough body bags in all of the kingdom to hold the dead. In Yemen, we simply got lucky. A *Cole*-like assault on a U.S. Navy destroyer, *The Sullivans,* failed when the attack vessel sunk in the mud under the weight of its own explosives.

By the afternoon of December 31, 1999, the FBI's Strategic Information and Operations Center, or SIOC, was already full. Representatives of every relevant governmental body were on hand, from the CIA to the Department of Defense, the White House, and on down the line—not necessarily the directors, the George Tenets and Bill Cohens, but senior people in a position to get things done in a hurry if necessary. The attorney general was there. So were all my top people. The place was packed. Every desk was taken, every room was full. It was the only time I would ever see the place bursting at the seams like that. And we weren't just sitting on our hands. At one point, we needed to throw together an electronic surveillance warrant related to the Ahmed Ressam investigation just then breaking open on the West Coast. I can remember picking up a pencil, hurriedly sketching out what the affidavit should say, and handing it over to the lawyers to begin processing.

Terrorism was on all our minds, and we all breathed with relief as word came in of the foiled plots and as networks and operatives related to them began to be rolled up. Each new midnight that passed east to west around the globe without major incident was a cause for minor celebration.

By a little before four that morning, when we finally stood down and had a quick debrief, every one of us at SIOC, I'm sure, felt good about what hadn't happened that night. We had put ourselves on a war footing, and because we had, we had dodged whatever horrors the bad guys had intended for us. But rather than celebrate that fact, I found myself worried about what would happen when we went back to business as usual. For one evening, New Year's Eve, we had seen the enemy for what it was and stared it down, but we had neither the will nor the resources to keep up the alert level. That's what really frightened me: not December 31, 1999, but January 1, 2000, and beyond.

It was not only the threat of terrorist attacks that had occupied our attention in the crisis center that long day and night. The fact is, we worried equally about the information infrastructure as we did about bombs, as much about databases lost as we did about people killed. That's where the bulk of the government's focus and the White House's attention rested: information security, not national security. Would computers fail to roll over to 2000 because of some fatal programming flaw? And if so, what would happen to the data stored within them? How about if banks, hospitals, insurers, and a whole raft of other data-dependent entities, private and public, lost their records? And how vulnerable were all these things to attack? For weeks we had had an entire SIOC wing set up as a 24/7 "watch center" to monitor and react to Internet attacks, infrastructure intrusions, anything that would threaten major components of the Internet or of critical-data business, government, or private sector continuity.

In retrospect, with 9/11 behind us, that seems foolish. How can we worry as much about a database as about an enemy who would eventually fly commercial aircraft into office towers and the Pentagon and kill Americans by the thousands? But that's the point I'm trying to make here: You can't read history backward.

All of which gets me to the self-appointed Paul Revere of 9/11, Richard A. Clarke. To hear Dick Clarke tell it, he was everywhere in the months, even years before September 11, 2001, prophetically warning of what was to so tragically befall this country. Presidents, cabinet secretaries, agency heads, national security advisers, leaders of Congress—they all had the benefit of his wisdom, apparently, and almost to a person they failed to heed it. I must have been among them because Clarke includes ten references to me in the index of his best-selling book *Against All Enemies*. But here's what I remember about Dick Clarke: almost nothing of any significance.

A career bureaucrat who began as an analyst in the Defense Department back in 1973, Clarke had been plucked off the National Security Council staff in May 1998 by Bill Clinton and appointed the first National Coordinator for Security and Counter-terrorism. As titles go, it has a golden ring, but access is what counts in Washington, and Dick Clarke had very little.

Janet Reno, myself, and others who were charged with monitoring and reacting to terrorist threats convened regularly with Sandy Berger to discuss national security issues. The deputy national security adviser would be on hand. So would other deputies at times, it wasn't just top dogs. But Dick Clarke was almost never included in these so-called principals meetings. Given the grandeur of his title, I found his absence conspicuous.

In his book, Clarke recounts a critical "principals" meeting close to the millennium celebration when Sandy Berger looked hard at Janet, George Tenet, and me, and said, " 'We have stopped two sets of attacks planned for the millennium. You can bet your measly federal paycheck that there are more out there and we have to stop them too. I spoke with the president and he wants you all to know . . . this is it, nothing more important, all assets. We stop this fucker.' "

Nice tale, but I was never at such a meeting, and Sandy Berger never would have spoken like that in front of the attorney general.

Clarke tells another nice tale that seems to have him at the epicenter of activity the night of the millennium, nervously monitoring activity around the globe from the Y2K Coordination Center at the White House, then darting up to the White House roof to watch the fireworks on the Mall, then back downstairs to keep an eye on midnight as it crept west toward Los Angeles, and finally back to the roof to pop a bottle in celebration at 3 A.M. East Coast time. Maybe it all happened exactly as he writes. But I know for a fact that everyone who really mattered, the serious people, were all in SIOC on December 31 from 1:00 in the afternoon until past 3:00 the following morning, and Dick Clarke wasn't among them. As for me, I was too tired to have champagne when the night was over. I just wanted to get home.

The same was true during the Bush administration. If he was rushing around the executive branch, trying to make a case that we were in imminent danger of a terrorist attack on our shores, he wasn't trying to make that case with me. He never spoke to me, never contacted me, never sent me a memo. I met often with Condoleezza Rice just as I had met often with Sandy Berger, and once again, Clarke was never there.

Clarke's portfolio shifted slightly in the Bush administration to information security, but in both roles he was basically a second-tier player. The only time he ever became visible was after a crisis. I'd turn on the secure television from the White House, and there Clarke would be, wanting to know in a very bureaucratic fashion what everyone was doing so he could report back to his superiors. As far as my senior associates and I were concerned, he never had a reputation as someone who pushed for things no one else wanted to do. That's the persona he created for himself post-9/11.

Nor is the other hero of Clarke's book, John O'Neill, the John O'Neill I knew. O'Neill, Clarke writes, was too aggressive for my tastes; he thought too much outside the box. He was so willing to break crockery in his pursuit of Osama bin Laden that we essentially drove him out of the Bureau, which is how he happened to be director of security at the World Trade Center complex on September 11, 2001.

I think I know why Clarke wrote those things. He and John O'Neill were very close, and he felt his death deeply, as I did. But the John O'Neill I worked with was never proposing anything different from what we were already doing. There was no notion within the Bureau that we were holding him back from any course of action. He did have authority over counterterrorism issues, and he was very good at supervising criminal investigations in places like East Africa. We could investigate, do forensic exams, interview witnesses, recruit informants, collect intelligence, but we couldn't go where the law wouldn't allow us to go. O'Neill knew that, and he acted accordingly.

One more thing: John O'Neill didn't quit the FBI in disgust

over our alleged temerity in fighting the terrorists. That's another myth that Clarke created after the fact of the 9/11 attacks.

For good measure, by the way, Clarke repeats in his book the rumor that I was a member of Opus Dei. Had he called me, I could have told him that was my brother, but he didn't bother. To me, that about says it all: bad facts and no access.

Epilogue

September 11, 2001, did change everything—for the FBI and the CIA, for the nation and the American people, even for the world generally. All of us live today with a fundamentally different mind-set than we woke up with on that awful morning. But 9/11 didn't change everything retroactively.

On the day before we could no longer ignore the war we were in, the FBI couldn't beg, borrow, or steal from Congress the funding necessary to fully upgrade and enlarge our counterterrorism manpower and operations. Far better to bankroll some new pork-barrel project back home where the voters are than to strengthen America's defenses against such an amorphous and undeclared enemy. On the day after we could no longer ignore war, Congress couldn't give us enough money, at least temporarily, and it couldn't pass the Patriot Act quickly enough either. Congress, too, could finally see in the aftermath of 9/11 that the old paradigm no longer held.

It wasn't as if we didn't have successful models of active intervention in front of us. In 1980, the Drug Enforcement Agency and the FBI obtained arrest warrants for Manuel Noriega, a narco-terrorist who also happened to be the head of a sovereign state. Nobody could have expected even heavily armed DEA and FBI agents to drive up to the presidential palace in Panama City and arrest Noriega. Yet that's essentially what happened after the *political* decision was made to invade Panama and support the arrest with overwhelming U.S. military force. Consequently, Noriega, whose years of drug trafficking killed at least as many Americans as died on 9/11, was brought back to the United States, tried, and convicted.

As with Noriega, so with Osama bin Laden. We were drowning in legal authorities to pursue him. We had warrants for his arrest; we had tried and convicted his lieutenants in heinous crimes against American citizens. Bin Laden was on the FBI Most Wanted List; he was all over Interpol. What we lacked wasn't the authority to pursue bin Laden and al Qaeda to the far corners of the earth. What we lacked was the spine to do it and the vision to see bin Laden and al Qaeda for what they were, and are.

By mid-August of 1998, Osama bin Laden had issued his fatwa against Americans everywhere. His forces had savaged the U.S. embassies in Dar es Salaam and Nairobi. Yet even then, the thought of going after him in his Afghan redoubt with anything more than an offshore Tomahawk attack seemed to pose unacceptable risks, politically and militarily. As late as 2000, the Clinton administration was considering and ultimately rejecting other plans to launch preemptive strikes against al Qaeda and their Taliban hosts and confederates. Again, the cost was too high, the political will lacking. By noon of September 11, 2001, with the World Trade Center towers reduced to rubble and the Pentagon still burning, everyone could see that the preemption had all been on the enemy's side. But the reality of September 10 and before is just not the same as the reality of September 11 and afterward.

September 11 was the difference—the bright line seared between a nation that sought to prosecute terrorists in its courts and one that hunted down and destroyed them using its global military might along with every available executive power.

In a grim sense, 9/11 brought order out of chaos. Sifting through the millions of bits and bytes of intelligence gathered every day by the FBI, the CIA, the National Security Agency, and many other outposts is like drinking from a fire hydrant. But war concentrates the attention in a way that peace never can. War begins to tell you what to look for and who to look for and where to go looking. The same intelligence data that had little or no context before 9/11 was crawling with it afterward.

September 11 also forced us, finally, to clarify the message we sent abroad to those who would be our enemies. For years, we had been feeding the terrorists' embedded belief that the United States lacked the fortitude to fight a real war against them. In 1983, when Iran's henchman surrogate, Hezbollah, murdered 243 marines in Beirut, Ronald Reagan responded by withdrawing U.S. military forces from the region. U.S. Navy divers, military attachés, CIA station chiefs, disabled cruise boat tourists, hundreds of innocent victims—Americans, Israelis, and Arabs—they all had been slaughtered wholesale for over two decades by ruthless terrorists virtually without fear of ever having to face American justice or military might. Iran's most senior leaders planned, furnished, and carried out the 1996 murders of nineteen U.S. servicemen at Khobar Towers. As I've already shown, we had the goods on them, cold, yet the Clinton administration miserably failed to seek any redress. When the fascist Ba'ath regime in Baghdad tried to assassinate the first President Bush, our government responded by firing a few missiles into the Iraqi Intelligence Service's headquarters, and by doing so after hours, to assure that we punished the cleaning staff of that genocidal organization rather than its leadership. Even Colonel Qaddafi's mass murder of Americans over Lockerbie, Scotland, would ultimately be resolved with the trial of two token henchmen and the payment of cash to the victims' families in lieu of real justice.

The image of a lumbering giant stumbling around with a sign on its back reading "Kick Me" was not lost on our enemies. Nor was the message hard to miss. From al Qaeda's risk analysis, what was there to lose in going after our embassies, our Aegis-class U.S. Navy cruisers, our citizens, even our homeland?

I think it's safe to say that we've gotten past that now. We send a different message these days, and America is a safer, not a more endangered, place for it. As individuals, we Americans may disagree on what battles to wage and where, for how long and with what resources, but as a nation we know we are at war.

It's no solace to the many, many families who lost loved ones on 9/11, but because of those attacks, we have begun to view the world as it is, not as we in our wonderful American naïveté hope it might be. That, I'm convinced, is the beginning of wisdom—but only the beginning. So much more remains to be done.

With respect to the FBI in particular, Congress must provide both the legal authority and significant new funding so that the Bureau and its agents can manage encryption technology. Of course, privacy advocates are going to worry, but there's no need for this technology to be any more intrusive than a wiretap on a phone line. Of course, the telecommunications industry wants to hold on to its trade secrets, but as I wrote earlier, it's mind-boggling—insane in the extreme—that the lead agency in the war on terror lacks the legal standing and the technology to intercept and decrypt coded communications. It's mind-boggling, too, that instead of legally compelling companies to hand over the keys to their encryption products, the Clinton administration actually permitted, with few restrictions, their shipment overseas.

Hezbollah, Hamas, the Abu Nidal organization, and al Qaeda all use data scramblers to support their operations. A decade ago, Ramzi Yousef, the mastermind of the World Trade Center bombing, was storing detailed plans to destroy United States airliners on encrypted files on his laptop computer. Yet even today, the FBI and other agencies are forced to conduct investigations of such groups and individuals with procedural devices forged in the last century during the infancy of the information-technology age. In all, it amounts to a huge gap in our public safety matrix.

Congress also needs to significantly increase the number of FBI special agents and support positions devoted to counterterrorism. It needs to provide additional funding so that the Bureau and its experts can have access to emerging technologies and to research and development work going on in the private sector. And it needs to exempt the FBI from congressionally mandated compensation restrictions that forbid the Bureau from paying more than a low-level government salary to critically needed experts—Arabic and Farsi speakers, to cite only two obvious examples—who can command far greater pay in the private marketplace. As of the end of 2004, the FBI had on the order of 120,000 hours of intercepts that it lacked the manpower to translate. Does Congress think they're going to magically transform themselves into English?

I know this is an old refrain, from me and everyone else who ever headed up a major Washington bureaucracy: give me money, give me bodies, give me legislative authority. By the time you read these words, much of what I have advocated here might already have been seen to, but recent past history is not altogether promising. The simple fact is that when I testified before the 9/11 Commission in April 2004, two and a half years after the attacks on the

World Trade Center and the Pentagon, the FBI had been granted the authority to expand its pre-9/11 workforce by all of two hundred people, an increase of less than 2 percent—to do battle in a world we all agree has been fundamentally altered. That, too, is flat-out nuts. It's time to get real.

It's time also for Congress to throw its full support behind the expansion of the FBI's Legat offices overseas and behind its international training programs. That's how we get eyes and ears abroad. That's how we build the bridges and create the contacts that help us combat crime and terrorism in an increasingly borderless world. That's how we spread our own system of justice and its built-in protections to a world hungry for fair play. Of all the FBI's programs, these two give American taxpayers the greatest ultimate return on the dollar.

One more thing Congress needs to do: it needs to restructure the budget process so that the FBI director, the head of the Central Intelligence Agency, and the attorney general have greater authority to determine *on their own* the allocation of funding and resources as missions evolve and new threats emerge. The genius of so much of American industry is its suppleness, its ability to turn on a dime as economic and business conditions change here and around the globe, to pursue opportunity wherever it arises. America's intelligence agencies, its crime fighters, and its lead counterterrorism forces need that same flexibility. Oversight, yes—the more, the merrier. Make the attorney general and the directors of the FBI and CIA defend their choices. Hold them accountable when they fall short. But enough with micromanagement. That's how you turn horses into camels.

I don't think it does much good here to get into the specifics of some of the sweeping legislation that has been passed in the wake of 9/11: the Patriot Act and its extension, and the intelligence bill that President George W. Bush signed at the end of 2004, in particular. The courts, including the Supreme Court, will be deciding the merits of the various provisions of those acts and their mandates for years to come. As a lawyer and prosecutor, I've learned to wait until judges have had their say. But a few general thoughts on the rush to restructure and strengthen our intelligence gathering in the face of the global terrorism threat.

First, I believe that establishing a separate Domestic Intelligence Service would be a major mistake. We Americans are rightly suspicious of a state secret-police force, even with all the constitutional protections we would still be entitled to. Standing up such a vast new division would also take at least a decade. These things just don't happen overnight, and in the interim valuable time would be lost and valuable resources squandered when they are most needed. Rather than encourage cooperation between intelligence gathering and law enforcement—a vital necessity—the proposed new service would inevitably raise still more barriers and lead to still more turf wars. As I told the 9/11 Commission in response to a question from Chairman Thomas Kean, "If you thought the wall was a big one before, this would be a fortress."

What's more, domestic intelligence divisions of the sort proposed simply don't have much of a track record. The long-standing British domestic secret-police force, the model most often cited by proponents of a similar U.S. body, has had a multitude of problems, including its failure to spot would-be shoe bomber Richard Reid. I see nothing to convince me that our experience on this side of the ocean would be dramatically different. Give FBI agents the tools and the budget authority to do the job they have been assigned to do, and they'll do it very well, and without having to skulk about in the dark. That's not the American way, and it shouldn't be.

Contending that the FBI and CIA couldn't or wouldn't work to-gether in the run-up to 9/11 might sell books and get you on the Sunday talk shows, but it simply is not true. George Tenet and I worked together extraordinarily well, as did the men and women who served under us.

Courageous agents and officers from both services apprehended Ramzi Yousef from his fleabag Pakistani hotel and brought him back to stand trial in New York City. The joint bin Laden task force known as Alex Station gathered and disseminated to both agencies invaluable information about al Qaeda. No, we were never able to arrest Osama bin Laden and bring him back to the States for trial. No one has managed to do that yet even with the backing of a powerful military force. But thanks to Alex Station, we were able to identify and in many cases apprehend and disable al Qaeda's leader-ship and its operatives and disrupt its plans, including plans to stage high-profile attacks on the eve of the millennium.

To be sure, the Capitol was filled with yelping after 9/11 about the CIA and the FBI failing to communicate. Washington is never short of politicians willing to off-load their own share of the blame. But as far as I know, from the mid-1990s until the day I retired as di-rector in June 2001, not a single member of Congress, including those on the various intelligence committees, ever once said to George Tenet or to me that there was any issue about our agencies not cooperating with one another.

The FBI and the CIA did their job prior to 9/11, separately and in unison, and they are still doing their job today. Give them the free-dom to be creative in pursuing terrorists, stifle the instinct to smother them both under some new überbureaucracy—a perfect Washington answer if ever there was one—and continue to back them up with the political will that was so tragically lacking in the years before

September 2001, and both agencies will continue to do their jobs in the future. And Americans and America will be safer because of it.

W e also have to fight against the tendency to prepare for the last war when the world is changing constantly around us. September 11 was a horrific spectacle, full of pyrotechnics, and with a body count and audacity that guaranteed it would lead every newscast and every paper in every corner of the world for weeks and weeks to follow, but that doesn't mean the next attack will look like the last one, at whatever magnitude greater or smaller.

Yes, we have to be hypervigilant for attacks by land or sea, for nuclear backpack bombs, for reprises of the hijackings that turned our own passenger jets into enemy missiles, but we have to constantly think outside those boxes as well. Just before he stepped down as secretary of Health and Human Services, Tommy Thompson took a pasting in the media for warning about the vulnerability of America's food chain to terrorist assault, but he was absolutely right to raise that red flag. Our food chains are vulnerable. So is our water supply. Spend all our energies protecting against high-explosive attacks, and we might miss an act of bio-terror with potentially far greater consequences.

Anyone who has sweated through a summer brownout or blackout in a place like New York City knows the extreme discomfort that follows when the energy infrastructure fails, but a multiprong attack on the power grids that serve, say, the five largest U.S. metropolitan areas would have economic consequences that would dwarf the physical ones. Stock markets would close, traffic of all kinds would be in chaos, emergency services would disappear. That list could go on and on. Terrorists know as well as we do that homeland security begins with economic security. We have to do a better job of protecting on that front as well.

America's information infrastructure might be the most vulnerable point of all. Find a back door into the databanks of our financial institutions, our health-care providers, the accounting and ordering departments of our Fortune 500 companies, and the U.S.—and global—economy could take years to fully recover, with devastating effects for everyone. Unlike an attack on the energy grid, too, this one could be launched from anywhere on the globe. Some of the most troubling assaults that the FBI's Infrastructure Protection Center dealt with during my time as director originated with an Internet service provider in Turkey, but ISPs are everywhere.

"Information warfare" equally threatens our national security. We know that a number of foreign nations have developed information-warfare doctrine, programs, and capabilities for use against the U.S. and other nations. Aware that they can never match our military might with conventional or "kinetic" weapons, our enemies see cyber attacks on our critical infrastructures as a way to hit what they perceive as America's Achilles heel: our growing dependence on information technology in government and commercial operations. Not long ago, two Chinese military officers published a book that called for the use of unconventional measures, including the propagation of computer viruses, to counterbalance the military power of the United States. A Russian official has also commented that an attack on a national infrastructure could, "by virtue of its catastrophic consequences, completely overlap with the use of [weapons] of mass destruction."

(The global reach of computer-launched terrorism and of white-collar computer crimes is another good reason as well for Congress to support the expansion of the Bureau's Legat offices.)

We also need to constantly expand our understanding of who and what a "terrorist" can be. Post-9/11, the word inevitably conjures up a Middle Eastern jihadist bent on bringing the Great Satan down, but some of the most devastating pre-9/11 terrorist attacks within the United States were planned and carried out by our own citizens: Timothy McVeigh in Oklahoma City, Eric Rudolph in Atlanta, and Unabomber Ted Kaczynski perhaps most notable among them. The publisher Forbes, Inc., the National Library of Medicine, and dozens of other businesses and organizations have all suffered crippling attacks on their data systems not by outside powers but by disgruntled former employees bent on revenge.

In February 1999 remarks to a subcommittee of the Senate Committee on Appropriations, I warned of " 'lone offender' and extremist splinter elements of right-wing groups" that the FBI had "identified as possessing or attempting to develop/use chemical, biological or radiological materials." I also spoke about the threat posed by "religious/apocalyptic sects that are unaffiliated with far-right extremists." Those dangers are no less real today than they were then, and the more we concentrate our counterterrorism attention solely on external enemies, the more vulnerable we are to violent assaults homegrown under our nose.

We need to remember, too, that an idea can be more powerful than an entire arsenal of missiles and bombs. The terrorist brief against the United States includes our superpower status and our determination to continue guaranteeing the presence of a Jewish state in Israel, but what the terrorists really hate is America's diversity and its traditions of individual liberty. They are violently opposed to free ideas, to freedom of religion, to free markets and freedom for women. Worse, and what makes their acts increasingly desperate, they know that they are on the wrong side of history. From Athens to the Covenant of Abraham, from the Magna Carta to the Warsaw Uprising, men and women have shown beyond any shadow of a doubt that they want to be free; and increasingly, they are acting on that desire.

Today, the authoritarians who hold power in Damascus and Tehran are more threatened by the nascent democracy taking root next door in Iraq than they are by any army, however powerful. With its restive, youthful, Web-based population, Iran is virtually certain in my mind to overthrow its fundamentalist mullahs within a decade. Millions of Iranians will soon be free, and great Iranian-American patriots like my good friend Nasser Kazeminy will have served the cause of peaceful democratic transition. Likewise, the fascists running Damascus have to be more preoccupied with their own exit strategies than they are with clinging to the levers of power.

In their place, I'm convinced, self-government will rise—flawed at first, as new systems are always flawed, but powerful all the same. Indonesia is living proof that a largely Muslim nation can establish a working democracy. (Any suggestion to the contrary is pure prejudice.) That and Turkey will be the model of the future for the Islamic world, not Iran and Syria. And as democracy takes root and grows, conflict will die down and terrorism abate because that is an odd feature about true self-government. Nations that practice it, ones that aren't in the grip of authoritarians, of dictators, of theocratic zealots rarely, if ever, wage war on or seek to destabilize one another. Millions of newly free people will demand free markets, enterprise, and opportunity, and then rule of law, once established in the Middle East, will work the same revolution there that it did in the 1960s in the American South when a tiny group of federal judges had the courage to enforce the Fourteenth Amendment to our Constitution.

That gets me to my final and most critical point. We cannot allow ourselves to imitate our enemies in the pursuit of defeating them. War always breeds excess, even in a Constitutional democracy such as ours. Abraham Lincoln suspended the writ of habeas corpus during the dark days of the Civil War. More than one hundred thousand Japanese-Americans were taken from their homes and interned in substandard camps during World War II. In the aftermath of 9/11 and the invasion of Afghanistan, hundreds of enemy combatants have been held indefinitely at the U.S. Navy base at Guantanamo, Cuba, which tests the limits of established rules of war. In Iraq, some prison guards at Abu Ghraib and elsewhere employed interrogation methods that most Americans consider reprehensible. These things happen in war, but the true glory of America is that, under the rule of law, they are essentially self-correcting.

Our predisposition to obtain an arrest warrant for Osama bin Laden or to give Miranda rights to the Nairobi embassy bomber Odeh upon his arrest in East Africa might slow down the administration of justice, but both acts go to the bedrock of our democracy. Unrestrained state police power has never succeeded in permanently suppressing terrorism, or liberty for that matter.

I remember a newspaper photo that appeared right before the November 2004 incursion into Fallujah, showing young soldiers taking notes at a briefing by military lawyers who were spelling out the terms of engagement for the upcoming battle. That's the rule of law at work. In a similar spirit, the most controversial sections of the Patriot Act were approved by Congress only after inserting sunset provisions that require reapproval to remain effective. At one point after 9/11, the Pentagon quietly proposed funding for what it called the Total Information Awareness Program. Once Congress understood that the project called for the creation of a massive database in which millions of Americans' names along with their travel and purchase habits could be profiled and mined, the idea was smothered without even a hearing.

Think back to those prisoner abuses in Iraq. What other superpower in global history would have allowed them to be so publicized? More important, what other one would have tried the perpetrators and punished those found guilty? Beginning with the Supreme

Court's ruling that the executive branch's detention of military combatants was unfair unless a judicial hearing was provided to determine the basis for detention, federal judges have taken the lead in applying the rule of law to the war against terrorism. Judges have thrown out convictions in major terrorism cases. They've required the appointment of attorneys for detainees captured on the battlefield and ordered public hearings in immigration procedures.

Just as important, judges and their courts have also validated the authority of the executive and the Congress to fight the war against terrorism in an effective but lawful manner. Witness the November 2002 decision by the Court of Review that reversed years of incorrect application of the Foreign Intelligence Surveillance Act by holding that the wall raised by the Department of Justice between criminal and intelligence information was contrary to the plain meaning and intent of the statute.

The bottom line is that we are one of the few nations in the history of the world to have ever exercised its natural right of self-defense against the most violent and unrestrained enemy in a lawful manner. Doing so can be messy. It can be slow. But if my nearly thirty years as a street agent, as a federal prosecutor, as a U.S. district court judge, and finally as director of the FBI taught me one thing above all others, it is just this: the uniquely American formula that underlies the rule of law can never guarantee that we'll make no mistakes along the way, but abiding by the rule of law will always ensure that we succeed in the end and that we do so honorably. And so it will with this war, too. Learned Hand, the legendary Southern District judge, said it best many years ago: "The spirit of liberty is the spirit which is not too sure that it is right."

AFTERWORD

fter leaving the FBI, I resigned myself to the fact that I would never again find the friendships and dedication that I had come to know in more than twenty-six years of public service.

It turned out that I had resigned myself to this prematurely. When I first met MBNA's founders, Charlie Cawley and Al Lerner, I was, like everyone else, greatly impressed by their legendary charm and success. One of my FBI colleagues, Jules Bonavolonta, had introduced me to Cawley, a fellow student at St. Benedict's High School in Newark, New Jersey. Jules also made the connection to Lerner, for whom he'd done private investigator work in New York City after leaving the FBI.

Cawley and Lerner had been phenomenally successful in growing MBNA America Bank overnight from a hundred-person operation in an abandoned A&P store into one of America's largest and most important financial institutions, but what struck me most about these men were their integrity and patriotism. Both were devoted to their families and to the people who worked for them. The decent core values that they practiced, even in the cutthroat world

315

of retail credit, carried over into all of their business dealings and into their lives generally. It was their bedrock principles, which so reminded me of the FBI values, that led me to MBNA.

Once I got there—coincidentally, my first full day of work was 9/11—it became clear that the men and women Charlie and Al had chosen to populate MBNA were people of equal measure and principle. Over the last four years I have had the privilege of working with Bruce Hammonds and John Cochran, who know the nation's credit card business better than anyone and who lead the company with honor and skill. MBNA's chairman, Randy Lerner, a great patriot and business leader like his father, constantly displays the integrity and humility always hoped for in a great leader. This leadership and integrity is also amply reflected in the other people who oversee MBNA and its business on behalf of the shareholders.

The entire senior management team of this great company—Lance Weaver, Ric Struthers, Ken Vecchione, Doug Denton, Chuck Krulak, John Scheflen, Ken Boehl, Michael Rhodes, Dave Spartin, Frank Bramble, Janine Marrone, Jack Hewes, Shane Flynn, Michelle Shepherd, Gregg Bacchieri, Becky Cahill, Robert DeSantis, Jim Donahue, Randy Black, Jeanne McClafferty, Eileen Leach, Thomas Wren, Dave Hirt, Omar McNeill, John Stanton, John Collingwood, Brian Dalphon, Pat Gallagher, Tim Naughton, Henry Moncure, Regina Mullen, Walt Donaldson, Kevin Gimlett, Al Scarpitti, Charlie Manelski, Richard Willis, Mike O'Hagan, Pete Romano, Brian Gimlett, Charlie Devita, Matt Neels, Terri Murphy, Jim Murphy, John Reinhardt, Lanny Edelsohn, and many others, including Howard Kessler, MBNA's longtime partner and brilliant sales agent—displays the virtues and qualities of wonderful leaders and business innovators. The law department, government affairs, corporate governance, special investigations unit, and ethics offices, which I oversee, are filled with incredibly talented and good people.

Most important, the 28,000 people of MBNA, working in

seven countries, have given the company its major and unequaled success. (Not surprisingly MBNA employees last year devoted 600,000 hours to pro bono community service.) It has been a great pleasure to work with them all and to be a part of this wonderful organization. My own success has in its largest part been the good fortune of being part of great organizations like the FBI and MBNA.

As I close, MBNA is slated to become part of Bank of America, one of the nation's finest financial institutions. Although I have been with MBNA for just four years, the process of conducting this sale and playing a key role has given me a deep insight into the leadership of this remarkable company. On June 17, 2005, a Friday afternoon, in the midst of discussions relating to the sale of MBNA, our helicopter crashed into the East River returning from New York City minutes after takeoff. Aboard were my friends and colleagues, Bruce Hammonds, Frank Bramble, Ric Struthers, Lance Weaver, Doug Denton, Tom Wren, and our two pilots, Blair Payton and Mark Schaberg. The tail of the Sikorsky broke off upon impact and the cabin immediately filled with water. Working as a team, remaining perfectly calm and looking out for one another, Lance and Ric managed to open the cabin door against immense water pressure while almost submerged. Had they not opened that door, all six would have perished. Once Lance and Ric exited, Tom and Frank were next to the door. The helicopter was now completely under the river's black water, and both men looked up toward the light, indicating the equally treacherous surface with its killer currents. Frank could have safely reached the surface without delay. Nevertheless, and in the most heroic fashion, he stayed behind in order to pull Bruce and Doug to safety. Without his valor, both men would probably have been lost.

Once on the surface, all six passengers and our two brave pilots worked together selflessly to keep one another afloat in one of the country's most dangerous rivers. All were rescued and safely returned to their families and friends. I am immensely proud of all eight of these men and still amazed at their courage, calm, and grace under pressure. And I almost thought that my action days had been left behind at the FBI.

Led by these fine men and by Randy Lerner, in particular, MBNA is being merged into one of the premier companies in the world—Bank of America—and our shareholders, employees, customers, and communities will be the beneficiaries of their good stewarding.

ACKNOWLEDGMENTS

First, for encouraging and allowing me to write the book I never contemplated, my sincere appreciation to Howard Means, a gifted writer, analyst, and wonderful human being who devoted countless hours, talent, imagination, and perspective to this book. I will always be thankful to him for the immense patience and kindness that he continuously showed to me. To the incredibly talented and dedicated people at St. Martin's Press, who helped me produce the book I finally wanted to write for the FBI, my gratitude to Sally Richardson, the excellent president and publisher; Charlie Spicer, my executive editor of inexhaustible patience; John Cunningham, associate publisher; George Witte, editor-in-chief; John Murphy, publicity director; Joe Cleemann, associate editor; Amelie Littell, managing editor; Elizabeth Catalano, production editor; Susan Yang, designer; and Eric Gladstone, production manager. I know that the men and women of the FBI will appreciate their fine efforts in this endeavor. And my deep appreciation to Jon Liebman, my friend at the U.S. Attorney's Office and the agent for this book.

What success I have enjoyed over the years has been the proximate result of surrounding myself with people more competent than I. My twenty-six years of public service are the best example of this very simple formula. From working the streets of New York City with FBI agents to prosecuting cases in the nation's premier United States Attorney's office in Manhattan to the storied Southern District bench and finally back to the world's very best investigative agency—our FBI—I had the recurring good fortune to be in the company of the very best. My streak continued at MBNA, then the largest, independent credit-card company in the world and recognized leader in affinity marketing.

More enduring than my public service, the love and incredible strength of my wife, Marilyn, and our six sons—Justin, Brendan, Sean, Connor, Liam, and Colin—has enabled me over two and a half decades to face the big challenges of my work life with competence, humor, and true satisfaction. Because of their support and sacrifice, I never had a day when I went to work without total commitment, focus, and the motivation to do the right thing. During some incredibly busy and even critical times on my government watches, we always managed to enjoy and celebrate our wonderful family, shuttering out the public winds that tried to buffet us but never succeeded. If at any time I thought my family would have suffered from my public service, I would have promptly quit. Government service should not be an alternative to participating in one's family life and their well-being.

My family and faith in God allowed me to stay comfortably and strongly in the *arena* immortalized by the words of Teddy Roosevelt. I never during my public service or afterward felt the slightest inclination to respond to the group of witless and mostly idle FBI critics who all believe they should lead this important government agency but would not have the fortitude or skill to do so. This assortment of knuckleheads—who inhabit government roles in some cases but mostly just stand on the sidelines—are wont to tell the real athletes, coaches, and referees what should be done in the arena without ever having put on a jersey themselves. Their impact on things continues to be *de minimis* and for that reason they won't find their names in the index here. That being said, I hope they buy multiple copies of *My FBI*.

My first debt of gratitude is owed to my parents, William and Bernice. Their love for me was unconditional, the best kind parents can give. From them I learned sacrifice, kindness, honesty, humility, and love for God. My brothers, Bill and John, resonated our parents' love and they have been lifelong friends. My grandparents confirmed the circle of love, and cousins like Claudia Cositore supported me over many years.

My mother- and father-in-law, Mary and Roger Coyle, also deserve great recognition. They are two of the kindest and sweetest people I have known. On almost every foreign trip and emergency that required my sudden absence from home, they would take a bus from Pittsburgh to help their daughter and grandsons cope while I was away. I often thought how a small part of our national security depended on them.

Many good people helped me grow up in the melting pot of Hudson County in the shadows of New York City. Sam Maniscalco, my Scoutmaster at Troop 19, taught me a lot about public service on my way to Eagle Scout. The wonderful Franciscan nuns from Peekskill, New York, who served at Immaculate Heart of Mary Grammar School in North Bergen, like Sister Sebastian, taught me to read, think, and pray. At St. Joseph's Boys High School in West New York, La Salle Christian Brothers such as Jerome Sullivan made it easier to be a teenager. In the summer of 1970, Father Ralph Beiting of the Christian Appalachian Project in Beria, Kentucky, gave me the chance to understand poverty, hope, and charitable works. At Rutgers College, Professor Richard McCormick took me back through exciting histories while Arthur Kinoy at Rutgers Law School taught me the sacred nature of dissent and liberty.

With rare exceptions the wonderful men and women of the FBI have taught and impressed me for over thirty years now. Starting with my exciting arrival at our New York office in August, 1975, legendary agents like Tom Emery, Jim Nelson, Bob Sweeney, Leo McGillicuddy, Jules Bonavolonta, Jim Kallstrom, and Tom Sheer were fortunately our leaders. My many talented colleagues there—Bob Cassidy, Martin Bilder, Jack Barrett, Bill Andrew, Phil Deutsch, Jim Abbott, Bob Lennek, Lew Schiliro, Vaughn Antab, Rich Reinhardt, Walt Stowe, Bill Lynch, Mark Mershon, John Klochan, Ray Kerr, Pat Colgan, Dennis Collins, Joe Spinelli, John Pritchard, Charlie Rooney, Pat Luzio, Carmine Russo, Bob Ward, Mike Slattery, Clare Murphy, Maureen Mallon, Lorraine Pregdnzer, Jane Johnson, Morfia Papain, Kathy MacGowan, Peggy Gawley, Barbara Gormley, and countless others—allowed me to succeed.

At the U.S. Attorney's Office at the Southern District, Bob Fiske, John Martin, Rudy Giuliani, and Otto Obermaier were great U.S. attorneys under whom I was privileged to serve. My dear friend and mentor, Benito Romano, also served with distinction as U.S. attorney, and I was honored to be his deputy. It was at that moment in our lives we both realized that the "kids" had taken over the Office. Luckily, Southern District greats like Bart Schwartz, Tom Fitzpatrick, Larry Pedowitz, Denny Young, Jane Parver, Fred Virella, Walter Mack, Shirah Neiman, Mike Devorkin, Dan Bookin, Steve Frankel, John Kenney, Jo Ann Harris, Pat Hynes, John Kaley, Gerry Lynch, Bob Litt, Audrey Strauss, Rusty Wing, and others were there to protect us from ourselves.

The many amazingly gifted lawyers who served in the Southern District U.S. Attorney's Office with me over ten years are too many to mention. Barbara Jones became one of my closest colleagues and friends. Her patience and generosity to me will always be treasured. Our Organized Crime Unit achieved historically significant victories against entrenched criminal enterprises. Bob Bucknam, Alan Cohen, Mark Hellerer, Bruce

ACKNOWLEDGMENTS

Baird, Aaron Marcu, Dick Martin, Adam Hoffinger, Fran Fragos-Townsend, Mike Chertoff, Andy McCarthy, Jim Bucknam, John Savarese, Joan McPhee, Tom Souther, Bob Stewart (from the New Jersey U.S. Attorney's Office), Mark Feldman, Gil Childers, Ken McCabe, Carl Bogan, Mike Fahy, and Tom Loreto all made major contributions to this success.

Another Southern District colleague, the truly impressive and talented Mary Jo White, deserves special mention along with Barbara Jones. Both as assistant U.S. attorney and then as U.S. attorney in Brooklyn and later Manhattan, Mary Jo was simply outstanding as a leader, thinker, and model public servant. My only regret for her yet uncompleted public career is that she was not the attorney general while I was at the FBI. No law enforcement leader in either the Clinton or Bush administrations better understood terrorism or had the skill to prosecute its most important cases.

My fellow judges from the Southern District and elsewhere provided great counsel and friendship for me, particularly through my years as FBI director. I am immensely grateful to Milton Pollack, Mike Mukasey, John Martin, Kevin Duffy, John Keenan, Ken Conboy, John Sprizzo, John Walker, Constance Baker Motley, Bob Sweet, Bill Conner, Loretta Preska, Barbara Jones, Charlie Brieant, Kimba Wood, Dick Casey, Miriam Goldman Cederbaum, Tom Griesa, Shirley Wohl Kram, Peter Leisure, Larry McKenna, Lenny Sand, Sonia Sotomayor, Louis Stanton, Bob Ward, Edmond Palmieri, Ken Starr, Gene Sullivan, Ed Devitt, Gerry Tjoflat, John Conway, Fred Lacey, Ralph Thompson, Tom Hogan, Royce Lamberth, Frank Johnson, Sterling Johnson, and many others. Pierre Leval, one of the nation's foremost jurists, is a dear friend from the court who I will always treasure.

Our family dog, Reni, a sweet golden retriever from the Guiding Eyes of New York was not with us in Washington, but despite President Truman's maxim about that combination, Marilyn and I had many friends in official Washington and in our neighborhood in Great Falls, Virginia. Our special thanks to Bill and Lynda Webster, Dick and Patricia Carlson, Antonin and Maureen Scalia, Floyd and Carol Clarke, Chris and Linda Wilcox, John and Caroline Oakes, Adam and Liz Hoffinger, Maggie and Ransom Parker, Jamie and Dee Jesse, and many others who were always there for us whether it was raining or shining.

Another special word of thanks to the several stalwart secretaries who, despite my failings, managed to keep me afloat over the many years: Kathy MacGowan, Lydia Quintana, Maria Morales, Brenda Bumgardner, Wanda Siford, Judy Leeper, Carol Williams, and most enduringly, the very magnificent Noreen Gawley, who has been propping me up since 1991.

322

ACKNOWLEDGMENTS

Long before he was kind enough to come to the FBI with me as chief of staff, Bob Bucknam has been one of my closest friends and colleagues since the Southern District. An outstanding prosecutor, administrator, world-class diplomat, media and congressional expert, Bob was the consummate COS and is largely responsible for my success as director and for preventing my self-destruction at key points. Another major ingredient for my survival in D.C. was Bob's equally talented brother, Jim Bucknam, who distinguished himself at the U.S. Attorney's office and served the FBI as my senior counsel. To Howard Shapiro, our outstanding first FBI general counsel and VANPAC co-counsel, I owe a great deal of thanks for his good service. And John Collingwood will always be the master on judgment and success in dealing with the media and Congress.

Over the many years, I have had the pleasure of working with another cadre of excellent lawyers who made my various government offices possible. Joyce Levowitz, Eileen Minnefor, Burke Doar, Lisa Jonas, and Lynn DeLisi were wonderful colleagues and remarkable lawyers with whom I was fortunate to work.

At FBI Headquarters a thankfully endless roster of superbly talented and dedicated people have served and continue to serve the Bureau. First and foremost for me is John Behnke. This extraordinary and simply wonderful agent was for many years my right arm. Religiously humble, quiet, and constantly working behind the scenes, John is probably the FBI's single best case agent/investigator. Working both VANPAC and the Rudolph cases, John was the quintessential agent's agent who does it all with remarkable grace and skill. Among a constellation of dedicated agents and FBI heroes, John in my experience was the best of class. His skill as an agent and support to me as special assistant were matched only by his courage and perseverance in battling an aggressive illness to a fortunate victory.

An able squad of agents and support professionals joined with John in working with me as director. These are the prototypic all-stars who make their principals appear to be prepared, on time and on message. My deep thanks here to Todd Letcher, Tom Almon, Artie Grubert, John Griglione, Bob Jones, Rick Todd, Mark D'Attilio, Lou Caprino, Ray Morrow, Sean Joyce, Bob Hunt, Ed Kahrer, Lisa Keller, Dean St. Dennis, Paul Blumberg, Lynn Hoffman, Charlotte Betts, Karen McCarron, Dave Markley, and Linda Sue Khachi. My appreciation to Wade Jackson and Mike Perry of the Quantico Firearms Unit whose dedication and friendship mean a great deal to me. Thanks to their diligence in keeping my firearms qualifications timely as director, I never had to take my gun away from myself. Many others helped me serve as director, like those brave officers who protected our children over eight years: Haejun Park, Mark Lewis, Allen Kittrell, Jacqueline Haynes, Eugene Grays, Bradford Walker, Shawn Melvin, Noel Gleason, Jaqueline Wilson, Richard McClendon, Dwain Johnson, Amy Riddick, Amy Cherry, Bryan Latham, and Roger Nickell. To our FBI photographers/receptionists Patti Jo Cotton, Suzette David, Margaret Sullivan, and Tracy Miner, and to Beverly Knight and all the 24×7 operators at the FBI's Strategic Information and Operations Center, my enduring thanks and respect.

I was extremely fortunate to have a truly impressive group of senior FBI leaders who enabled me to lead this remarkable institution. They include Floyd Clarke, Dave Binney, Larry Potts, Bill Esposito, Bob Bryant, Tom Pickard, Larry Parkinson, Bob Reutter, Dale Watson, Mike DeFeo, Milt Ahlerich, Don Kerr, Tom Kelley, Sean McWeeney, Charlie Prouty, Paul Daly, Joe Genovese, Lance Emery, Mike diPretoro, Mike Pyszczymuka, Ralph Horton, Bassem Youssef, Eliska Tretera, Lee Flosi, Raul Salinas, Jim DeSarno, Steve McCraw, Paul Phillips, Mike Rolince, Walt Wilson, Barry Mawn, Mike Kortan, Charlie Steele, Andrea Simonton, John O'Neill, Carolyn Morris, Dave Kirkpatrick, Hector Pesquera, Les Kaciban, Weldon Kennedy, Manny Gonzalez, Bob Dies, Neil Gallagher, Bill Perry, Wiley Thompson, Rueben Garcia, Grant Ashley, John Pistole, Chris Swecker, Lew Schiliro, Ed Bodigheimer, Jack Eckenrode, Jeff Lapinski, and Jim Kallstrom.

The courageous and devoted agents who make up the FBI's world-renowned Hostage Rescue Team (HRT) will always command my loyalty and respect. Roger Nisley, Bob Hickey, Chuck Pierce, and a continuing lineage of heroes have given by their service and expert competence an unprecedented advantage to the FBI and our country in combating and preventing serious crimes. This skilled team of selfless and brave operators is the archetypal "tip of the spear" for America's law enforcement. The courageous and honorable men who serve us there, like Lon Horiuchi, deserve the nation's praise and lasting gratitude. I will also forever appreciate the support given to HRT by two friends and skilled lawyers, Adam Hoffinger and Seth Waxman.

Throughout my public service in law enforcement, I always believed that my constituency was the victims and potential victims of crimes. These included the special agents who were killed in the line of duty while I was director. I will always feel personal responsibility for the tragic deaths of these brave agents: Martha Dixon Martinez, Mike Miller, Chuck Reed, Billy Christian, and Kevin Kramer. The FBI and our nation will forever honor their sacrifices and those of their wonderful families. Another special group of victims for me is the survivors of those killed while protecting all of us in the line of duty. To all the men and women inscribed on the Law Enforcement Memorial in Washington, D.C., and always to their families, I express my deep thanks and reverence. And to all the survivors of our military heroes, especially the brave and wonderful families of our nineteen Khobar Towers heroes, I will always have the deepest love and admiration for all of them. America and the liberty we cherish would vanish without the long but vulnerable line of defense provided by our many law enforcement and military guardians posted dangerously around our perimeters.

I am immensely grateful to former President Bush and his wondrous wife, First Lady Barbara, for their friendship and support over many years. President Bush's confidence in me to serve as a federal judge was one of the highlights of my professional life. Their many kindnesses to me and Marilyn and our six sons, from Kennebunkport to Washington, D.C., to Texas, will always be treasured by our family. As for the current President Bush, under whom I was FBI director for five months, it was a pleasure to serve a president of honor and integrity, just like his father. I regret that I did not have a longer opportunity to work with Vice President Cheney, Andy Card, Condi Rice, and Colin Powell, all public servants whom I greatly admire.

Last and most important, I am grateful for my Roman Catholic heritage and faith in God. For this special gift I have many to thank, beginning with my parents. Cardinals John O'Connor, Theodore McCarrick, Bernard Law, and Bishop Saltarelli have all contributed to and strengthened my faith over the years. Other dear friends, who have been spiritual and moral leaders for me, like Elie Wiesel and Abe Foxman, will always be remembered in my heart and prayers.

INDEX

INDEX

INDEX

INDEX